Order and Disorder

ORDER AND DISORDER

Anthropological Perspectives

Keebet von Benda-Beckmann and Fernanda Pirie

Berghahn Books
New York • Oxford

First published in 2007 by
Berghahn Books
www.berghahnbooks.com

© 2007, 2011 Keebet von Benda-Beckmann and Fernanda Pirie
First paperback edition published in 2011

All rights reserved.
Except for the quotation of short passages
for the purposes of criticism and review, no part of this book
may be reproduced in any form or by any means, electronic or
mechanical, including photocopying, recording, or any information
storage and retrieval system now known or to be invented,
without written permission of Berghahn Books.

Library of Congress Cataloging-in-Publication Data

Order and disorder : anthropological perspectives / [edited by] Keebet von Benda-Beckmann and Fernanda Pirie.
   p. cm. -- (Monographs in German history)
Includes bibliographical references and index.
ISBN 978-1-84545-198-1 (hbk) -- ISBN 978-0-85745-148-4 (pbk)
 1. Political anthropology. 2. Order. 3. Social conflict. 4. Political violence.
I. Benda-Beckmann, Keebet von. II. Pirie, Fernanda, 1964-

GN492.O73 2007
306.2--dc22

2007049153

British Library Cataloguing in Publication Data

A catalogue record for this book is available from
the British Library.

Printed in the United States on acid-free paper

ISBN 978-1-84545-198-1 (hardback)
ISBN 978-0-85745-148-4 (paperback)
ISBN 978-0-85745-002-9 (ebook)

Contents

List of Plates		vi
Preface		vii
1.	**Introduction** *Keebet von Benda-Beckmann and Fernanda Pirie*	1
2.	**Order and the Evocation of Heritage: Representing Quality in the French Biscuit Trade** *Simon Roberts*	16
3.	**Pride, Honour, Individual and Collective Violence: Order in a 'Lawless' Village** *Aimar Ventsel*	34
4.	**Order, Individualism and Responsibility: Contrasting Dynamics on the Tibetan Plateau** *Fernanda Pirie*	54
5.	**Vigilante Groups and the State in West Africa** *Tilo Grätz*	74
6.	**Imposing New Concepts of Order in Rural Morocco: Violence and Transnational Challenges to Local Order** *Bertram Turner*	90
7.	**Law, Ritual and Order** *Peter Just*	112
8.	**The Disorders of an Order: State and Society in Ottoman and Turkish Trabzon** *Michael E. Meeker*	132
9.	**Anthropological Order and Political Disorder** *Jonathan Spencer*	150
Notes on Contributors		166
Index		169

List of Plates

7.1	United States Supreme Court	120
7.2	Courtroom, Otter-Tail County Minnesota	121
7.3	Justice Moore and His Monument	122
7.4	British Colonial Judge	125
7.5	Ama Balo	126
7.6	Chief Justice Rehnquist	127

Preface

This volume developed from a conference held at and funded by the Max Planck Institute for Social Anthropology on 26 and 27 November 2004. With the exception of the contribution by Michael Meeker, all the chapters in this volume originated as papers presented during that conference. The organizers are grateful to Michael Meeker and Tsypylma Darieva, who were discussants during the conference, and to Franz von Benda-Beckmann, who gave encouragement and advice during both the preparations and the conference itself. For assistance in preparing the manuscript for publication we are indebted to Gesine Koch and Sung-Joon Park. But most of all we wish to thank the participants. They took part in some lively discussions of both individual papers and general themes, and we have benefited from these in the preparation of this volume, in particular the Introduction, for publication.

INTRODUCTION

Keebet von Benda-Beckmann
Fernanda Pirie

The issue of order and how it is generated and maintained is one to which considerable sociological attention has been directed over the decades. Many early ethnographic studies were concerned with the question of how order was produced in small-scale, acephalous societies, those beyond the control of any state. More recently, however, anthropologists have tended to turn their attention away from the issue of how order is maintained in isolated communities to relations of power and domination in more complex societies – the effects of colonialization, domination and resistance, inter-state relations and globalization. Forms of hierarchy, hegemony and the unequal access to resources have received more attention than structures of order. At the same time, anthropological analyses of conflict and violence have proliferated.[1] The focus has been on the violent, the illegitimate and the immoral while order, it seems, has almost disappeared from the anthropological picture.

The question that arises, then, is whether the issue of order is still relevant as an object of anthropological enquiry. Can questions about order still lead to valuable insights? The analytic value of the concepts of both order and disorder, we suggest, needs to be reconsidered, along with the theories elaborated during the first decades of sociological and anthropological thinking and the extent to which they are still relevant. To consider such questions the contributors to this volume were invited to a workshop hosted by the Max Planck Institute for Social Anthropology in November 2004. The papers that resulted, reproduced here, all take a fresh look at the question of order. They do so in the context of wider configurations of power and politics, including commercial competition, and recent anthropological analyses of the state and political relations. They suggest, among other things, that the notion of order can have different meanings in different contexts. The term may refer to the absence or containment of violence, to the existence of a shared set of norms, but also to a sense of predictability and feeling of security. It can, thus, be used in both an objective and subjective way. Several chapters indicate that the existence of disorder, in the sense of a lack of peace and security, does not necessarily imply a lack of shared norms or sense of predictability for those caught up in it. Indeed, most chapters address the issue of how order emerges out of disorderly contexts and discuss the creative ways in which people create small spaces of order in situations of disorder and disruption.

The role of the state emerges as a central theme in the volume. It is shown to be a source of disorder as much as a guarantor of order, especially where it is weak or retreating. Where it does assert the primary role of creating and maintaining order, as in the case of the nation states of the developed world, it may do so through elaborate symbolism and ritual, while local spheres of order are simultaneously established in ways that have little to do with the state's legal system. In this introduction we highlight some of the ways in which this is done, picking up the threads that run through the individual chapters. We then turn to consider some of the themes that emerged when anthropologists were more explicitly concerned with the principles according to which societies do and should function and reassess these in the light of the case studies.

The Role of the State

Many anthropological discussions have concerned the maintenance of order apart from the state. They have examined the processes and structures found in small-scale, acephalous societies, those which had hardly, or very lightly, been touched by the controlling hand of the state or the administration of a colonial power. In the present volume the emphasis is, by contrast, on order despite the state, that is on the order that is created by those whose social worlds are deeply affected by a state, but one that does not guarantee them peace and stability. Indeed, in many of the case studies the state is portrayed as a cause of disorder. It is described as a source of instability or, at the very least, as failing to guarantee order. The chapter by Meeker develops such an analysis by portraying the state as an inherently disorderly institution. His case study concerns the Ottoman Empire of the nineteenth century which, he argues, prefigured processes by which the nation state developed in Europe. He suggests that the Ottoman regime can only be understood as a disorderly conjunction between the order of the state and that of society. The nature of that conjunction changed over time, but it remained a source of tension and conflict, an inherent disorder in the power structures of the Empire. In Meeker's analysis this illustrates the order of the state and that of society acting upon one another. Some states overwhelm their subject societies, transforming them to their own order, while some societies have the potential to penetrate the colonizing officers, classes and institutions, undermining and corrupting them. However, the relationship between state and society is, in principle, 'touched by instability', precisely because states operate through rationalized and codified institutions designed for supervizing a subject population. The order that the Ottoman rulers attempted to create bore the very seeds of its own instability.

Spencer, in his chapter, addresses the assumption found in much political anthropology that we can look to the realm of the political as the location of social order. Like Meeker, he examines the disorderly relations between state and society, here as they play themselves out in the political realm in Sri Lanka. This field, he suggests, simply cannot be understood without paying attention to processes of disorder. The state itself can be regarded as just one amongst several warring parties. Politics is identified with divisions and trouble by his informants in Sri Lanka. It is regarded as a kind of 'collective moral disorder', an agonistic space of disorderly activity. Spencer thus dissociates the issue of order from that of politics. Ideologies and images of order and nationality are constructed within the practices and discourses of the political, but they are also ideologically distanced from it. As he puts it, the political in Sri Lanka contains within it both order and disorder.

Also discussing the role of the state, Just, in his chapter, points out that the nation state is the paradigm of 'legitimate' governmental control and its order is symbolized in the grandeur, the ritual and the moral symbolism of the parliament chamber and the court room. We might add to this the elaborate ceremonies and regimentation of military parades. These symbols of an abstract, all-encompassing order present to the public the need for a functioning nation state as the necessary condition for the possibility of social life. However, they also celebrate the fact that the state is the source of organized violence, the chaos of war and the agonism of adversarial politics and judicial processes. Such activities are legitimated by explicitly equating them with order and justice. Their disorderly consequences are transformed into symbols of the legitimate order of the state. The state here is simultaneously a guarantor of order and a source of disruption and disorder.

Roberts, in his chapter, considers not so much the state as the workings of the free market and the commercial struggles that are supported and encouraged by it. He likens the interwoven processes of competition and rule breach found in the commercial world to the struggles for political ascendancy described by Victor Turner in his studies of chieftainship in Central Africa (Turner 1957, 1967). His study suggests that if we look beyond the state, we find commercial manufacturers appealing to consumers by creating a sense of a locally-rooted order, using images of local history and interweaving them with more widely-shared cultural images and idioms. All these studies indicate that the state itself is often responsible for conditions of social or political disorder and they highlight the different ways in which this can occur and with what consequences. As Meeker's case study most graphically illustrates, it is the disorderly conjunctions between state and society that create the framework, or the arena, in which processes of order can and must be creatively established by its citizens.

Order Despite the State

We must, therefore, look beyond the state for sources of order, but without ignoring the defining role it plays. The papers in the volume edited by Ferguson and Whitehead (1992) concern patterns of disorder, in particular the disruption of warfare, that are brought about by the proximity or intrusion of an expanding state. In the current volume, by contrast, several papers are concerned with conditions of disorder brought about by a weak or retreating state. Subtle shifts and balances then characterize the construction of order, especially amongst unstable social groups.

Grätz, in his chapter in this volume, discusses the gold-mining communities that have been established in West Africa, whose actions the state is unable or unwilling fully to control. The rapid growth of these new communities has disrupted patterns of social and economic life for resident populations, while also giving rise to problems of order and stability for the incomers. This has, in part, been due to the new mixture of established residents and recent arrivals in and around the mining camps. The consequent problems were answered by the establishment of vigilante groups who initially provided a welcome and more deliberate measure of regularity and predictability for both residents and incomers. Grätz describes how they acquired legitimacy in the eyes of the local population by upholding and enforcing their norms of retributive punishment.

This study demonstrates that the establishment of legitimacy is crucial to the ability of local institutions to guarantee regimes of order, particularly when these are alternatives to the order of the state. Such legitimacy has to be established in the context of local notions concerning social order. As Grätz describes, when one of the vigilante groups in West Africa began to use excessive violence, its activities became not only unpredictable and arbitrary but also illegitimate in the eyes of the local population. At the same time, having been tolerated by state authorities in the interests of stability, this group came to be perceived as a threat to the sovereignty of the state. The authorities then branded it as illegitimate and took steps to curtail its activities.

The authority of those who seek to maintain order in a society can also be undermined if their actions infringe the norms of a moral or religious order, which likewise renders them illegitimate in the eyes of the local population. As described by Bertram Turner in this volume, Islamist Salafiyya groups were able to introduce new forms of control into small communities in south-west Morocco because they claimed to be promoting the law of Islam to legitimate their form of social order. Such claims were initially accepted and allowed these groups to impose new controlling elements. However, their subsequent recourse to violence infringed local notions of order, rendering their activities unacceptable to the local population. They were seen to have transgressed local ideas concerning descent and social relations and to have generated unacceptable levels of conflict within the community. In this way, local notions of order became more reflected and contested, and at the same time they became the basis for a challenge to the legitimacy of the external actors who were seeking to establish a position of dominant control.

Like Grätz's and Turner's chapters, Ventsel's case study from Siberia indicates the importance of a shared set of norms when it comes to establishing order in a community in which state institutions are weak. The population of a Siberian village, established by a strong (Soviet) administration, found itself having to adapt to conditions of weak central control left by a retreating state. Like Grätz, Ventsel illustrates the way some sections of society, in this case elder men and former prison inmates, had brought a certain structure to the local community by establishing the authority to control violence. Among adolescents and young men status and honour were defined by displays of physical aggression. Although this behaviour was in principle tolerated, people were aware of the threat that unrestrained violence posed to the precarious social order. The elder men had to invest considerable effort in containing the violent behaviour of the youth through practices of restraint and disapproval. Although different views were often expressed about the justification of violence in this community, the success of these practices depended upon certain influential members deciding that a fine line had been crossed between acceptable forms of violence and that which threatened to undermine the local order. Their efforts in limiting excessive or disruptive violence were only successful because they actively established and maintained such standards of acceptability.

While Turner's chapter, thus, demonstrates the force of underlying, unreflected notions of order, Ventsel illustrates the deliberate establishment of normative standards. In the Siberian village members of a certain age group claimed that much of the violence in which they engaged was justified as a way of 'proving themselves'. The enforcement of social norms was thus the prerogative of particular members of the community and a certain amount of rule breaking was expected on the part of the young men. It seems that it is not so much that the youth did not share the norms enforced by the elders, but rather that they gained social capital by defying and discursively rejecting them. As Ventsel notes, these young men were expected to accept the punishment that they knew would follow from their behaviour. By accepting punishment they indicated their acceptance of the norms they had violated.

This case study also demonstrates the need for the anthropologist to dissociate the issue of order from that of violence. As Ventsel illustrates, people can develop a range of responses to deal with the perceived threat that the violence of certain sections of society, here the 'kids', poses to their social order. Order is not so much found in the absence of violence in such societies, as in the appropriate nature of the response to violence and in the ongoing processes of containment and adjustment by which people react to and limit its effects.

Among the nomads of Amdo, in north-eastern Tibet, Pirie also found that certain individuals were expected to breach the norms. She describes, in her chapter, the way in which the nomads simultaneously invoked a set of shared norms in order to resolve blood feuds, while granting a grudging respect to those who defied the imposition of such norms. In her analysis it is not so much that the members of the group did not share and enact a common set of norms, as that there was an inherent tension between the norms of order and the norms which applied to individual male behaviour. These incorporated a certain valorization of rule breaking and defiance. This case study indicates that while certain forms of violence were obligatory, according to the norms of feuding and reciprocity, elaborate methods of conflict resolution were also undertaken in order to resolve the blood feuds that escalated to dangerous proportions or threatened to do so. A certain form of order was thus reimposed within these groups by means of established responses to anticipated and predictable forms of disruptive behaviour. Nevertheless, the outbreak of violence remained a constant source of concern. Violence, therefore, can be normatively sanctioned, it can even be obligatory as a matter of individual or group action; however, it may also be negatively evaluated and feared for its socially disruptive consequences.

All these studies illustrate the very fine line that is drawn between acceptable and unacceptable forms of violence. The new, localized power regimes described by Grätz gained acceptance, despite being disadvantageous or even oppressive for some, because they were predictable and people felt able to adapt to them. However, when the vigilantes' use of violence came to be perceived as arbitrary and terror-like it created fear instead of peace and security and the vigilantes lost the trust of the local population. A thin line between acceptable and unacceptable violence and coercion had been crossed. In this case, as in many others, it was also a line between predictability and uncertainty. This is just one indication of the close connection between the issue of order and that of predictability, which recurs in other chapters. Ventsel's and Pirie's studies, for example, both show communities adapting to and developing methods to control a certain amount of predictable violence.

These studies also illustrate the imposition of shared norms, both reflected and unreflected. While Grätz and Turner's chapters describe the regimes of order established as alternatives to that of the state, relying on a certain amount of violence or coercion, they also demonstrate that new power holders have to draw upon established norms to maintain their positions. Conditions of disorder can also be created from within. While the importance of shared norms in creating the conditions for order has been highlighted, several case studies indicate that such norms may simultaneously be challenged from within. Ventsel and Pirie, for example, both describe societies in which a certain amount of rule breaking is both feared and expected. Bertram Turner, in his chapter, explicitly considers the competing normative systems that characterize relations between territorial and kin-based groups in south-west Morocco. As he describes it, more than one set of ideas about order, law, justice and morality can be found among local groups in the region. Numerous notions of order, based on descent, territory, agricultural activities, religion and local and state laws, interact and intersect, each with its own mode of argumentation and standards for the evaluation of behaviour. He suggests that instead of searching for one fundamental way in which the order of a society is established, it is more fruitful to assume that societies may have several different notions of order, which may be invoked alternately or even at the same time.

Turner contrasts two dominant models of order, one based on the idea of harmony and one based on the principle of retaliation or reciprocity. The norms of retaliation are part of a logic of reciprocity, which is integral to relations between different constellations of territorial and kin-based groups. He describes these relations as generating a permanent state of tension, to which any form of final resolution would be inappropriate and, in practice, illusory. Paradoxically, it is the model of order based on the idea of harmony which is also responsible for generating social tensions. The model that incorporates violent retaliation, on the other hand, can serve more effectively to limit or even prevent the occurrence of violence.

The Location of Order

Almost all the examples given in this volume indicate an awareness on the part of those studied that order cannot be taken for granted. It has to be maintained, restored and reconstituted, or even actively constructed, in the first place. This is especially so when the state is weak and can no longer be relied upon, or has never been relied upon, fully to guarantee order. There may also be variety and inconsistency amongst the ideas about order expressed within what we might view as a single society or community. Its members may not fully agree on what establishes order and they may also disagree about what kinds of behaviour support or undermine it. The behaviour or conditions criticized by some as disorderly, illegitimate or oppressive can be neutrally, or even positively appraised by others or they may become unacceptable only in changing circumstances. These differences may follow age, class and gender divisions but also more complex cleavages, as Turner's case study demonstrates. This does not mean, however, that local concepts of order do not, at the same time, involve the idea of some absolute and encompassing ideal and a firm sense of the line that exists between order and disorder. In most situations discussed in this volume there is a line that people feel they can and must draw between order and chaos, and between acceptable violence and disorder. There are implicit boundaries beyond which disorder is felt to emerge, behaviour seems to threaten the conditions for social continuity and life ceases to make sense.

A focus on locality, we would suggest, is crucial to the analysis of order. This does not, however, mean seeking out a bounded, homogeneous sphere. Rather, it requires making sense of the disorderly conjunctions of social processes out of which people construct forms of regularity and predictability. Several chapters in this volume describe the ways in which people construct local structures to maintain order within the context of, but often in competition or uneasy alliance with, official structures of the state. The state shapes the arena but does not determine the patterns of order. This creates disorderly tensions which provide the context in the midst of which people have to establish a more localized sense of order. Interesting questions then arise about the interactions between different forms of ordering institutions and their respective authority. Grätz suggests that the political culture of the vigilante groups he observed is shaped by elements stemming from local tradition, but they do not act completely against the state. Nor do they reinvent the juridical process. As Pirie also shows, with her example from north-eastern Tibet, even in the context of a strong and dominant (Chinese) state local groups can maintain their own ordering institutions. On the grasslands of Amdo, tribes of pastoralists look to locally recognized orators or Buddhist lamas in order to resolve their blood feuds. Rather than rejecting the authority of the police and other agents of the state, however, the Tibetans draw, or attempt to draw, state agents into their own locally constructed patterns of order.

Local norms, therefore, shape the way patterns of order are negotiated between state and society. This has some relevance for recent academic discussions of the way in which people establish predictable patterns of social behaviour in complex situations in which they do not know all the individuals they are dealing with. Giddens (1998) has illustrated the importance of trust in such situations, emphasizing the time and space 'distantiation' characteristic of late modernity. He demonstrates the ways in which trust is established among strangers who are bound in relations of distant communication and have to relate to others they may never meet or get to know. While Giddens focuses on long chains of dependence, several of the chapters in this volume, however, demonstrate how a sense of locality is central to the creation of this sense of trust. Roberts, for example, addresses the question of how the political attachment needed to produce order is generated among the increasingly heterogeneous civil society of the developed world. He suggests that longings for a safe and ordered world are met, in part, by representations of culture and heritage. Images of a historical past grounded in a particular locality provide pattern and a sense of order. His case study concerns civil society, and more specifically the marketing of consumer goods, where authenticity is conveyed by creating an image of production methods based on long-established recipes and professional knowledge, enhanced by reference to local artists, and thus suggesting links with a locality that nurtures its valuable culture and heritage. Establishing trust among strangers, the producer and the buyer, may thus involve more that the rational, detached reliance on professionalism that Giddens describes. Rather, the producers can rely on a yearning for an apparently fugitive 'authenticity'. Roberts likens this to the relations between subject and polity or the commitment to norms which anthropologists have described as being central to the creation of order.

The chapters by Grätz, Turner, Ventsel, Pirie and Roberts, thus build on the discussions of the state found in the chapters of Meeker, Spencer, Just and Roberts by illustrating some of the other ways in which order is generated at the interstices of state and society. They all take a processual approach, discussing the ways in which order is actively generated and maintained. Order, like any other structure, does not simply exist: it becomes, emerges, settles and disappears. The case studies illustrate the disorderly processes of state and society while also revealing the endlessly creative ways in which order is constructed. They describe inherent tensions and competition in social processes which do not, however, negate the possibility that those caught up in them can lead ordered lives. Even within conditions of instability, people can create a sense of regularity and predictability.

The Perception of Order

In most situations there is, therefore, a line that people feel they can and must draw between order and disorder. They have a sense, possibly only implicit, of the boundaries beyond which disorderly behaviour threatens the conditions for social life. This highlights the fact that both order and disorder can be regarded as social constructions. To some extent we must treat them as matters of perception, as understandings as much as processes or states of affairs. A distinction must, therefore, be drawn between order as an objective quality of society, as a state of peace, stability and security, on the one hand, and order as a matter of perception, on the other. As the studies of Ventsel, Pirie and Turner demonstrate, for example, even when rule breaking or violent retaliation is expected of some sections of society, leading to a continual apprehension of violence and disruption, a sense of order can be created by the established responses by which its effects are contained and limited. These societies would hardly be called peaceful or secure for those liable to be caught up in the recurrent violence, yet they are not without order.

What is also apparent is that ideas of order may not be clearly conceptualized by those we study. As Pirie describes, in a remote Ladakhi village the communal ideal of order is only ever negatively expressed in the moral condemnation of antagonism. The villagers, as a body, make concerted efforts to resolve disputes and suppress conflict and there is considerable consensus about what destabilizes the normal flow of life. There is a strong, albeit implicit, ideal of peaceful cooperation between all members of the community, but there is no local concept translatable as 'order'. In this, and many other cases, the boundaries of order only become apparent when an event appears to threaten them. Ventsel's and Grätz's studies, in this volume, illustrate the very fine line that is drawn between acceptable and unacceptable forms of violence and Turner's example shows how such a boundary is only crossed after a series of incremental steps have created a sense of disorder. In the end, it may be only the most minor event which marks the shift from the acceptable to the unacceptable, or the legitimate to the illegitimate, and which arouses concern and prompts people to take counter-measures. The case studies in this volume thus indicate a pervasive concern with disorder and a firm idea of the existence of boundaries. However, they also illustrate that such ideas may be only implicit and unreflected.

Victor Turner (1957) emphasized the role that ritual can play in symbolizing and re-establishing order when social norms have been challenged. Analysing the social and political order of Central African communities that are driven by periodic struggles for political ascendancy, he showed competition and rule breach to be integral to the negotiation of the political order. As he describes it, ritual can be used to symbolize and reaffirm the social order at times of unrest. Referring to this discussion, however, Roberts's paper in this volume describes the way in which symbolic resources can be employed within such struggles, in this case the competition for commercial ascendancy. He uses this example to highlight what he considers to be an overemphasis in the social sciences on the significance of ritual and cosmological symbolism in upholding political or 'traditional' authority.

The performance of a ritual may, therefore, explicate the order of a society, but rituals can also symbolize order indirectly. Bertram Turner describes the way certain forms of trance dancing undertaken during annual festivals in Morocco represent social chaos or the inversion of the social order. In this way the local order receives supernatural affirmation. It is ritualized chaos, in such a case, that highlights the order of daily life to the local population. As other anthropologists have noted, the passage of time, normally unmarked, can be indicated in rites of passage that mark the transition to a new year (Leach 1961, Gell 1996). In a similar way, we would suggest, an underlying, normally unrepresented, form of social order may be marked at times of licensed disorder, such as the ritualized disorder of the carnival.

Just, in this volume, describes legal processes among the Dou Donggo of eastern Sumbawa, Indonesia, during which ritual is used to symbolize disorder. A certain type of behaviour that breaches the social norms, in this case obligations towards kin relations, is formalized and expressed in ritual ways. Instead of challenging the offender by claiming that rights have been infringed, the offended party performs a ritual breach of the norms. This ritual serves as a performative alternative to a discursive method of drawing attention to a serious breach of order. It is not that the ritual symbolizes disorder in the way that carnival does as an inversion of the overall order. Rather, the ritual elements symbolize to the community the occurrence of events that threaten the social order and which require redress, as well as the existence of the underlying cosmic and social order which must be restored by the process of resolution. The judicial proceedings themselves are extremely informal. The most minute signs indicate to the local population the fact that judicial authority is being exercised, conflict has been resolved and order has been restored. If we consider order as a social construction or perception, then, it is apparent that important though they are for a sense of security some forms of order are essentially unreflected. It is this taken-for-granted sense of order that is highlighted by Just's case study of the Dou Donggo. As he describes it, the ritualized, but informal, processes among the Dou Donggo are possible because the elders are known to be restoring the underlying cosmic and social order, which is taken for granted by the community.

In the U.S., by contrast, the judges of the higher courts obtain their authority from the status of their office, which is symbolized in the clothes and trappings of grandeur. Here, as Just points out, order is something that has to be created and imposed on a heterogeneous population. There is no assumption of an underlying social order. The rituals and moral symbolism of the parliament chamber and the court room stand for the elaborately-maintained, all-encompassing order that is guaranteed by the state. Symbols of order can also serve to legitimate the state's authority to use force and violence, of course. It is also now well accepted that engendering a fear of disorder in a population – the imminent threat of terrorism, for example – can successfully legitimate an increase in governmental control in the name of security (Nader 1997). What might otherwise appear as political oppression comes to be accepted as legitimate social control.

Theories of Order

As Roberts points out in his chapter in this volume, two models of order recur in sociological theory, that of the leader and the following, often over-simplistically attributed to Weber, and that of the shared, articulated repertoire of norms, generally associated with the theories of Durkheim. Individual chapters affirm the continuing importance of such models. Social norms remain integral to the construction, maintenance and apprehension of social order and so do institutions, such as the state, that set out to guarantee or impose order. Moreover, as Roberts emphasizes, the issue of attachment between subject and polity and of commitment to norms remains important. What many of the chapters in this volume illustrate, however, is not just the ambiguous role frequently played by the state, but also the parallel institutions that arise, flourish and, often as not, disappear having established a more limited sphere of order. As many chapters illustrate, and as Roberts in this volume demonstrates, the issue of legitimacy, extensively analysed by Weber (1980), and his categories of traditional, charismatic and rational forms of legitimation, continue to be central to the analysis of such cases. They can be extended to informal ordering institutions and even to understand relations between consumers and producers in a complex civil society.

As well as the importance of ordering institutions, there is a persistent notion in the social sciences that, as Roberts puts it, commitment to a shared, articulated repertoire of norms is indispensable to stable social arrangements. Many conceptions of society are based on the notion that society cannot exist without law and norms, and that without them there is disorder or a state of anomie (Durkheim 1930). Any society must develop patterns of behaviour that produce a certain level of predictability. Patterns and regularities in behaviour lead to reliance and expectations on the part of others, so that they inevitably acquire a normative character. These norms, then, come to reflect not only what people generally do, but also indicate how people should behave. In their study of the Tswana, for example, Comaroff and Roberts (1981: 47) illustrated the way in which the basic principles for inclusion in and exclusion from a social group are laid out in its normative system, in particular in kinship rules. These rules define the structure of the society and form the constitutive order underlying its socio-cultural system. However, Comaroff and Roberts also emphasized the importance of social processes, in this case the legal, in maintaining a dynamic social order. Many of the case studies in this volume have similarly illustrated the continuities and changes in normative orders as they develop in practice, and the existence of different or even multiple understandings. They highlight the presence of ambiguity and the space this allows for manoeuvring and negotiation. They thus complement a number of studies in legal anthropology (Moore 1978,

Nader and Todd 1978, F. von Benda-Beckmann 1979, K. von Benda-Beckmann 1984) that have also considered the dynamic characteristics of normative systems, focussing on processes as much as on rules. The chapters in this volume do not, therefore, cast doubt on the fact that normative systems, contested and changeable as they are, can provide a sound basis for social order. Indeed, several chapters underline the importance of shared norms in generating a sense of predictability and order even, or especially, in cases where state law is distant and unreliable.

Georg Simmel (1908) long ago suggested that convergent and divergent currents are inseparably interwoven in all social units. As Roberts points out in this volume, he suggested that an absolutely centripetal and harmonious group could show no real life process. A viable social order cannot exist without a considerable amount of predictability but it also has to allow for a certain amount of indeterminacy and creativity, lest it become suffocatingly rigid (F. and K. von Benda-Beckmann 1994: 7). We have already mentioned the competition between social norms that characterizes many societies. In very few social situations are spontaneity, creativity and accident unambiguously condemned and even deliberate rule breaking may be valorized. Such studies are complemented by the chapters of Meeker, Spencer, Just and Roberts, which all analyse dynamics of disorder. These are shown to be inherent features of the societies being studied which deserve an explicit focus of attention.

The models of order attributed to Weber and Durkheim thus continue, as Roberts points out, to inform much modern social theory. They are also inherent in the assumptions and models which underlie the decisions of many policy makers and opinion formers in the modern world (Quarles van Ufford and Roth 2003). The anthropologist should not, therefore, be too quick to abandon their analytic legacy. As Spencer, in this volume, suggests, however, another important, but largely unacknowledged, model of order has arisen in the recent literature on violence and disorder. As he points out, the irreducibility of disorder can be a disturbing and analytically problematic element for the anthropologist, whose task unavoidably involves trying to make sense of another social world. Spencer points out that anthropologists of politics have, since the 1980s, seemingly abandoned their attempts to construct models of political order. The political arenas and processes of the societies they study have, rather, been depicted as sites of instability and contradiction (Taussig 1984, 2003, Nordstrom 1995, Scheper-Hughes and Bourgois 2004). Nevertheless, Spencer suggests, such writers have not abandoned the notion altogether: their analyses do not proceed without any model of order. The structuralist models may have disappeared in their works, but a sense of moral or ethical order has replaced them. Their depictions of violence and oppression, or domination and resistance in particular, set up new dualities and frameworks for analysis. The order of morality may only be implicit but, as Spencer demonstrates, it underlies their depictions of chaos and disorder.

Conclusion

As the chapters in this volume demonstrate, classic paradigms concerning the role of norms, the legitimation of power and the significance of ritual continue to prove their relevance for an understanding of both order and disorder in the modern world. Moreover, order has not disappeared as a matter of concern for those we study. The anthropologist may graphically illustrate the instability and disorder in which his or her informants are struggling to survive, but simultaneously these same informants will be trying to construct spaces of order out of the chaos of their surroundings.

Most of the chapters in this volume reveal the extent to which the state represents a source of disorder as much as of order. However, even in situations of chaos, and even in a social milieu where there are competing sets of social norms and a lack of state control, people can create spaces and processes of order. The case studies reveal the endlessly creative ways in which they do so, through the establishment of relations of trust, by drawing on images of locality, through appeals to 'ancient' tradition and religious norms, by allowing a certain latitude to those who defy the norms, as well as by employing violent and coercive tactics. Processes of order can be found in the interstices between state and society, in the spaces left by a weak or retreating state or in the disorderly dynamics of the political realm. When asking about order, we would suggest, the question of location is all important. Order is not necessarily a quality of society as a whole.

The case studies also demonstrate the fragility of many of these dynamics of order, the thin line that can be drawn between order and disorder and the centrality of the notion of predictability. They also indicate the deep-seated, underlying ideas about order that many social groups share, ideas that may be unreflected until an event occurs to disturb them, possibly the excessive use of force on the part of those who purport to guarantee order. Such notions of order are not necessarily synonymous with a state of peace and security, which explains why in many situations people can live with violence, competition and rule breaking. Order can be analysed as a state, but it can also be approached as a matter of perception, as a social construction. The anthropologist must pay attention to both and it is the relationship between the state of society, viewed objectively, and local perceptions of order that is one of the most fruitful avenues for enquiry.

Notes

1. Five years have produced at least six volumes: Aijmer and Abbink (2000), Schmidt and Schröder (2001), Stewart and Strathern (2002), Eckert (2004), Scheper-Hughes and Bourgois (2004) and Whitehead (2004).

References

Aijmer, G. and Abbink, J. 2000. *Meanings of Violence: a Cross Cultural Perspective*. Oxford: Berg.
Benda-Beckmann, F. von 1979. *Property in Social Continuity: Continuity and Change in the Maintenance of Property Relationships through Time in Minangkabau, West Sumatra*. The Hague: Martinus Nijhoff.
Benda-Beckmann, F. and K. von 1994. 'Coping with Insecurity' in *Coping with Insecurity. An "Underall" Perspective on Social Security in the Third World*, special issue *Focaal*, 22/23, eds F. and K. von Benda-Beckmann and H. Marks, 7–31.
Benda-Beckmann, K. von 1984. *The Broken Stairways to Consensus: Village Justice and State Courts in Minangkabau*. Dordrecht, Leiden, Cinnaminson: Foris Publications, KITLV Press.
Comaroff, J. and Roberts, S. 1981. *Rules and Processes: the Cultural Logic of Dispute in an African Context*. Chicago: University of Chicago Press.
Durkheim, E. 1930 [1897]. *Le Suicide: Etude de Sociologie*. Paris: F. Alcan.
Eckert, J. ed. 2004. *Anthropologie der Konflikte: Georg Elwerts konflikttheoretische Thesen in der Diskussion*. Bielefeld: transcript.
Ferguson, R.B. and Whitehead, N.L. eds 1992. *War in the Tribal Zone: Expanding States and Indigenous Warfare*. Santa Fe, N.M.: School of American Research Press.
Gell, A. 1996. *The Anthropology of Time: the Cultural Construction of Temporal Maps and Images*. Oxford: Berg.
Giddens, A. 1998. *The Third Way: the Renewal of Social Democracy*. Cambridge: Polity Press.
Leach, E.R. 1961. *Rethinking Anthropology*. London: Athlone Press.
Moore, S.F. 1978. 'Uncertainties in Situations, Indeterminacies in Cultures' in *Law as Process: an Anthropological Approach*, ed. S.F. Moore, London: Routledge and Kegan Paul, 32–53.
Nader, L. 1997. 'Controlling Processes: Tracing the Dynamic Components of Power', *Current Anthropology*, 38(5), 711–37.
Nader, L. and Todd, H. eds 1978. *The Disputing Process: Law in Ten Societies*. New York: Columbia University Press.
Nordstrom, C. 1995. 'Creativity and Chaos: War on the Front Lines' in *Fieldwork under Fire: Contemporary Studies of Violence and Survival*, eds C. Nordstrom and A. Robben, Berkeley: University of California Press, 129–53.
Quarles van Ufford, P. and Roth, D. 2003. 'The Icarus Effect: the Rise and Fall of Development Optimisms in a Regional Development Project in Luwu District, South Sulawesi, Indonesia' in *A Moral Critique of Development: in Search of Global Responsibilities*, eds P. Quarles van Ufford and K. Giri, London: Routledge, 76–100.
Scheper-Hughes, N. and Bourgois, P. eds 2004. *Violence in War and Peace*. Oxford: Blackwell.
Schmidt, B. and Schröder, I. eds 2001. *Anthropology of Violence and Conflict*. London: Routledge.
Simmel, G. 1908. 'Der Streit' in *Soziologie: Untersuchungen über die Formen der Vergellschaftung*. Frankfurt am Main: Suhrkamp, 186–255.
Stewart, P. and Strathern, A. 2002. *Violence: Theory and Ethnography*. London and New York: Continuum.
Taussig. M. 1984. 'Culture of Terror – Space of Death: Roger Casement's Putumayo Report and the Explanation of Torture', *Comparative Studies in Society and History*, 26(1), 467–97.
——— 2003. *Law in a Lawless Land*. New York: New Press.
Turner, V. 1957. *Schism and Continuity in an African Society: a Study of Ndembu Village Life*. Manchester: Manchester University Press.
——— 1967. *The Forest of Symbols: Aspects of Ndembu Ritual*. Ithaca N.Y.: Cornell University Press.
Weber, M. 1980[1920]. *Wirtschaft und Gesellschaft. Grundriss der verstehenden Soziologie*. Tübingen: J.C.B. Mohr (Paul Siebeck).
Whitehead, N. ed. 2004. *Violence*. Oxford: James Currey.

Chapter 2

ORDER AND THE EVOCATION OF HERITAGE: REPRESENTING QUALITY IN THE FRENCH BISCUIT TRADE

Simon Roberts

'Tradition is more than a particular form of the experience of temporality; it represents the moral command of 'what went before' over the continuity of day-to-day life.'
A. Giddens (1984: 200)

'... our experiences of the present largely depend on our knowledge of the past, and ... our images of the past commonly serve to legitimate a present social order.'
P. Connerton (1989: 3)

'... there probably exists no social unit in which convergent and divergent currents among its members are not inseparably interwoven. An absolutely centripetal and harmonious group ...not only is empirically unreal, it could show no real life process.'
G. Simmel (1908; 1955: 15)

Introduction

Inviting us to reflect on the themes of 'order and disorder', the editors direct our attention back to a vast agenda of unfinished business.[1] Some items on that agenda have been exhaustively considered, even if they remain unresolved. Among those items, two durable if contested assumptions are generally lurking somewhere in the background when we think about the constitution and reproduction of the social world. First, is an idea that a large part of the regularity we see around us can be attributed to the willed achievement of those in power. Second, is the persistent notion that commitment to a shared, articulate repertoire of norms is indispensable to stable social arrangements. In the anthropology and sociology of law, the dominance of these understandings of order has led, in broad schematic terms, to two preoccupations. One of these has been with the conditions of survival of centralized government, and so with the nature of legitimacy claims and lines of 'attachment' between subject and polity. The other has been a related concern with the conditions under which 'rules' acquire and retain validity as law, and more generally with questions surrounding 'commitment' to norms. Associated with both of these questions has been an equally durable idea that different answers to them are required in opposed, imagined contexts respectively labeled 'tradition' and 'modernity'. In this respect, there has also been a strong, and largely unchallenged, tendency – at least over the last thirty years – to think about ritual and symbolic productions, with their predominantly 'illocutionary' as opposed to 'propositional' qualities, as exclusively associated with the legitimacy claims of political hierarchies, and more specifically as a strategic resource associated with 'traditional authority'.[2]

Arguably just as important in marking out pattern and providing social continuity, yet far less fully explored, are our understandings about provenance and 'quality' in the things with which we surround ourselves in the material world. These understandings – closely linked to 'the past', to locality and to a particular cultural heritage – inform what we choose to use and consume, and hence significantly shape any social group.[3] Much of the time – as is the case with other aspects of culture – such understandings remain implicit, visible in and transmitted through practice, without necessarily receiving discursive formulation at all. However, in all but the simplest arenas of production and consumption, two features are likely to be present. First, we very generally come to rely on others to make decisions about quality for us. Second, we have to choose between competitors for our trust in making those decisions. Under such conditions, understandings about quality are likely to be made explicit as those others seek to justify our trust and claim their superiority over competitors. So one important context in which these understandings receive discursive formulation will be in representations made in the course of complex interactions between producers/suppliers and consumers.

In addressing this perhaps neglected dimension of order, it is certainly not intended here to deny the importance of 'command' or of 'rules' in shaping the social world. Today, to be sure, command can be found everywhere, and almost everything we read about tends to reflect it. The shrinkages and failures of 'the state' provide a pervasive backdrop to discussion in this volume, whether we are reading about drunken youths in Siberian villages or out of control paramilitary men in West Africa. But there is the danger that, as Clifford Geertz memorably insisted in *Negara* 'impressed with command, we see little else' (1982: 121). Again, discursive formulation of 'rules' is an important phenomenon in any polity; but we must not lose sight of other dimensions of articulated cosmologies. There is also the further point that we can claim too much for discursive formulation generally if we take it as our starting point, as Durkheim perhaps did when he claimed – in what now must also be seen as a terribly politically incorrect formulation – that: 'even the humblest have their cosmology' (1976: 428). In doing so he marginalizes implicit, unstated understandings. An increasingly strong message from cognitive science suggests that in many respects deployment of such an explicit cosmology is peripheral to the way we learn and the way we act.[4] If we begin the discussion of order with cosmology, we risk neglecting really interesting questions surrounding the circumstances under which unspoken understanding becomes replaced by explicit, discursive formulation and the manner in which we should interpret the presence of such formulations.

In summary, I am proposing for the purposes of this paper a fourfold shift of focus, rather than any direct challenge to powerful, long established orthodoxies:[5]

- From the 'legitimacy' claims of government to the 'authenticity' claims of producers and suppliers of goods in civil society;
- From areas of the cosmology dealing with normative prescriptions to those concerned with identifying and representing quality in the sphere of consumption;
- From a conception of tradition as a more or less discrete precursor of 'modernity' to one under which tradition constitutes a central element of the life world in the present;
- From ritual and symbolic representations as a property of traditional authority to ritual as a general feature of society.

In doing so I am also intent on relocating the discussion to explore those points at which implicit, unsaid cultural understandings give way to explicit formulation.

In bringing this proposed shift down from abstraction to a concrete level, it would have been possible to use representations drawn from almost any sphere of production and consumption in the West – we could have begun with Frank Cooper's 'Original' Oxford thick cut marmalade or with stories of the European wine trade.[6] But this paper draws upon an apparently simple story of commercial competition in one tiny area of the French grocery trade, that concerned with the manufacture and marketing of biscuits known as *les galettes bretonnes*. I look in the first instance to the nature of representations made about provenance and quality in the course of this competition, as two firms struggle to present themselves as originating, and their products as exemplars of, a particular culinary tradition. Their discursive productions draw explicitly on local culture and heritage in representing these biscuits as linked to a 'traditional' Breton life world – an Arcadian association presumed to make them, at the beginning of the twenty-first century, more desirable objects of purchase and consumption.

Representing Authenticity in the French Biscuit Trade

In France, the foundation of gastronomic authenticity claims in 'tradition' and through invocation of local cultural heritage is reflected everywhere in explicit links between 'tradition' and 'quality'. The phrase *tradition et qualité* appears again and again in the advertising and on the packaging of an enormous range of food products. In memory, the olden days (*l'antan*) are characterized by food of local provenance and manual, craft production (*fabrication/production artisanale*). These memories – of *le vrai* and *l'authentique*, 'the real' and 'the authentic'(English gloss/translation after foreign terms) – are energetically invoked by suppliers and woven into the cultural fabric of the present through their produce.

A Tale of Two Firms

In the south Finistère town of Pont-Aven, small round butter biscuits known as *les galettes bretonnes* have long been made. These biscuits have two conventional forms – the thin, crisp *galettes fines* and the thicker, crumbly *galettes épaisses*. Today, a majority of the *galettes* baked in Pont-Aven is produced by two local companies, SA Biscuiterie Penven and SA Biscuiterie Traou Mad.[7] Their principal local outlets are their own shops, close together near the *le port* on the estuary at the bottom of the town; their modern factories also lie directly opposite each other, alone in the fields, in a *zone artisanale* above the Aven valley.

At least from the mid 1980s, any attentive visitor would have quickly recognized Biscuiterie Traou Mad as the apparently larger, more vigorous manufacturer: they have a second shop near the bridge at the town centre; their factory is bigger; their *galettes* are sold in the principal national supermarkets (Leclerc, Intermarche and Ecomarche), on the ferries out of Brittany ports and through some luxury food outlets across Europe and North America; text in six languages appears on the packaging of their products. Biscuiterie Penven presents itself deliberately as a small, 'family' firm, intent on delivery of 'quality' rather than on capturing a mass market. In Pont-Aven itself, their biscuits are sold only in their own shop and in one other outlet (on the site of the original Penven *boulangerie*). This strategy is also reflected in its approach to the market outside Pont-Aven – until recently limited to a few specialist outlets.[8] Their exclusive approach to marketing is epitomized in their link with the well-established specialist grocery distributor Albert Ménès.[9] That firm supplies a range of three hundred and eighty 'produits d'épicerie fine issus de la tradition',[10] under the guarantee of its own label, to a nationwide network of food retailers. Albert Ménès also sells these lines – among them, Biscuiterie Penven's *galettes épaisses* – directly through its own boutique in the 8th *arrondissment* of Paris.[11]

Viewed in the summer of 2001, the window displays of Biscuiterie Penven and Biscuiterie Traou Mad also revealed apparently contrasting types of authenticity claim. Penven displayed faded sepia photographs of Isidore Penven and the granite building at 4 Rue des Abbés Tanguy in the centre of town where, as a local baker, he is said to have started to make and sell *galettes* in 1890. His recipes for *galettes*, 'au beurre frais de baratte Breton', were claimed to be 'conservées intactes par ses descendants'. Traou Mad, on the other hand, placed in the foreground of their display a large printed notice drawing the public's attention to the fact that 'nos specialités Traou Mad et Les Galettes de Pont-Aven sont des marques déposées a L'Institut de la Propriété Industrial (INPI).' The notice also claimed these marques to be 'confirmé par La Cour d'Appel de Rennes dans son Arrêt de 14 Mars 2001.'

At first sight, these respective appeals – to long establishment, the use of local ingredients and a 'family' recipe on the one hand; and to the support of a modern regulatory standards agency and contemporary jural authority on the other – suggest a simple 'tradition' versus 'modernity' opposition. Traou Mad undoubtedly wants to present itself as a large, up to date commercial enterprise, attentive to hygiene, with ambitions of global reach for its products.[12] In contrast Penven has deliberately presented itself as a small family enterprise, offering a traditional, handcrafted product in a predominantly local market. Holidaymakers at that time were already encouraged to visit the Penven factory, taste the butter and dough from which *galettes bretonnes* are made, and watch two busy cooks preparing biscuits by hand for the oven, with the aid of some quaint, apparently early-nineteenth-century, machinery. Public viewing of the supposedly more mechanized operation across the road at Traou Mad was not then permitted; maintenance of hygiene and the safety of members of the public in a work place were the reasons given for this prohibition.[13]

However, that first impression conveys only one element of complex strategies through which this market competition is pursued. The very name Traou Mad – in Breton literally 'good things' – has a deep traditional resonance. That corporation also joins Penven in making direct, self-conscious appeals to tradition. It describes its product on the wrapping as made 'tout au beurre frais *a l'ancienne*' [their italics] and as representing an 'Authentique Tradition de Pont-Aven'. Their packets and tins at the same time identify the company as '*Fondée en 1920*'.

In common, Biscuiterie Penven and Biscuiterie Traou Mad also make strong attempts to advertise their products by linking them with the local cultural past on a visual level. Two particular sources representing that heritage are relied on heavily. The first lies in the famous local *faience* work, pottery and porcelain hand painted with Arcadian scenes of peasant life. Second are the paintings of Breton landscapes and country people by Paul Gauguin and other members of the School of Pont-Aven. In the case of Biscuiterie Penven, the claim of a direct link is made on their packaging: 'Les peintres de l'école de Pont-Aven, nombreux à cette époque, fréquentaient souvent la Maison Penven.' On some of their biscuits too, the names and dates of leading members of the School of Pont-Aven are impressed ('P. Gauguin 1848–1903'; 'E. Bernard 1868–1941'; 'P. Serusier 1863–1927'). In the case of Biscuiterie Traou Mad, a reproduction of Gauguin's *Breton Girls Dancing* (1888) provides the centrepiece of their contemporary (2005) presentational design.

A visitor returning in the summer of 2002 would have noticed a new element to Penven's presentational strategy. In that year the firm also made an appeal to modern legal authority, in a typed notice attached to the door of its shop. This notice drew attention to the fact that the Court of Appeal at Rennes, in its *arrêt* of 14 March 2001, recognized the generic character of the term *galette* and the historic priority of Penven in manufacturing it. The notice went on to relate that the court at the same time ordered Biscuiterie Traou Mad, at that company's expense, to publish the whole judgement in a newspaper chosen by Penven. It turned out that this order represented the concluding moment of an action commenced by Traou Mad against Penven in 1997 on the ground that the packaging of their products constituted a *contrefaçon* (lit. 'forgery'; perhaps to be translated as 'passing off' in the terminology of English common law).

At this point, what might so far have appeared to the outsider as a straightforward story of commercial competition in the French biscuit trade becomes visibly a 'dispute'. That dispute turns out to have a complex history, involving a bitter family quarrel.

A Consequence of Two Marriages

It is generally acknowledged in the locality that the Penven family, local bakers, were making and selling *galettes* in the town by the end of the nineteenth century. Isidore Penven took over from his father at the family bakery on Rue des Abbés Tanguy around 1890 and is credited by his descendants with starting to make these biscuits. But Isidore, who was married to Francine Le Gall, died young in 1914. He left Francine with their son Robert, at that time aged seven.

Traou Mad's origins lie in Francine's second marriage to Alexis Le Villain. Together they started to make biscuits in 1920, apparently according to the Penven recipe, from their house in Rue Rosmadec. In 1924, Robert, on leaving school, joined his step-father when the latter moved production to new premises on Rue du Port. This arrangement continued for many years with Robert working alongside members of the family of his mother Francine's second marriage. Robert's role in the enterprise became an important one, overseeing the kitchen and carrying out the specialist task of preparing *la pate*, the dough from which the biscuits were made.

It seems that there were long-term tensions between Robert Penven and children from 'the house' of his mother's second marriage. Anyway, in 1952 Robert left to start his own firm nearby on Quai Théodore Botrel. He formed a company, SA Biscuiterie Penven, selling biscuits made according to his own recipe under the label 'Les Délices de Pont-Aven'. Following Robert's death in 1970, his widow continued the firm, hiring an expert *patissier* Albert Lamande. Soon the management passed to their daughter Annie. Annie Penven actively expanded the firm, moving production to modern factory premises in a newly designated *zone artisanale* outside the town on the road to Rosporden in 1974.

On Robert's departure, the management of the Le Villain business remained in the hands of his youngest half-sister, Marguerite Le Villain, who registered the enterprise as SA Biscuiterie Le Villain (1952). Marguerite seems to have developed that firm actively, emphasizing the specifically Breton character of the enterprise and particularly promoting one of their lines, the thicker *galette épaisse*, sold under the label *Traou Mad*, the name under which the firm itself was subsequently reregistered. Biscuiterie Le Villain also moved to modern factory premises, immediately opposite those of Penven, in 1974. The Le Villain family eventually sold the company to M. Jean Mentheour in 1985. A period of energetic expansion of sales across France and abroad has followed,[14] latterly under Jean's son Thierry. The sale of Biscuiterie Traou Mad 'out of the family' provided the context for the ensuing transformation of the conflict between the two firms into the public sphere of litigation.

The Construction of Separate Histories

The promotional literatures of the two firms present apparently separate 'histories', giving few clues to the kinship linkages and family quarrels between them. Biscuiterie Penven explicitly dates its origins to the establishment of Isidore Penven's bakery on Rue des Abbés Tanguy in 1890. A portrait of Isidore and a contemporary photograph of the granite building at 4 Rue des Abbés Tanguy appear on packets and tins of Penven's biscuits today. The Penven story continues with the opening of Robert's shop on Quai Théodore Botrel in 1952, the move to the *zone artisanale* in 1974 and subsequent growth thanks to the energy of Isidore's granddaughter Annie Penven.

The Traou Mad story is presented very differently. It postpones the commercial production of *les galettes* in Pont-Aven to the entrepreneurial energy of the spouses Alexis and Francine Le Villain in the period immediately following the First World War.[15] As noted above, the legend '*Fondée en 1920*' appears on Traou Mad's packaging. The story continues with

Francine's efforts to sell the biscuits at country fairs during the difficult times of the 1930s, the incorporation of the firm in 1952 as SA Biscuiterie Le Villain by Marguerite, the move to the *zone artisanale* in 1974, the subsequent sale of the enterprise to Jean Mentheour and its continued growth till the present under his own son, Thierry.

Conspicuously, both firms write each other firmly out of the story. The link with Isidore, the hiatus following Isidore's death and Robert's long involvement is ignored in the Traou Mad story. Similarly the enterprise of Francine and her second husband in the post-war period receive no recognition in the Penven account.

Yet, what would an account of evolution in the biscuit trade around Pont-Aven be worth without an understanding of the consequences of Isidore Penven's early death? What would that trade look like today if M. Penven had not died young, opening the way to conflict between the issue of Francine's successive 'houses'? We simply cannot understand this history without knowing of Francine's first marriage to Isidore and her second one to Alexis. The palpable, predictable tensions arising between the two 'houses' born to Francine's successive marriages, publicly revealed in Robert's initial rupture with Marguerite in 1952 and then living on in the subsequent rivalry between Marguerite and Robert's daughter Annie, shape much of this story.

Analysis

While recognizing the care taken by those aspiring to be 'in charge' to secure provenance, construct genealogies and deploy 'tradition' instrumentally[16] as a basis of legitimacy, and the extensive scholarly attention given to these strategies, this paper turns instead to kindred strategies in civil society. Here two French biscuit manufacturers are seen to claim authenticity for their products by representing them as heritage objects linked to local cultural tradition. In that respect, this story also forces us to prise the discussion of ritual and symbolism away from questions of political domination because here, the 'symbolic resources' of locality, local culture and heritage are invoked in the context of civil society to underpin the marketing strategies of these two firms. On another level, this story illustrates in the context of civil society the very complex relationship between competition and rule breach more fully explored in struggles for political office.

From Legitimacy to Authenticity

A central strategy of both Biscuiterie Penven and Biscuiterie Traou Mad is to provide their *galettes* with charters of quality and authenticity by anchoring these products to supposedly deep traditions of Breton produce and cookery. A particular picture is evoked of local produce and cuisine – the fresh butter made on local farms, the wholesome flour ground from locally grown wheat in the once numerous mills of the tiny town of Pont-Aven,[17] and the longstanding continuities of local craft production (*la fabrication artisanale*) traced through the 'lineages' of the 'ancestral' figures of Isidore Penven and his widow in her second marriage to Le Villain. These material dimensions are concurrently supplemented in the representations of both firms by symbolic resources, as wider features of local culture and heritage are drawn on for presentational purposes, linking the products in to a mythical, Arcadian past on a visual level.

At the heart of these presentational constructions is the represented association of *les galettes bretonnes* with time past. The marketing assumption is that these biscuits must be good because the producers have been making them for a long time. Biscuiterie Penven claims to have been making biscuits '*Depuis 1890*', reproducing on their packets a sepia photograph of the premises at 4 Rue des Abbés Tanguy with the Penven name painted on the wall. The same association is sought by Biscuiterie Traou Mad with the claim '*Fondée en 1920*'.

Central also is a notion of locality – 'Pont-Aven' itself. People will want to buy these biscuits because of their association with a particular place – a picturesque village with a rushing boulder-strewn stream and many water mills, built around a bridge at the bottom of a steep, wooded valley. This is part of what SA Biscuiterie Traou Mad is trying to capture in registering the marque 'Les Galettes de *Pont-Aven*', and Biscuiterie Penven in using the label 'Les Délices de *Pont-Aven*' (original italics).

With that notion of place is linked local agriculture and the handcrafted production involved in simple country cooking. In making their biscuits 'au beurre frais de baratte Breton' and local wheat flour, Penven claims to respect 'scrupuleusement les ingrédients d'origine'. Traou Mad's biscuits, 'tout au beurre frais *à l'ancienne*', 'subliment le saveur authentique de la farine de froment'. The latter corporation, in registering the marque 'Traou Mad', seeks to capture and exclusively exploit the wholesome essence of traditional local produce and cookery.

A further dimension of the marketing strategies of both firms is to invoke, and associate their biscuits with, representations of Breton cultural tradition re-assembled – 'invented' in Hobsbawm and Ranger's sense (1983) – during the latter part of the nineteenth century. This representation of tradition appears to have originated concurrently in the local *faience* industry around Quimper and in the work of painters of the School of Pont-Aven. The packaging of both firms has reproduced country scenes and people in traditional dress used to decorate the local *faience* work – in earthenware and porcelain – for which this part of Brittany is famous. The use of Breton rural scenes on crockery does not apparently go back very far historically. The great Quimper firm, H.B. Henriot, claims that the now familiar Breton peasant figures first appear in the 1860s and that the firm started using these decorations on their earthenware and porcelain only in the 1880s.[18] In this context, it is an interesting question how far M. Isidore Penven was in 1890 – like his compatriot M. Henriot down the road in Quimper – already self-consciously exploiting his Breton cultural heritage to satisfy the cravings for 'authenticity' of that early wave of artistic visitors?

At the same time, both Penven and Traou Mad use reproductions of landscape and farming scenes recalling the style of Gauguin, who lived and worked in and around Pont-Aven between 1886 and 1890.[19] So, in this instance, idyllic representations of Breton culture created for/and associated with an earlier wave of visitors to Brittany are re-exploited at the end of the twentieth century. SA Biscuiterie Traou Mad claims in its own history[20] that M. Montheour had the 'brilliant idea' of harnessing Gauguin's artistic heritage to marketing *les galettes* in 1990 when reproductions of the latter's paintings begun to appear on the Traou Mad packaging (realizing 'la marriage de la peinture et de la gastronomie', as the firm puts it).[21]

Competition and Rule Breach

This long struggle between the Penvens and the Le Villains underlines Georg Simmel's early insistence (Simmel 1908) that, while competition and rule breach may be distinguished analytically, they are very often interwoven in the interactions of everyday life. The dispute underlines – in the different context of civil society – Victor Turner's now classical warning about any approach to the analysis of political conflict that relies on a simple opposition between competition and rule breach. The complexity of any such polarization, from an ethnographic perspective, is beautifully illustrated in his early monograph, *Schism and Continuity in an African Society* (1957). There Turner describes how the headship of Ndembu community must devolve on a male member of the senior matrilineage in the village; but no detailed rules specify which member this is to be – that is a matter of individual achievement and acceptance. So whenever an existing head shows signs of growing old and loosing his grip, younger members of the matrilineage compete among themselves for the headship. Bitter quarrels attend this competition, typically involving claims of wrongdoing and accusations of witchcraft and sorcery. It is only as the new head manages to establish his ascendancy that this all subsides and disappointed competitors either knuckle down under the new regime or leave the village and found their own communities. In Turner's vivid ethnography we see these general processes being acted out through the career of a particular aspirant for headship, Sandombu. In the poignant story of successive failures to achieve the headship of his village, structural features and Sandombu's personal frailties are brought inextricably together.

Through that account Turner reveals a process in which claims about wrong are closely interwoven with struggles for political ascendancy and competition for resources. In the constantly negotiated nature of Ndembu life, we cannot usefully view conflict as somehow in contrast to normal life processes – assertions of rule breach simply represent one means through which competition for political ascendancy is taken forward.

The present case history makes exactly the same points in the context of commercial competition. Biscuiterie Penven and Biscuiterie Traou Mad are struggling to sell a virtually identical product, initially within the limited market created by the tourist season in Brittany and then across a wider field. In the course of this competition, trademarks are registered, a 'dispute' over these is generated and litigation undertaken by Biscuiterie Traou Mad to protect them. Behind this competition, Isidore Penven's early death sets the scene in structural terms for his widow's second marriage to Alexis Le Villain and subsequently the ensuing opportunity for conflict between the issue of the two 'houses'. Underlying all this, at the micro level, we see Robert Penven's break with his half-sister Marguerite and the bitter personal enmity subsequently continuing between Marguerite and Robert's daughter Annie, hostility carried over in relations between M. Mentheour and Penven following the sale of Biscuiterie Traou Mad out of the family.

More generally, this small case study brings into the foreground the (perhaps obvious) micro human complexities that may underlie apparently straightforward, macro processes associated with culture, heritage and commercial competition. From a starting point provided by the careers of individual bakers in Pont-Aven, both general features of the French biscuit trade and the constitution of consumer life worlds are examined. In attempting to integrate these micro and macro levels of analysis, I draw gratefully on the theoretical resources provided by Cicourel and Collins in the last decades of the twentieth century.[22]

Concluding Remarks

I have argued here that this discourse of grocers about authenticity is, on the level of 'civil society', an analogue of the legitimacy claims advanced by government in any contemporary polity. Just as the claim to domination in the political sphere inevitably calls up a justificatory discourse, so too do the exigencies of commercial competition. Thus even though I am trying to move the discussion away from the hegemonic grasp of centralized 'command', these correspondences make it sensible to treat explicitly as one starting point Weber's treatment of legitimacy in *Economy and Soci-*

ety (1978). The authenticity claims dealt with here immediately appear to match Weber's threefold typology – the traditional, the charismatic (exemplified in the sepia photograph of a founding father, Isidore Penven) and the rational/legal (the foundation of Traou Mad's litigation). Similarly, the equally dominating clutches of normative order exerted by Durkheim's foundational discussion in *The Elementary Forms of the Religious Life* (1976) must not distract us from counterparts in other areas of the cosmology discussed here. Moving on, we need to orient ourselves self-consciously to this intellectual heritage; there are hidden dangers in the formative, partially clandestine legacy of classical social theory.

Exploring here, in a very preliminary way, representations about quality and 'authenticity' in a tiny sector of the French biscuit trade, we have found the self-conscious invocation of 'tradition', at the end of the twentieth century and the beginning of the twenty-first, as a means of providing a charter of authenticity for a commercial product. This is done in a particular way, by giving explicit, discursive formulation to common cultural understandings about quality, generally residing in – and transmitted through – practice. In making these representations, the producers seek to ground that product symbolically, associating it with a locality, that locality's heritage of production and cuisine, and the Breton culture of the region.

Thinking about this, we need to understand 'tradition' in senses distinguishable from that used in, say, the work of Weber and Luhmann (1970). There tradition appears primarily as no more than a thinly characterized, largely unexamined foil where exploring the nature of 'modernity' is the central interest. We are looking here at contemporary, self-conscious appeals to tradition in which elements of an exemplary, even idealized, Arcadian past are explicitly evoked to form part of the lifeworld of the present.

So we are dealing with – and need to distinguish between – two dimensions of tradition, identified long ago by Pocock (1972) and Giddens (1979). First, just as some of our foundational assumptions around authority and normative understandings remain on an implicit level – they 'go without saying' – the same is true of corresponding understandings about 'quality'. *Some* practical sense of appropriateness, of fitness for purpose, will inform the selection of things we own, use, and consume in everyday life. Such understandings, culturally determined and probably quite localized, embody some notion of 'provenance' – a matter of where it came from, who made it, and what materials they used – whether or not this is subject to discursive formulation. That will be so even where trust and confidence in a particular source has been built up through repeated transaction between particular suppliers and consumers over a long period of time. In analytic terms, such tacit understandings about quality are founded in 'tradition' in the simplest sense (Giddens 1979: 200).

We are concerned here with 'tradition' in a different sense, focusing on the moment when such unspoken understandings are co-opted and transformed into explicit, discursive representations of 'tradition' as a marker of quality. Here we have moved to an arena of production and consumption in which we have come to rely on others to make decisions about quality for us. In doing so we have to choose between competitors for our trust in making those decisions. With growing complexity, or where we find ourselves in an unfamiliar context, the identity of a particular producer (a 'brand') itself provides a guarantee of quality, not just in respect of a single product but in making generalized choices about quality for us. That is what M. Ménès is doing here (and compare the related role occupied by, for example, Heinz's '57' Varieties). In some sectors these understandings are, of course, hedged about – even in part constructed – by dense, complex regimes of regulation. Obvious examples are provided by the regulatory frameworks of the cheese and wine trades in European states.

In this universe, a dual transformation has taken place. First, the latent continuities inherent in the simple notion of tradition discussed first are superceded by the allocation to 'tradition' of explicit, articulated *value* as the basis of quality. Second, as understandings about quality come to receive discursive formulation, these 'native' articulations are utilized in instrumental ways by both producers and consumers.

This transformation needs to be looked at from the perspectives of both producers and consumers. Whatever the commercial strategies and imperatives of the corporations behind them, the local producers, self-consciously working with recipes used in the past, in an explicitly designated *zone artisanale*, arguably feel themselves a part of an enterprise akin to the Arts and Crafts Movement that spread across Europe and North America in the late nineteenth century (just as their compatriot M. Henriot with his *faience* pottery in Quimper had at the time undoubtedly been). In that movement, rural life, craftsmanship and the beauty of natural materials were re-evaluated in terms of a response to consequences of industrialization. Here a Breton culinary heritage is explicitly invoked, to provide a cultural charter, in the formation and practice of an artisanal lifeworld in the present.

Looking to the purchasers and consumers of these biscuits, given the general point that they may need specialist help in choosing a product, why do they seek 'tradition'? Why do they crave this added substance, this extra thickness that the discursive link with cultural heritage purveys? What is it that the artifacts of *biscuiteries* Penven and Traou Mad provide? And why do French buyers want intermediaries like M. Ménès to locate, identify, and certify 'le produit le plus vrai' for them? Why is it not enough for them just to go out into the market place, prod the cheeses, nibble the biscuits, ask the seller which she thinks are 'the best' and then make their own decisions? One argument here must be that specialist producers like Penven and Traou Mad, and intermediaries like M. Ménès, not only sell 'good' biscuits but fulfill a more important, if latent, function in redressing an experienced cultural deficit in the lifeworld, satisfying a yearning for apparently fugitive 'authenticity'.

There is the additional complexity that many buyers of these biscuits will have travelled to Brittany from abroad. For them, of course, Breton cultural understandings *have* to be made explicit if they are to have any resonance at all. But beyond that, what are they looking for, in choosing to appropriate these elements from beyond their own cultural inheritance? In buying *les galettes*, and taking them back to eat far away, they too are refreshing their lifeworlds. But they are doing so vicariously, reinventing themselves at more than one remove through co-opting material and symbolic links with somebody else's (in this case the Bretons') reconstructed genealogies and cultural representations. For those who buy these delicacies outside Pont-Aven – by courtesy perhaps of the efforts of M. Ménès – the link is more remote; but what is happening is essentially the same. They are acquiring a bit of someone else's cultural heritage to furnish their own lifeworlds, in the present, with meanings inherent in a borrowed genealogy and claimed associations with a foreign Arcadian past. This does not make the practice and the associated understandings any less real as a component in the lifeworld of those involved. This is just something tourists 'do' – just as members of the gentry and aristocracy went to Venice in the eighteenth century and came back with Guardi's *vedute* to hang on their walls.

Obviously, critiques of this overall approach and of my specific account of what is going on here could readily be mounted. First, the very argument that this discourse of grocers about authenticity is, on the level of 'civil society', an analogue of the legitimacy claims advanced by government in any contemporary polity may be questioned. So too may my effort to see correspondences between what is going on here to that larger cosmology of which legal rules form another part. Looking first to the idea of an analogy between the authenticity claims of biscuit manufacturers in 'civil society' and the legitimacy claims advanced by government in the public sphere, there are quite strong strands in sociological theory that encourage us to see the rationalities/understandings/discourses of the public sphere as radically different to those of the private. Certainly, for example, Jürgen Habermas consistently maintains such a position in postulating 'system' and the 'lifeworld' as separate spheres across the long journey from *Legitimation Crisis* (1976) to *The Theory of Communicative Action* (1987). Again, some authoritative readings of Weber's classic discussion of legitimate authority in *Economy and Society* (1978) confine us to thinking about tradition, as well as the field of ritual and symbolism, not only as a feature of 'the past' but also as having to do exclusively with political domination. Maurice Bloch (1974, 1986), for example, in his pathbreaking ethnography of political language and oratory in the Merina kingdom in Madagascar, insists upon linking ritual productions to processes of political domination. He argues further that the invocation of ritual and symbolic representations is a characteristic of a traditional rather than a modern world.

Again, the 'authenticity' of the associations made in the representations discussed here, and the purposes for which the understandings behind them are being evoked, could undoubtedly be questioned along the lines famously undertaken by Hobsbawm and Ranger in *The Invention of Tradition* (1983). The 'traditions' involved here are openly recognized as being of quite limited historical depth. Complex issues of colonial domination perhaps also surround the co-option of Breton culture in an essentially 'French' biscuit trade. Again, Mlle Penven and M. Mentheour are astute people of business, selling luxury goods in a modern, stratified society. The same questions surround their customers, some of whom may be snobbish, wealthy tourists anxious to bring home gifts that will impress their friends. In this context, it can be no accident that M. Ménès' one boutique should be located in the expensive 8th *arrondissment* of Paris, at the point where les Boulevards Haussmann and Malesherbes meet. M. Ménès' shop is in that very *quartier* of Paris where Marcel Proust spent his life – and we hardly need to be reminded here of the vast literary, sociological and psychological construction that Proust built around the capacity of French *patisserie* to furnish the present by evoking the past.[23] But none of these potential worries seem to me to undermine the simple point I am making here, that memories of our material surroundings in the past – whatever their provenance and mode of transmission – significantly inform the order of the present.

Coming back to the links I began by making between legitimacy claims associated with political domination and the claims as to quality advanced for commercial products in civil society, there is perhaps one further interesting correspondence. Weber advanced his original arguments in the troubled atmosphere of late-nineteenth-century and early-twentieth-century Europe. Today, anxieties are expressed once again as to the means of generating political 'attachment' to increasingly heterogeneous aggregations at both national and transnational level.[24] The representations of culture and heritage at the level of civil society in late modernity, revealed in this fragment of ethnography, can also be understood as direct counterparts – responding, in both their propositional and symbolic dimensions, to the same anxious longing for a safe, ordered world.

Acknowledgements

I am very grateful for the sensitive and expert editorial help of Keebet von Benda-Beckmann, Fernanda Pirie and Gesine Koch in Halle; and for the comments of Tatiana Flessas, Nicola Lacey, Martin Loughlin, Alain Pottage, Marian Roberts, Edite Ronnen and Ting Xu in London.

Notes

1. Any return to this agenda needs to acknowledge the magisterial survey of the field provided by Wrong (1994).
2. Bloch (1974, 1975).
3. For an early, rich exploration of the manner in which general understandings of the past configure our experience of the present, see Halbwachs (1925, 1992).
4. See generally, Bloch (1998).
5. But I shall firmly follow Hobsbawm and Ranger (1983) in arguing both that we can find 'tradition' widely employed instrumentally in the representations of all 'modern' polities; and that we can safely, profitably have a discussion of ritual and symbolism away from the question of political domination.
6. An interesting start in that direction is made in the acclaimed documentary *Mondovino*; see www.Mondovino-Lefilm.com
7. Numerous brands of *galettes* manufactured further afield are also sold in Pont-Aven. A third local producer, Biscuiterie de Pont-Aven, now also provides increasingly energetic competition.
8. Biscuiterie Penven now claims export links with Japan, Germany and Ireland: http://www.galettes-penven.com.
9. http://www.albertmenes.fr/index.php
10. A range that Albert Ménès boastfully presents as 'un véritable "Conservatoire" des produits d'épicerie fine'.
11. At 41 Boulevard Malesherbes, Paris 8. Albert Ménès, himself a Breton, established his own business selling exotic groceries in 1921 after an earlier career at sea. Set upon 'La Quête de l'Authentique', the firm's mission is to find and market groceries made by 'les meilleurs producteurs artisanaux ... au savoir-faire ancestral', to 'recherche du produit le plus vrai, élaboré selon des criteres de qualité et de maitrise du savoir faire'.
12. This ambition is stated explicitly on the corporation's web site and in its promotional literature.
13. But note that this policy has changed and visits are now advertised (June 2005: http://www.finisteretourisme.com).
14. In the current promotional literature of SA Traou Mad Francine and Alexis Le Villain are credited with the idea of making and selling *galettes*. No mention is made of the fact that Francine was the widow of Isidore Penven; she first appears under her maiden name, Le Gall. The foundation of the firm in 1920 is simply described in these terms: 'Les époux Le Villain on l'idée de fabriquer les galettes dans leur maison familiale et de les vendre sur les marchés de Bretagne' (Traou Mad promotional statement, 2003).
15. Biscuiterie Traou Mad's packaging states: 'A Pont-Aven, les bonnes choses ont une historire ... En 1886, le peintre Paul GAUGUIN fit chanter les couleurs de cette petite cité bretonne ... Quelques années plus tard, en 1920, un autre artiste, gastronome celui-là, créa de nouvelles gourmandises'.
16. Such representations can be found widely in modern political oratory, in institutional design and in the public built environment. Take, for example, the recurring, unambiguous references to classicism in North American court architecture. Similarly, when the Royal Courts of Justice in London were relocated in the 1860s as part of a larger move to modernize the administration of justice, the architect G.E. Street's winning Gothic design chose to make 'consistent use and adaptation of the English style of the C13' (Pevsner 1973: 321).
17. A local saying has it that there used to be fourteen mills and fifteen houses in Pont-Aven.
18. Pamphlet on H.B. Henriot firm history available at their Lochmaria Pottery.

19. The Post-Impressionist painter was living at Pension Gloanec (now 5 Place Paul Gauguin) in the centre of the town when he and a group of colleagues, including Emile Bernard (1868–1941), resolved to form 'the School of Pont-Aven' in 1888.
20. See the corporation's home page of June 2005 at: www.traoumad.com/fr/default-detail.html
21. On the packets of *les galettes épaisses* the firm tells this story: 'En 1886, le peintre Paul GAUGUIN fit chanter les couleurs de cette petite cité bretonne, pleine de caractère et de lumière. Quelques années plus tard, en 1920, un autre artiste, gastronome celui-là, créa des nouvelles gourmandises: LES TRAOU MAD (bonnes choses en Breton) et LES GALETTES DE PONT-AVEN'. Traou Mad's present packaging reproduces Gauguin's 'Breton Girls Dancing' (1888).
22. An account of these resources appears in Knorr-Cetina and Cicourel (1981).
23. 'And suddenly the memory revealed itself. The taste was of that little piece of Madeleine ....' (Proust 2002: 53).
24. See, for example, the discussion in the 1998 Special Issue of *Public Culture*, particularly Appadurai (1998: 443–49).

References

Appadurai, A. 1998. 'Full Attachment', *Public Culture*, 10(2), 159–66.
Biscuiterie Traou Mad. http://www.traoumad.com/fr/default-detail.html (accessed June 2005).
Bloch, M. 1974. 'Symbols, Song, Dance and Features of Articulation: Is Religion an Extreme Form of Traditional Authority?', *Archives Européennes de Sociologie*, 15(1), 55–81.
—— 1986. *From Blessing to Violence: History and Ideology in the Circumcision Ritual of the Merina of Madagascar*. Cambridge: Cambridge University Press.
—— 1998. *How We Think They Think: Anthropological Approaches to Cognition, Memory and Literacy*. Boulder, Colorado: Westview Press.
—— ed. 1975. *Political Language and Oratory in Traditional Society*. London: Academic Press.
Connerton, Paul. 1989. *How Societies Remember*. Cambridge: Cambridge University Press.
Durkheim, E. 1976 [1912]. *The Elementary Forms of the Religious Life*. 2nd edn. Trans. J. Ward Swain. London: Allen and Unwin.
Finisteretourisme. http://www.finisteretourisme.com (accessed June 2005).
Geertz, C. 1982. *Negara: the Theatre State in Nineteenth Century Bali*. Princeton: Princeton University Press.
Giddens, A. 1979. *Central Problems in Social Theory: Action, Structure and Contradiction in Social Analysis*. London: Macmillan.
Giddens, A. 1984. *The Constitution of Society: Outline of the Theory of Structuration*. Berkeley: University of California Press.
Habermas, J. 1976. *Legitimation Crisis*. London: Heinemann.
—— 1987. *The Theory of Communicative Action*. 2 vols. Boston: Beacon Press.
Halbwachs, M. 1992 [1925]. *On Collective Memory*. Trans. L.A. Coser. Chicago: University of Chicago Press.
Hobsbawm, E. and Ranger, T. eds 1983. *The Invention of Tradition*. Cambridge: Cambridge University Press.
Knorr-Cetina, K. and Cicourel, A.V. eds 1981. *Advances in Social Theory and Methodology: Toward an Integration of Micro- and Macro-Sociologies*. London: Routledge and Kegan Paul.
Luhmann, N. 1970. *The Differentiation of Society*. Trans. S. Holmes and C. Larmore. New York: Columbia University Press.
Ménès, Albert. http://www.albertmenes.fr/index.php
Mondovino. http://www.Mondovino-Lefilm.com

Penven. http://www.galettes-penven.com
Pevsner, N. 1973. *The Buildings of England: London I: The Cities of London and Westminster*. 3rd edn. Harmonsworth: Penguin Books.
Pocock, J.G.A. 1972. *Politics, Language and Time*. London: Methuen.
Proust, M. 2002 [1913]. *In Search of Lost Time, I: Swann's Way*. Trans. C.K. Scott Moncrieff and T. Kilmartin. London: Vintage.
Simmel, G. 1955 [1908]. *Conflict*. Trans. K.H. Wolff. New York: Free Press.
Turner, V. 1957. *Schism and Continuity in an African Society: A Study of Ndembu Village Life*. Manchester: Manchester University Press for the Rhodes-Livingstone Institute.
Weber, M. 1978 [1917]. *Economy and Society*. Trans. E. Fischoff et al. New York: Bedminster Press.
Wrong, D. 1994. *The Problem of Order: What Unites and Divides Society*. New York: Free Press.

Chapter 3

PRIDE, HONOUR, INDIVIDUAL AND COLLECTIVE VIOLENCE: ORDER IN A 'LAWLESS' VILLAGE

Aimar Ventsel

This chapter is about the maintenance of order in a post-Soviet Arctic village not far from the coast of the Arctic Ocean. Siberia as a region and legal anthropology as a field of study are only weakly linked. Soviet ethnography, like Tsarist Russian, post-Soviet and recent Western scholarship, has, among other things, described and analysed legal norms and the social structure of researched groups (Popov 1946, Dolgikh 1960, Shirokogoroff 1976, Gurvich 1977, Boiko and Kostiuk 1992, D'iachenko and Ermolova 1994, Grant 1995, Krivoshapkin 1997, Fondahl 1998, Ziker 2002). However, there is no literature on how these norms and concepts are maintained and violation is either prevented or punished. Another topic under-represented in Siberian anthropology, is the role of violence in the structures and methods of maintaining order. Some works show that violence and violent death is quite common in the everyday life of Siberian people (Pika 1993, Ziker 2002) and used to be part of their ritual and social behaviour (Batianova 2000), but violence as social behaviour is not discussed in Siberian anthropology.

Conflict resolution, mechanisms of social control and the ways in which these are related to honour, shame and violence have been discussed much more outside Siberian anthropology. The development of informal governance structures and an increase in the use of violence is typical for transition societies, including those of the former Soviet Union (e.g., Nash 1994, Koehler 2000, Humphrey 2002). In addition, several studies show that in a small face to face community the importance of reputation and honour increases and is directly linked to the economy (Peristiany 1970). In a small community, reputation has a practical utility: the lack of trustworthiness and prestige of a family may have serious economic consequences (Baroja 1970, Bourdieu 1970). Informal structures carry their own norms and these can be controlled through non-violent means. Gossiping (Gluckman 1963) and informal negotiations (Todd 1978) are often enough to motivate people to follow the general rules of the community. However, in some societies peaceful methods have limited success and can give way to violence. Similar to the urban Asian setting, in a Siberian village it is only one step from dispute to violence (c.f. Alexander 2000). However, violence also has its rules, 'it is also very much a discursive practice with symbols and rituals' (Whitehead 2004: 2). In this paper I explore these rules and the ways in which violence is discussed in the community.

Studies in other regions show that not only are informal methods of maintaining order different from formal legal methods, but also that the notion of crime differs from 'official' notions (Ruffini 1978, Rausing 1998). In this paper I show not only that crime is understood differently by people and the state but also that various age groups have their own understandings of what crime is. Discussing crime in an Arctic village I show that age groups are linked to each other by informal kinship-based networks and these networks play a central role in maintaining order in the village. Positions of such networks and other people's obligations toward an individual are again linked to personal reputation and an individual's wish to maintain or increase their honour (cf. Romanucci-Ross 1973).

Political and Geographical Background

The village of Uurung Khaia lies in the Anabarskii district, the most northwestern part of the Republic of Sakha, eastern Siberia. The Republic of Sakha is the largest region of Russia, with a territory of 3,103,200 square kilometres, but the population numbered only about one million in 1999 (Pakhomov 1999: 4). This republic is famous for its diamond industry and produces around ninety-nine percent of Russian and thirty percent of the world's diamonds. However, northern regions are officially considered to be 'agricultural', which means that the main occupation of the inhabitants is the hunting of wild reindeer, domestic reindeer herding and fishing. In 1994 the incomers, mostly represented by Russians, Belorussians and Ukrainians, formed approximately fifty-five percent of the population. The titular ethnic group, Turkic speaking Yakuts or Sakha (their own ethnonym, which has gained popularity in the last ten years), were the second largest group with around thirty-nine percent of the whole population (ca. 350,000). The rest were so-called northern indigenous minorities: Evenki, Even, Chukchi, Yukagir and Dolgan (Argunova and Habeck 1997).

Uurung Khaia is the only village in the republic in which the majority of the 1,200 inhabitants are Dolgan. There are just a few dozen incomer Sakha and only five Russians among them. All indigenous people of the district speak Sakha as their first language and have adopted many elements of Sakha culture, having been in contact with ethnic Sakha over many centuries. I spent eight months in the Anabarskii district in

2000–2001, living either in the tundra or staying in Uurung Khaia and another of its villages. The district is locally referred to as 'Anabarskii district' or just 'Anabar'; both expressions will be used in this text without any difference in connotation. Despite the fact that during the fieldwork period I became quite fluent in conversational Sakha, many young people preferred Russian when speaking with me. Therefore most interviews and discussions, presented below, took place in Russian.

The Setting

The native population of the Anabarskii district has traditionally been engaged in hunting wild reindeer and fur bearing animals, domestic reindeer husbandry and fishing. The region was seldom visited by scholars or even state officials and thus there is very little information about its economy and social structure or the legal ideas of its inhabitants. At the core of their social organization in pre-revolution times were extended families led by elders. These families were a loose collection of households that used to migrate together. The Anabar region was controlled only to a certain extent by the regional centre in Yakutsk up to the 1950s. In the 1920s, small villages, more like trading posts, with schools and other governmental institutions, were established by the Soviets in Anabar. In 1941 these small settlements were united into two villages: Saaskylaakh and Uurung Khaia. To achieve full control over nomads in the region, Soviet officials began establishing reindeer herding and hunting collectives which, at the end of 1940s, were united into two collective farms (later state farms) with centres in both villages (Gurvich 1977, Poligrafia Anabarskogo raiona 1987, Neustroeva 1995, Tokarev 2000).

During the period of collectivization, the native economy was restructured. The indigenous people of the Anabarskii district continued to be engaged in hunting, fishing and reindeer herding but now also as workers for the state enterprise (*sovkhoz*). Uurung Khaia became a location for the border station; this in practice meant a half-closed village and heavy police control over the movement of its inhabitants as well as everyday life in the settlement.

The collapse of the Soviet Union affected the life of the inhabitants of Uurung Khaia. The state farm was transformed into a district farm and known as MUP 'Il'ia Spiridonov'. This enterprise was subordinated to the district administration but lost its economic monopoly over the tundra. Since the late 1990s, new hunting and reindeer herding enterprises have been established in the village. All reindeer herders and hunters have been engaged in hunting wild reindeer and Arctic fox but also in fishing for private ends and in order to sell their produce to private entrepreneurs. The management of the MUP had little impact on these activities; nor was the district administration in a position to control the hunters' and reindeer herders' use of land in the tundra. Since there were no reliable formal control structures, the significance of kinship networks for monitoring the resource use in the tundra increased in importance (Ventsel 2004).

When the border guard station was closed in the mid 1990s, most incomer Sakha and Russians left the village. Unemployment increased because many former state farm facilities as well as schools, workers cantines and so on were either closed or reduced their number of employees. Transport connections to nearby Saaskylaakh became unpredictable and the village became difficult to access.

State Law and Local Law

Many people in Uurung Khaia proudly told me that their village is 'even more dangerous than Chicago' and that there are no laws. Pride in being from a dangerous place was often expressed by men, especially young men, and it was part of their masculinity, of 'being a tough guy'. This pride was shared in many cases by women as they stressed the difficult living conditions and the peculiarities of their community.

Although criminality and violence is a common problem in Sakha, the northern districts are seen as especially dangerous and rough, where people drink a lot and carry weapons. State power is weakly represented in the villages such as Uurung Khaia. There was one local constable, but he was neither able nor willing to maintain 'order' in the village. As far as I could observe, he tried to keep himself out of trouble in the community. The lone police officer's motivation to get involved in local conflicts and to take sides was low because he knew that he could always be accosted and beaten up on a street during the long polar night. This had happened quite a few times and, as a result, the village police officers were popularly called 'kamikaze' (*smertniki* in Russian). As one of my friends said to me, 'Cops won't survive here!' The state was more present in the district's central village, Saaskylaakh, where a small post of police officers was located. Saaskylaakh is also the location of the district court and the district attorney. The court and police forces were present in Uurung Khaia's daily life only when a violation of the law was especially severe. In the cases of fights involving weapons, stabbings, murders, rapes, and similar crimes, police officers were flown in from Saaskylaakh and the arrested persons transported back to Saaskylaakh.

According to public opinion across the district, Uurung Khaia has always been a dangerous place, but the situation became worse at the beginning of 1990s alongside growing inequality. Villagers feel that before *perestroika* the social life of the village had a 'more meaningful structure and an aura of social well-being and communitas' (Gambold-Miller 2003:

15, referring to Turner 1969). Despite its reputation as a lawless place across the district, in Uurung Khaia there are concepts of what is right and what is wrong. Many commonly accepted rules are linked to property: nobody should touch another person's traps in the tundra; there are certain people who have more right to use resources in certain regions than others ('masters' or *khoziain* in Russian); stealing from dwellings and storages in the tundra is a crime; private reindeer should not be used without the permission of the owner, and so on. However, there are no clearly fixed legal concepts which all people know and follow. Many norms and their violation are matters for discussion, and in many cases people's opinions depend on their own point of view in any particular case or on how closely they are related to the persons involved.

The Male Age System in Uurung Khaia

To understand the functioning of kinship networks in Uurung Khaia one has to have some knowledge of the male age system in the village. The male population of Uurung Khaia is divided roughly into three categories: elders (*stariki* in Russian; *ogonn'onnor* in Sakha, singular form *ogonn'or*), adult men (*vzroslye muzhiki* in Russian; *kihiler* in Sakha) and young men or 'kids' (*patsany* in Russian; *uollattar* in Sakha). These groups are not comparable with the classic East African age groups (e.g., Legesse 1973, Bernardi 1985, Spencer 1988, Bassi 1996), where the membership of one or another age category and entry into the group is strictly fixed and ritually celebrated, and the whole structure functions as a 'discrete kind of political organization' (Bernardi 1996: 9). Nevertheless, in the context of Anabar's social structure there are also age groups that appear to have their own particular position within the indigenous social hierarchy with specific rights and obligations towards family, decision-making power in community life, places in the division of labour and so forth.

When a person becomes a pensioner he usually leaves the 'adult' category and will be referred to as an elder or old man. Because different professions have different rules as to the age at which one can retire, the group of pensioners contains people of different ages. In Russia women normally retire at the age of fifty and men at the age of fifty-five. In Siberia some professions (including reindeer herders and hunters) have the right to retire earlier. Therefore, most pensioners in Uurung Khaia stop working at the age of forty to fifty and are then called either 'old man' (*ogonn'or*, Sakha) or 'old woman' (*emeeksin*, Sakha).

The border between adults and 'kids' is less clear than that between elders and adults. Young males usually leave the category of 'kids' after their army service, at the age of twenty to twenty-two. Even when they do not go into the army, young people tend to get married in their early twenties (young women even earlier, at the age of seventeen to nineteen) and this change in their status transfers people into the group of adults. However, a man of twenty to twenty-five years of age can sometimes belong to the 'kids' category, sometimes to the adults. If he is unmarried, he can be accepted by youngsters as part of their group and participate in their entertainment. At the same time he has same responsibilities toward his parents as the adult men have and is incorporated in family's decision making processes. 'Kids' have more freedom in their daily life: they drink and party more and come home late. As an adult, one is expected to have more responsibility, to contribute more to the household's income and to show initiative in looking for possibilities for extra income. Adult men must also stay away from 'kids' entertainment', especially petty crime and hooliganism.

Adults are the main stabilizing social group who maintain at least some kind of order in the streets and other public spaces of Uurung Khaia. One reason they feel themselves obliged to keep the 'kids' under control is their status as 'family men'; they have an obligation to support their children and older parents and take care of their security. Adults also have considerable property to lose if stealing and robbery become uncontrollable. As one of my informants told me, 'We people over the age of thirty keep the order here in the village. We make sure that the "kids" don't do anything evil.' Leaders among the adults who take it upon themselves to maintain order are very often *zeki* or a few so-called *avtoritety* ('authority, very respected person' in Russian). *Zek* is a person who has been in prison. Life in a Russian prison is hard, and a person who survives many years of imprisonment has gone through many tough situations.[1] The *zeki* are easy to recognize by their use of specific slang, their behaviour and tattoos. The crueller the crime a person has been sentenced for, the more respect he enjoys in his home village. For many adults, this respect is negative, that is it is caused by fear. *Zeki* usually keep together and support each other. Therefore hardly anybody wants to get into conflicts with them. However, in a small community like Uurung Khaia it is nearly impossible not to interact with a person, either in private, or in public. Therefore *zeki* are not seen as an immediate danger and they are embedded in various extended family-based social networks. At the same time, for young men, *zeki* often have a positive image as outlaws because the former convicts were often avoided and feared by state officials (including the constable) and other adults.

The institution of *avtoritety* developed with the appearance of private businesses in the post-Soviet period. Local entrepreneurs bribe local authorities to give them a green light for their semi-illegal businesses in the tundra villages and became suppliers and main business partners for local population. In every village there are a few *avtoritety* (singular *avtoritet*). They are mostly well known as cruel thugs or half-criminal entrepreneurs with not-so-honest business methods. One *avtoritet* in the village of Uurung Khaia was a man called Tsempion (Champion). He was a successful entrepreneur, owned a shop, traded bootleg alcohol and supplied people with guns and ammunition. Tsempion used to be a real champion of the Republic of Sakha, in kick boxing, and was famous for his ability to knock out much larger foes with a kick in the face.

Similar to the 'bosses' in 'street corner society' (Whyte 1993: 113–22), the *avtoritety* in Sakha villages are not only able to control and influence life in the village and thus guarantee an undisturbed space for their own businesses, they also have social obligations toward the community. These obligations involve taking care of the general welfare and order in the community. Thus, one friend of mine told me how local *avtoritety* in Chersk, in north-eastern Sakha, organized a supply of basic groceries for the settlement in the middle of the 1990s during the general economic crisis and the collapse of transport networks. As a result, prices in Chersk were much cheaper than in Yakutsk for a long time. Such activities are useful for all sides; the community accepts and supports the illegal or semi-legal business of the *avtoritety*, while the latter profit from it.

'Kids' are young males aged between seventeen and their early twenties. Young females are usually called 'girls' (*kyrgyttar* in Sakha) and form a different social group. These young people – in local perception male youth, because girls are seen as boys' satellites – are usually either high school students or dropouts and they are seen by adults and by older people as a group which causes constant trouble. Drinking, violent behaviour and the criminal activity of 'kids' is condemned by the wider community, but it is also regarded as a kind of leisure and as a means of 'proving themselves' by the 'kids'. These different notions about the violation of norms frequently resulted in conflicts between 'kids' and adults. Though 'girls' are seldom involved in a direct violation of social norms, according to my observations, because of their personal relations with the 'kids' and their similar age, 'girls' share the 'boys' views on the meaning of 'improper behaviour' and in conflict situations with adults support and assist the 'kids'.

At the top of this informal hierarchy are old people or elders who, as a rule, are able to control adults and even the young 'kids' of their own family, and in some cases even their friends. Old men are the unquestioned heads of the family, able to mobilize their male relatives and friends to take punitive action, but also able to use their authority to resolve disputes. The respect that elders enjoy in Siberia has been described by many Soviet ethnographers (Popov 1946, Dolgikh 1960, Vasilevich 1969, Gurvich 1977, Boiko and Kostiuk 1992, D'iachenko and Ermolova 1994, Piliasov 1998). I came across many situations in which the respect for old people was clearly demonstrated, most remarkably on one occasion when one harsh word from the old father stopped an intense dispute between his adult children and forced them to withdraw to other rooms.

These extended families are spread over social and geographic space, which means that members of same family live in the tundra, village and towns of Sakha. Altogether the family forms a network which enables its members to gain access to various resources and distribute them among nuclear households. As in many large families, the children gather at least once a day in the house of their elders to eat, socialize and watch TV. In this way the patterns of sociability keep people informed about what is happening in and beyond the community but also about family affairs. Therefore, in a similar way to Mexican business families, such gatherings are essential to the 'family economy' (Lomnitz and Pérez-Lizaur 1989). By attending these informal gatherings, younger family members hear elders' opinions about local happenings and whether they condemn or applaud particular incidents. Traditional values and norms are transmitted through these discussions: younger people are either encouraged or discouraged to behave in certain ways, including undertaking or desisting from violent action.

Violence, Masculinity, Honour

According to my observations, in the Anabarskii district there are two principal ways in which order is violated: theft and individual or group fights. However, not all such incidents are characterized as 'crimes' by the community.

Theft is regarded as a violation of an individual's or a family's property rights and has a broad meaning. Hunting on someone's hunting ground without informing the 'master' of the territory or breaking into a garage and stealing a snowmobile or parts of it are considered theft. Theft does not only mean the appropriation of property but is also an offence against personal and family pride. In the economic crisis that has occurred after the collapse of the Soviet economy, when many people lost their jobs and incomes, and in the harsh conditions of the Arctic, theft can endanger one's livelihood. But it also indicates that the victim is not able to protect his family and property. Therefore, reaction to theft is closely connected to a concept of masculinity.

Violence is not always interpreted as a crime but can often be regarded as a reaction to crime. As demonstrated by some authors, violence is not 'senseless', it has cultural and social meaning, but this meaning is not automatically the same across societies (Yablonsky 1962: 4, Blok 2001: 104). Bourgois defines the term 'street culture' as a 'power-charged belief system' that organizes the 'common sense' of the street (1999: 316). He describes many 'cross-cultural confrontations' which were caused by the difference between concepts of good behaviour and gender roles in Puerto Rican immigrant working-class and white middle-class culture. One part of the Puerto Rican male attitude was the will to demonstrate masculinity through a readiness to violence, a certain 'body culture' (Bourgois 1999: 319–20).

Likewise, aggressive behaviour in the Anabarskii district is a part of the everyday life of the male population and is bound up with a local understanding of masculinity. In this sense, the attitude does not differ from that of Georgian street youth or Cheyenne Indians, where the man had to be loyal to his family and friends and to 'outface any man' (Llewellyn and Hoebel 1967: 267–68, Koehler 2000: 28–29). The ideal of a man in Uurung Khaia is a 'tough guy' who is able to defend his reputation and has no fear of physical conflict. A 'good reputation' usually means the man is reliable in a conflict and is able to 'take a stand' even when he is clearly outnumbered; that is, he does not run away but 'fights back'. He also supports his family and friends when they need help, whether in work or in a fight.

The virtue of being 'tough' (*krutoi* in Russian) is valued not only among young males. In discussions, women (and girls) strongly supported the idea that a 'real man' must fight when necessary. One young woman referred to a discussion she had with a German anthropologist she met outside the district. 'We talked about violence and fights. I asked him what he would do if someone provoked him and wanted to beat him up. He answered that he would run away. Then I told him that you cannot run away. You have to fight!' Violence is not categorically condemned by adults or elders either. During multiple discussions, adults told me stories about their past confrontations or expressed their opinions about the violent deeds of other people, and their judgement was not always negative. The crucial distinction is between kinds of violence that are 'bad' and those that are 'good'. I explore this in the next section.

I do not intend to imply that the streets of Uurung Khaia are always filled with fighting groups. Most of the time I spent in the community, the streets and homes were peaceful and people were extremely hospitable. However, aggression and violence as a mode of social interaction was always present in people's everyday life.[2] Pika (1993) shows that dynamics of violent death and homicides among Siberian native communities is strongly connected to seasonality and geography: thus most homicides are committed in the villages during the winter period. John Ziker has collected data about violent deaths in Ust-Avam and shows that 'violent deaths of various types are more common than natural causes of death' (2002: 97). Ziker includes not only violence and alcohol related deaths in this category but also all accidents. I do not have similar statistics for Uurung Khaia. However, my data shows that during my fieldwork there was approximately one violent death per month. There were three suicides, one drowning, one freezing to death while intoxicated and two stabbings. In fact, the rate of violent armed crime was higher than that because there were also a few knife fights in which at least one participant was seriously wounded but not killed. Similar to Ust-Avam, gun related violence is extremely rare in this heavily-armed village (Ziker 2002: 98). As is also the case in Ust-Avam, alcohol is seldom present in the tundra. In the village where, by contrast, alcohol is ever present, rifles and ammunition are locked up in steel cabinets. Many herders and hunters leave their rifles in the tundra at the brigade's base when they return to the village. Thus, spontaneous armed fights are usually limited to the use of hunting knives that many men carry, even in the village, and every family has dozens of these in the home.

Contact with violence starts at an early age. Children hear parents, other adults, and older children discussing recent violent encounters. The violent past of former convicts or some especially 'crazy fighters' are also a frequent topic of discussion. At every large event (holidays, discos and sporting events) alcohol is present and, as a rule, at least some minor quarrel breaks out. Children are always present at these events, even late at night. Some children also experience violence at home. According to my observation, violent games and sham battles are very much practised by children in the village.

Already as teenagers boys start to behave according to masculine ideals. Boys aged fifteen smoke openly at home. With the consumption of alcohol, boys start to get involved in fights. Young boys often have conflicts among themselves, especially on the weekends when, before or after the disco, they drink at somebody's home while the parents are out. Small fights are common when youths are intoxicated, are considered normal and usually do not spoil a friendship.

The first teenage experiences with violence are not only through such conflicts among young people but also sometimes involve the aggressive behaviour of adults, as the following recollection of Oko, one young reindeer herder, shows:

> Sometimes the adults themselves start a fight. It's not always the youths' fault. Last summer, I was still at school, and we were playing football in Uurung Khaia. Suddenly a drunken adult man came to us and started to provoke us. He said, 'Now I'm gonna show you, you bastards!' (*Ia vam pokazhu, urody!*) We, us boys, were a little drunk as well. Then we taught him! (*My ego nauchili!*)

Showing courage and being tough is already practised by the youngsters at school with their age mates and even with older people. The reputation one builds up during the later school years can follow a person through his entire life. Failing to be a 'real man' affects one's social position in a group and in the wider community. Some of my adult informants believed that after the beginning of the 1990s youth, both males and females, had begun to take the ideals of acting 'tough' more seriously. Youth criminality and violence in Uurung Khaia is, therefore, partly seen as a contemporary phenomenon.

Another reason for this perception is the different notions of violence and crime found among different age groups mentioned above; the concept of 'doing harm' is less connected to outright violence for young males and females, who often see provocative and aggressive behaviour as a way to 'show oneself' and maintain a good reputation (e.g., Riches 1991: 283–84). Violence against adults and old people, on the other hand, as is shown by Oko's story and the other examples below, is an issue of criticism in the village. On their side, teenagers mentioned, similar to Oko, that adults 'come and start' a quarrel: 'Always someone complains when we are too noisy on the street. Then you have to show them their place.' Another source of problems is stealing. During my fieldwork, all property was locked up, especially at night. Food was stolen by teenage 'kids' to consume during their drinking parties. I heard people complaining many times that somebody had stolen meat and fish when they happened to forget it outside over night on sledges or from nets near to the river. One of the 'kids' said to me: 'I do not know what people complain about. There is plenty of fish in the river. It is not my fault that somebody hasn't checked fish nets before me'. I also know that youngsters broke into garages to steal snowmobile parts to trade for alcohol. Such acts are usually committed when intoxicated and encouraged by the group as an act of courage. For adults this sort of breaking in was a very serious crime, particularly due to increasing prices.

Different Levels of the Maintenance of Order in the Village

In the second part of my paper I discuss the different levels on which order is maintained in the village of Uurung Khaia. I begin with the non-violent methods and move on to violent means of conflict resolution and order maintenance. In practice, borders between these levels are fluid and one action can shift over into another very quickly.

Gossip

I start with gossiping and rumours as one of the main non-violent means of social control in Uurung Khaia. Max Gluckman argues that gossip is a means to maintain unity, cohesion and the social values of the group (Gluckman 1963: 308). Scott shows, with the help of Kaufman, how every segment of society in an Asian peasant community had to mould its behaviour in order to avoid 'malicious gossip' and how the impact on one's reputation influenced one's social position (Kaufman 1960: 36, in Scott 1976: 42). Scott argues that gossip was a means of social control of poor against wealthy people. While he observed gossip as a tool which forced wealthy people into reciprocal relationships with their poorer village members, I want to show how gossip plays a role in maintaining order in the Arctic community and sometimes may prevent people from taking the 'wrong actions'. In the same way as Scott argues that the existence of social norms of reciprocity did not automatically push wealthy people to 'live up' to these norms completely (1976: 42), I do not want to argue that gossip in Uurung Khaia was something which prevents all crime and violence. Because legal concepts are embedded in social relations, gossip and rumours can decrease a person's reputation and therefore have an impact on behaviour (see Members of the Project Group Legal Pluralism 2001: 148, 152, 153).

When I spent a few weeks with the sixth reindeer brigade of the MUP "Il'ia Spiridonov", I spoke one night with a young reindeer herder, Oleg, about the people in the village. He told me that he studied in the same class with the MUP's director, Pavel, and they used to be good mates:

> But now Pavel has become arrogant. After he returned from Yakutsk [where Pavel studied agriculture], he became cocky. He never wants to talk to old friends. After he started as director [of the MUP] I met him in a disco. Pavel was completely drunk and came to me and said that he is tougher than me. He wanted to have a fight with me. I said to him, bring another bottle of vodka. It is not fair, because I am sober. If I beat you up then people will say afterwards, 'Oleg is such a bastard, he beat up drunken Pavel. It wasn't a fair fight!' And Pavel hung around with the girls and then disappeared. He said he was going to bring the vodka. He is so obnoxious (*naglyi*). He simply didn't return. When I go back to the village, I will punch him in the nose! (*ia dam emu po morde!*)

Even in violent behaviour one has to be 'fair'. There are certain rules to fighting which, according to public opinion, should not be violated. To beat up a drunken person when one is sober is shameful because it is seen as an unequal situation in which another has less chance to defend themselves. To use weapons is generally condemned. Oko said to me once, 'Only psychopaths fight with knives!' When it is rumoured that someone has won a fight with somebody who was more intoxicated, the gossip spreads quickly and the person can expect suspicious stares on the street, probably questions in the company of friends and, in the worst case, avoidance in social interaction, especially at festive events.

Another case is when a person has a reputation for being 'weak'. Therefore males were forced to behave as tough as possible in any conflicts where witnesses were present. A reputation for being a coward can cause social marginalization, from laughter on the street to harassment in the disco. Gossip is relevant insofar as being 'weak' is linked with 'being unreliable' and in a wider context it means that the person is not worthy of respect. Therefore males in any public situation try to avoid giving the impression that they cannot cope with problems of any kind. Being 'weak' not only means being unfit for physical conflicts but also implies a lack of skills or the strength to do hard or complicated work. I have seen sick men with a high fever catching reindeer and others repairing their snowmobiles in the freezing cold in order to show that they were strong and capable of controlling themselves.

Very critical gossip is spread about a person who 'lied'. A 'real man' is expected to keep the promises he gives to fellow villagers. Promising something and not fulfilling it is interpreted as lying in Uurung Khaia. A 'liar' is also 'unreliable' and this means that one cannot do any 'serious business' with such a 'weak' person. Such a person is often excluded from common fishing or hunting trips, and people are also reluctant to trade with him. In the community of Uurung Khaia, when somebody is looking, for example, for company to travel to the tundra he asks around for possible partners. Then he is warned not to co-operate with an 'unreliable' person. I documented a case in which a fisherman, N., wanted to sell a large quantity of fish to an entrepreneur. The potential deal was very lucrative because the entrepreneur promised to pay a good price. The only condition was that the trader wanted to buy several tons of fish at once. However, N. did not have a large enough quantity of fish and he asked people in the village if they wanted to get in on the deal with him. Speaking with N. later, he mentioned to me fishermen in the village he was warned not to cooperate with: 'People told me that they are unreliable. They promise a lot and then do not fulfil their promises.'

Gossip and consequent possible social marginalization are also connected to one's sexual behaviour in a small community. In Uurung Khaia, the 'question of morals' was relevant for both sexes. When I discussed sexual relations in the village community with one young man, Igor, he said: 'But the man should not sleep around too much. When people get to know that, no one takes you seriously.' It was difficult to draw the line where this 'sleeping around too much' started, but the older the person became, the less promiscuity was accepted. Having many sexual partners especially affects the reputation of married people and means that the person was not welcome in others' company. During my fieldwork I documented a few cases where somebody was not taken along when we went to a party in the village due to their not 'being serious'. In the case of one woman, my companion who arranged the party said: 'She is one who sleeps around. People say that a few years ago she was really into drinking and sleeping with men.' In another case, when refusing to invite a young man to his home, my friend said, 'I do not respect him!' When I later asked what was wrong with the man, he told me, 'He always drinks and has parties with different girls.' In both cases, rumours played an important role in creating the person's reputation.

People gossip a lot in Uurung Khaia and with passion. There are many other topics to gossip in addition to one's fights, personal business, drinking events and sexual behaviour, but these were the topics I encountered most often as reasons when somebody 'was not taken seriously'. Exclusion from social events was one consequence of rumours. To counteract rumours one had to prove that these were not true. One possibility was to act publicly in an accepted manner in order to convince others that the gossip was false. Another way, used especially by males but sometimes by females too, was to provoke a fight with the person who spread the rumours.

Group Violence and Social Order

It is difficult to distinguish different levels of social control and to categorize specific examples of problem resolution. Non-violent means (discussion) can develop into violent action (fights). An individual fight can suddenly become a group fight when friends come to help. Individual violent action can involve either revenge, demonstrations of masculinity, an attempt to restore 'justice' and one's reputation, or just a crime. In practice, it can be all at once. A brutal fight can be condemned by other people but could have been initiated by the desire for revenge against someone who has spread rumours or stolen something. A particularity of such a small settlement like Uurung Khaia is that it is very unlikely that a confrontation can take place where no other people are present: either on the street, at home or in the weekend disco, other people are always around. According to my observations, people of Uurung Khaia are quiet and controlled when sober and in a formal situation. They are quite different when under the influence of alcohol and in an informal atmosphere. This is the moment when many disputes are started and conflicts erupt. It is also very likely that at certain moments friends or other bystanders will intervene and the individual fight grows into a violent group action. For support in such a situation, one needs a large network of friends and relatives.

But I also encountered sanctioned violent action called *razborka* that exists as an informal institution of punishment and a means of maintaining order in the village. The name comes from the Russian verb *razbirat'*, 'to make things clear, to sort out'. *Razborka* is vernacularly understood as a (group) fight between persons who have some conflict to solve and belongs, in another setting, to a mafia repertoire of 'gangland sorting-out' (Humphrey 2002: 102). In Uurung Khaia, *razborka* had a specific meaning and was a name for planned, institutionalized, collective action.

While in the tundra I was talking with my host Vassili about violence in the village of Uurung Khaia. He told me that on New Year's Eve there was a big fight:

A brother of mine and two of his friends, all adult men, were at one of the friends' house. They were drinking vodka and celebrating the New Year. There was a disco in the club and some 'kids' came from the disco to this house. They were drunk and rude. As far as I know, they wanted money to buy vodka. The men told them to go to hell. But the 'kids' began mouthing off. My brother and the other men wanted to throw them out and there was a small fight. But the 'kids' had some girls with them and they ran over to the club and brought other ['kids'] in [to the house]. So, the boys came with Druzhba [Russian chainsaw] chains and beat my brother up. They didn't touch one of the men, the owner of the house, because they [the 'kids'] knew him. But my brother and the other man were badly beaten up, as I said. My brother was in the hospital for many months with concussion.

Then we, *tundroviki* [herders and hunters who spend most of the year in the tundra], gathered these boys in the club. The first time a few of them did not come. We told them we wanted to talk to all of the boys [who were involved in the beating] and told them to gather next week. Next week all the 'kids' came. We talked to them and warned them that next time we will punish them severely.

As I was told by other friends, *razborka* is quite common in remote Sakha villages as an informal institution to keep order and punish violators of communal norms. *Razborka* is not just a modern 'invention' here, which has arisen because state structures are unable to maintain public order. One of my friends who grew up in a Sakha village near the town of Lensk (Upper Lena river, southern Sakha), told me that certain conflicts were solved within the community even in Soviet times. *Razborka* in Anabar is a collective answer by the community to a crude crime, organized only in extreme situations when a group of youngsters has brazenly violated commonly accepted norms. According to my informants it is used when a group of boys beats up women or old people, when they break into a store or private house and ransack it or when somebody is brutally beaten up by a group.

In Uurung Khaia *razborka* is considered to be an intra-community event, humiliating for some families involved, which should not be discussed outside the village. Therefore people were, as a rule, extremely reluctant to speak about it. The following information was collected from short remarks and comments and two interviews I was able to have after one such event.

There seemed to be two groups of men in the village who act as the keepers of order and therefore take the initiative in organizing *razborkas*: *tundroviki* and *zeki*. Both groups have a strong sense of belonging to one group. The *tundroviki* have a separate group identity from village people. They share a common physical space, the tundra, where they can survive only by helping each other. The sense of belonging to a group is not only connected to a different economy and way of life but also to culture and social responsibility. This mutual tie and group identity persists when *tundroviki* are living in the village. In Russia, criminals also have a strong tradition of sticking together and an ideological explanation for it (Humphrey 2002: 102–4). In Uurung Khaia, their common biography – prison – unites them even in freedom. This sense among ex-convicts of being one group is supported by their marginalization. Men from both groups are mostly married adults with children and heads of independent households.

People from both groups told me, 'If we do not look after the "kids", then nobody will do it!' This sense of responsibility has different roots, however. The main reason expressed to me was just a need to maintain some order in the village and to guarantee a peaceful environment for their families, parents and relatives. Elders who, in many cases, have little authority among 'kids', especially when the youngsters are not members of their families, are able to convince adults to interfere when 'kids' grow 'out of hand'. *Zeki*, for their part, demonstrate through their initiative in a *razborka* that, despite their marginal position in the community, they have power as a group and that they, as do all other men in the village, have a sense of responsibility to the community.

One of my informants told me about a *razborka* in January 2001: 'People came together and they questioned all the persons involved. The men asked the "kids" why they beat the old man. The boys explained their point of view. Then the victim was questioned. Some fathers of the boys were there, but not all of them, only those who wanted to come. It is a great shame when your son is judged this way. And then they were punished.' This time the boys were not warned but beaten up. How justified and honest such a 'court' can be is a matter of discussion for outsider but not in the village. Many people who turned up that evening were already drunk. I can imagine that despite all the intentional 'neutrality', this 'process' was not as fair as a formal court. Most people were already of the opinion that the boys were guilty and should be punished before the discussion. But *razborka* is seen as a decision-making and punishment tool of the whole community and, for this reason, the decision of the collective is widely accepted by other families in the village.

I asked my friends why the boys went to the *razborka* when they knew that they would probably be beaten up by drunken men. Igor explained to me: 'The "kids" have their pride. When you have done something bad you have to answer for your deeds. They know it and are ready to accept the punishment. And you cannot hide yourself here in the village anyway. There is no place to hide. Even when you go to the tundra, people know which direction you went and where you are.' *Razborka* is seen as shameful for the 'kids' involved, but their reputation and social position in the community would suffer even more if they tried to avoid it. That would be 'running away'. To show that they are tough they have to face the beating from the crowd. When youngsters are openly presented in front of gathered villagers as criminals then they also demonstrate their masculinity according to the local ideal. *Razborka* is used by the community as a warning against further extreme violations of order and property. Through such 'constructive' violence the community protects its integrity, takes over the role of the state and reproduces the social order (Bowman 2001: 30–31).

Conclusion

The reason social control has come to be dominated by informal methods in the Anabarskii district since the 1990s is that formal institutions are unable to control order in the community (Just 1991: 107–9). For that purpose, the community has established a complicated system of rules and structures to enforce these rules. As I have demonstrated in this article, methods of social control include both violent and non-violent means. However, even when discussing non-violent means of informal governance, violence is always present, even if only in the background. I have demonstrated that violence, although having a traditionally important place in Siberian indigenous peoples' cultures (Batianova 2000: 31), increased after the collapse of state-governed control and punishment mechanisms. Although many non-locals believe that the indigenous population is criminal and violent and 'has no laws', I can cite only Robarcheck and Dentan's comment on violence and non-violence among Semai: 'Semai are only violent when there are sufficient external reasons to become violent. There is no need to postulate a biologically rooted, repressed, universal human drive to explain their behaviour' (1987: 361–62). My argument is that the high importance placed on violent behaviour is caused by the need to employ radical means to defend property rights and individual security in a situation of social, political and economic collapse.

Lederach (1991) shows that conflict is a cultural event, and knowledge of what is right and wrong is included in people's world-view and provides methods for how to proceed. Here I have discussed how perceptions of what is a violation of order differ on many levels. The point of view of the state does not overlap with the concept of crime within the community. Furthermore, there are remarkable differences between younger and older generations in their interpretations of violent behaviour.

The establishment of informal social control structures is closely linked to the economic transformation in the post-Soviet period. Due to the fact that the control and distribution of resources has moved into the family sphere, extended families have also become the main resource for defending one's property and security in the community. Local notions of right and wrong are based on family unity and the belief that one must solve one's own problems oneself, as well as on the ways in which a reputation is maintained in the community and its connection to one's social position.

The community, as a group, is interested in maintaining relative order and peace in the village and is able to mobilize itself as an entity in especially serious cases of violence.

Acknowledgements

This article is based on data collected during my doctoral fieldwork and was financed and supported by the Max Planck Institute for Social Anthropology, Halle/Saale, Germany. I am grateful to Chris Hann, Fernanda Pirie, Keebet and Franz von Benda-Beckmann for their comments and discussions wich helped to form this article.

Notes

1. One Russian friend, who spent five years in prison, told me that the grouping in a prison takes place on an ethnic basis. Russians, Sakha, gypsies, Ukrainians, etc. try to live in one cell with people of their own ethnic group and create so-called families. He told me that the relations in Sakha 'families' were especially brutal, where the boss had absolute right over the property and health of his 'family members'. One's position in the 'family' depended on the kind of sentence and the length of time one had already spent in prison.
2. Compare the analysis of honour, drunkenness and fun among Australian Aborigines (Tomsen 1997).

References

Alexander, C.E. 2000. *The Asian Gang: Ethnicity, Identity, Masculinity*. New York and Oxford: Berg Publishers.
Argunova and Habeck. http://www.spri.cam.ac.uk/resources/rfn/sakha.html (accessed October 2000)
Baroja, J.C. 1970. 'A Historical Account of Several Conflicts' in *Honour and Shame: the Values of Mediterranean Society*, ed. J.G. Peristiany, Chicago: University of Chicago Press, 79–138.
Bassi, M. 1996. *I Borana: Una societá assembleare dell'Etiopia*. Milano: Franco Angeli.
Batianova, E.P. 2000. 'Ritual Violence among the Peoples of Northeastern Siberia' in *Hunters and Gatherers in the Modern World: Conflict, Resistance, and Self-Determination*, eds P. Schweitzer, M. Biesele and R.K. Hitchcock, New York and Oxford: Berghahn Books, 150–63.
Bernardi, B. 1985. *Age Class Systems: Social Institutions and Politics Based on Age*. Cambridge: Cambridge University Press.
―――― 1996. 'Africa: East' in *Encyclopedia of Social and Cultural Anthropology*, eds A. Barnard and J. Spencer, London and New York: Routledge, 7–9.
Blok, A. 2001. *Honour and Violence*. Cambridge: Polity Press.
Boiko, V.I. and Kostiuk, V.G. 1992. *Evenki basseina Enisseia*. Novosibirsk: Nauka.
Bourdieu, P. 1970. 'The Sentiment of Honour in Kabyle Society' in *Honour and Shame: the Values of Mediterranean Society*, ed. J.G. Peristiany, Chicago: University of Chicago Press, 191–242.

Bourgois, P. 1999. 'From Jíbaro to Crack Dealer: Confronting the Restructuring of Capitalism in El Barrio' in *Anthropological Theory: an Introductory History*, 2nd edn, eds R.J. McGee and R.L. Warms, Mountain View, CA, London and Toronto: Mayfield Publishing, 315–29.

Bowman, G. 2001. 'The Violence in Identity' in *Anthropology of Violence and Conflict*, eds B.E. Schmidt and I.W. Schröder, London and New York: Routledge, 25–45.

D'iachenko, V.I. and Ermolova, N.V. 1994. *Evenki i Yakuty Iuga Dal'nego Vostoka. XVII–XX vek*. Sankt Peterburg: Nauka.

Dolgikh, B.O. 1960. *Rodovyi i plemennyi sostav narodov Sibiri v XVII v. Trudy Instituta Etnografii im. N.N. Mikluho-Maklaia*. New Series, tome 55. Moscow: Izdatel'stvo Akademii Nauk SSSR.

Fondahl, G. 1998. *Gaining Ground? Evenkis, Land, and Reform in Southeastern Siberia*. Boston, MA: Allyn and Bacon.

Gambold-Miller, L. 2003. *Interdependence in Rural Russia: the Postsocialist Mixed Feudal Economy*. Max Planck Institute for Social Anthropology, Working Paper No. 51, Halle/Saale.

Gluckman, M. 1963. 'Gossip and Scandal', *Current Anthropology*, 4(3), 307–16.

Grant, B. 1995. *In the Soviet House of Culture: a Century of Perestroikas*. Princeton, NJ: Princeton University Press.

Gurvich, I.S. 1977. *Kul'tura senernykh yakutrov-olenovodov*. Moscow: Nauka.

Humphrey, C. 2002. *The Unmaking of Soviet Life: Everyday Economies after Socialism*. Ithaca, NY and London: Cornell University Press.

Just, P. 1991. 'Conflict Resolution and Moral Community among Dou Donggo' in *Conflict Resolution. Cross-Cultural Perspectives*, eds K. Avruch, P.W. Black and J.A. Scimecca, New York, Westport, London: Greenwood Press, 107–44.

Kaufman, K. 1960. *Banghuad: a Community Study in Thailand*. Locus Valley, NY: J.J. Augustin.

Koehler, J. 2000. *Die Zeit der Jungs: Zur Organisation von Gewalt und der Austragung von Konflikten in Georgien*. Münster: Lit.

Krivoshapkin, A.V. 1997. *Eveny*. Sankt Peterburg: Prosveshenie.

Legesse, A. 1973. *Gada: Three Approaches to the Study of African Society*. New York: The Free Press.

Lederach, P. 1991. 'Of Nets, Nails, and Problems: the Folk Language of Conflict Resolution in a Central American Setting' in *Conflict Resolution. Cross-cultural Perspectives*, eds K. Avruch, P.W. Black and J.A. Scimecca, New York, Westport, London: Greenwood Press, 165–86.

Llewellyn, K.N. and Hoebel, E.A. 1967. *The Cheyenne Way: Conflict and Case Law in Primitive Jurisprudence*. Norman: University of Oklahoma Press.

Lomnitz, L.A. and Pérez-Lizaur, M. 1989. 'The Origins of the Mexican Bourgeoisie: Networks as Social Capital' in *Netzwerkanalyse. Ethnologische Perspektiven*, ed. T. Schweitzer, Berlin: Dietrich Reimer Verlag, 35–46.

Members of the Project Group Legal Pluralism 2001. 'Project Group: Legal Pluralism' in *Max Planck Institute for Social Anthropology. Report 1999–2001*, eds G. Schlee and B. Mann, Halle/Saale: Heinrich John Halle/Saale, 129–65.

Nash, J. 1994. 'Global Integration and Subsistence Economy', *American Anthropologist*, 96, 7–30.

Neustroeva, I.M. 1995. *65 let Anabarskomu ulusu. My darim severnoe siianie*. Saskylakh: Unitarnoe Gospredpriiatie 'Ogni Anabara'.

Pakhomov, E.A. 1999. *Respublika Sakha (Yakutia). Administrativno-territorialnoe delenie na janvaria 1999 goda*. Yakutsk: NIPK Sakhapoligrafizdat.

Peristiany, J.G. 1970. 'Introduction' in *Honour and Shame: the Values of Mediterranean Society*, ed. J.G. Peristiany, Chicago: University of Chicago Press, 9–18.

Pika, A. 1993. 'The Spatial-Temporal Dynamic of Violent Death among the Native Peoples of Northern Russia', *Arctic Anthropology*, 30, 61–76.

Piliasov, A.N. 1998. *Ot paternalizma k partnerstvu. Stritel'stvo novykh otnoshenii narodov Severa i gosudarstva*. Magadan: SVKNII DVO RAN.
Poligrafia Anabarskogo raiona. 1987. *K 70-letiiu Velikogo Oktiabria. Anabarskii raion*. Poligrafia Anabarskogo raiona. Saskylakh.
Popov, A.A. 1946. 'Semeinaia zhizn u dolgan', *Sovetskaia Etnografiia*, 4, 50–74.
Rausing, S. 1998. 'Signs of the New Nation: Gift, Exchange, Consumption and Aid on a Former Collective Farm in North-west Estonia' in *Material Cultures: Why Some Things Matter*, ed. D. Miller, London: University College London Press, 189–214.
Riches, D. 1991. 'Aggression, War, Violence: Space/Time and Paradigm', *Man*, 26, 281–97.
Robarcheck, C. and Dentan, R. 1987. 'Blood Drunkenness and the Bloodthirsty Semai', *American Anthropologist*, 89, 356–65.
Romanucci-Ross, L. 1973. *Conflict, Violence, and Mortality in a Mexican Village*. Palo Alto, CA: National Press Books.
Ruffini, J.L. 1978. 'Disputing over Livestock in Sardinia' in *The Disputing Process-Law in Ten Societies*, eds H.F.J. Todd and L. Nader, New York: Columbia University Press, 209–46.
Scott, J.C. 1976. *The Moral Economy of the Peasant: Rebellion and Subsistence in Southeast Asia*. New Haven, CT: Yale University Press.
Shirokogoroff, S.M. 1976 [1929]. *Social Organisation of the Northern Tungus*. New York: Garland Publishing.
Spencer, P. 1988. *The Masai of Matapato: a Study of Rituals of Rebellion*. Bloomington, IN: Indiana University Press.
Todd, H.F.J. 1978. 'Litigious Marginals: Character and Disputing in a Bavarian Village' in *The Disputing Process: Law in Ten Societies*, eds H.F.J. Todd and L. Nader, New York and Oxford: Columbia University Press, 86–121.
Tokarev, P.N. 2000. *Istoriia voennogo komissariata RS(Ia)*, vol. 1. Yakutsk: NKI Bichik.
Tomsen, S. 1997. 'A Top Night: Social Protest, Masculinity and the Culture of Drinking Violence', *British Journal of Criminology*, 37(1), 92–102.
Turner, V. 1969. *The Ritual Process*. Chicago: Aldine Publishing Company.
Vasilevich, G.M. 1969. *Evenki. Istoriko-etnograficheskie ocherki (XVIII – nachalo XX v.)*. Leningrad: Izdatel'stvo Nauka.
Ventsel, A. 2004. 'Reindeer, Rodina and Reciprocity: Kinship and Property Relations in a Siberian Village'. Unpublished Ph.D. Diss., Max Planck Institute for Social Anthropology/ Martin Luther University Halle-Wittenberg.
Whitehead, N.L. 2004. 'Rethinking the Anthropology of Violence', *Anthropology Today*, 20, 1–2.
Whyte, W.F. 1993 [1943]. *Street Corner Society: the Social Structure of an Italian Slum*. 4th edn. Chicago and London: University of Chicago Press.
Ziker, J.P. 2002. *Peoples of the Tundra: Northern Siberians in the Post-communist Transition*. Prospect Heights, IL: Waveland Press.
Yablonsky, L. 1962. *The Violet Gang*. New York: NKI Bichik.

Chapter 4

ORDER, INDIVIDUALISM AND RESPONSIBILITY: CONTRASTING DYNAMICS ON THE TIBETAN PLATEAU

Fernanda Pirie

The 'problem' of order in societies that sanction violence has posed an analytic challenge to anthropologists since Evans-Pritchard's (1940) classic work on the Nuer. More recently, studies of violence and conflict in Melanesian societies have been used to critique certain models of social order. Strathern (1985), for example, uses a Melanesian example to cast doubt on the idea that order is the proper state of society and needs to be imposed on individuals who are, by natural propensity, asocial beings, a model which is associated with state legal systems. It should not be assumed, she says, that such a view is shared by members of other societies, nor that disputes necessarily represent ruptured social relations, which need to be repaired through processes of conflict resolution. Harrison (1989: 585) develops Strathern's argument by questioning a model of order elaborated in the work of Sahlins (1968) whereby tribal societies view their political groups as moral universes whose normative values derive from shared membership in a group. In many Melanesian societies, Harrison points out, violence is regarded as a threat to physical existence but not, apparently, to conceptions of the social. It is amoral, not immoral behaviour.

In this paper I describe a Tibetan community in which violence is, under many circumstances, compulsory. Among groups of nomadic pastoralists in Amdo, the principles of revenge require that attack is met by violent retaliation and pressure is put upon members of the relevant group to combine to do so.[1] The resulting violence is regarded as a threat to the physical existence of the community, but not as immoral behaviour. The ideas about order and the attitudes to conflict and violence which are critiqued by Strathern and Harrison are not entirely absent among these groups, however. Within the nomads' encampments the headmen take responsibility for maintaining peaceful relations, for punishing certain forms of violence and for promoting cooperation within and between groups. Elaborate processes of mediation are undertaken in order to resolve blood feuds, during which shared moral values are expressed and enforced. There is an idea that disputes represent ruptured social relations and that order needs to be reimposed during such processes. Such ideas do not, however, dominate all aspects of social behaviour. The norms of restraint and compromise invoked by headmen and mediators in order to resolve conflicts have to be asserted in opposition to norms of violence and aggression, which are articulated by angry men bent upon revenge. The social order, in fact, incorporates more than one set of norms and there is a constant tension between them.

To illustrate this point I contrast the Amdo nomads with an agricultural village in Ladakh, at the opposite end of the Tibetan plateau.[2] The Amdo pastoralists and the Ladakhi farmers share many religious, cultural and linguistic features, despite their different forms of livelihood. Nevertheless, the villagers in Ladakh's mountainous terrain strive to achieve a harmonious community, condemning all forms of conflict within it. They combine, as a body, to reimpose order on any individual who displays overt aggression. Ideals of cooperation and peaceful coexistence dominate their moral universe in a way which resonates with Sahlins's model of an order based on shared moral norms. Such ideals are not, however, absent in Amdo. Similar ideas are expressed by both the Ladakhi villagers and the Amdo nomads during their processes of conflict resolution. Both groups regard order as something which has to be imposed on deviant individuals. However, they have very different expectations of the ways in which such ideals should and will be enacted and enforced, or ignored and flouted by the members of their groups. In Ladakh rule breaking is anticipated but unequivocally condemned. In Amdo a certain defiance of the norms of order is not just expected but, in certain circumstances, normatively valorized.[3]

Ladakh

The Himalayan region of Ladakh, now part of India, has always been a predominantly agricultural area, its sparse population clustered into small, widely spaced villages, where irrigation makes subsistence possible in the high, arid environment. The region was incorporated into the early Tibetan empire of the seventh to ninth centuries and thereafter retained strong religious and trading links with central Tibet. However, until the mid nineteenth century it was ruled as a substantially independent kingdom. The kings governed through ministers, whose families came to form a small aristocracy, elevated in the social hierarchy, but administrative control was mostly light, largely limited to tax collection and the periodic mobilization of the population for war. Buddhist monasteries of various sects were patronized by the kings and often became powerful landowners. These continue to maintain small temples in each village, attended by caretaker monks who carry out rituals for the local populations.

Ladakh was conquered by the Dogras, then rulers of Kashmir, in the 1940s and incorporated into British India as part of the Princely State of Jammu and Kashmir. A certain amount of bureaucratization subsequently took place in the capital, although the main experience of the villagers was of an increase in their tax burdens. Since Indian independence the region has been governed by administrators appointed in Jammu, while legal order is nominally upheld by the police force and regional courts. Taxes have largely been abolished and successive governments have pursued modernizing agendas in the region. New forms of trade and tourism have been introduced, along with an expanded market economy. People now generally see the state as a force for good and a source of material benefits, but the government's administrative control is barely visible within the remoter villages, where the people still largely depend on subsistence farming. Here, they continue to organize their own agricultural cycle, festivals and ritual events, to raise their own taxes, maintain internal laws and settle disputes within the boundaries of their own community.

Village Administration

My case study concerns Photoksar, one of the remoter Ladakhi villages with a population of around 200, divided into 22 households. These households form the basic units of village organization, paying local taxes and fulfilling rotating village duties. A network of ties links them into different groups for agricultural, ritual and social tasks, which ensures that the village is criss-crossed with alliances and hinders the formation of permanent factions. Individuals are ranked, for all social purposes, in the *dral-go* (*gral go*)[4] seating and dancing lines, which place the monks, aristocracy, and (now) visiting officials into separate, higher positions. However, apart from the *amchi*, the practitioner of Tibetan medicine and the astrologer, it arranges the villagers, who are all of the commoner class, solely according to age and gender. This social mechanism thus symbolizes (relative) equality amongst the villagers, while placing outsiders into superior and, thus, most distant positions.

The headman of the village, the *goba* ('*go pa*), controls the community's funds and represents the village vis-à-vis outsiders. He organizes meetings, liaises with the astrologer and is responsible for settling disputes. However, this post rotates annually between all the full households of the village and all important and innovative decisions are taken at the village meeting. This is made up of the *yulpa* (*yul pa*), explained to me as being 'everyone', although in fact only consisting of the adult men. It also firmly excludes outsiders. The *dral-go* does not apply here, thus denying even the superiority of age demonstrated on social occasions. Meetings are relatively informal: differences of opinion are expressed but, on the whole, people let an agreement emerge. In practice, certain men talk more than others at the meetings, some go to more meetings than others, some are listened to more respectfully than others, but afterwards the influence of such individuals is never acknowledged. Those who attended always report what 'we' agreed and documents drawn up to record their decisions invariably stress the fact of agreement between the *yulpa*.[5] This internal group of *yulpa* is the final arbiter in disputes within the village and it is the idea of unanimity amongst them that is thus the foundation of their authority.[6]

Formerly there was a stronger *goba* system in most parts of Ladakh, with a man selected on the basis of ability for a number of years. This was needed, people explained, during the Dogra period, when the demands of the tax collector were strong and skill was required to negotiate with him. As the tax demands lessened in the twentieth century, however, most villages changed to a system of rotation and more than one explained to me that this was because they could not find a 'good enough' man to be a permanent *goba*. Conversely, in recent years, the availability of benefits from the centre has made it more desirable to have an educated man as *goba*, someone who is able to deal with the administrators and the bureaucracies. Some villages are, therefore, again electing their headman for a number of years, although complaints about the difficulty of finding a 'good man' are still common. Selection by rotation, therefore, appeared as the default system for choosing the leader when centralized control was at its lightest. It is still the system used in Photoksar.

Social Capital

Small rules of hospitality define many aspects of daily social behaviour, the giving and receiving of food and drink, the paying of visits, attendance and performance at festivals and rituals. There is considerable conformity in dress, household management, the preparation of food, the treatment of children and babies, as well as in agricultural processes, which are coordinated under the directions of the astrologer. Little value is placed on innovation, individualism and eccentricity. The place of each individual within the village is, rather, determined by gender, age and household affiliation and superiority in personal abilities or household resources are rarely mentioned. Everyone is aware of disparities in wealth, for example, but resists discussing and even acknowledging them. It causes resentment, they told me, which can bring people into conflict. Personal qualities are, likewise, downplayed. The *amchi*, the Tibetan medical practitioner, is educated, clever and highly regarded by others, for example. When his term of office as *goba* came to an end, however, he strongly resisted attempts made by other men to involve him in the resolution of disputes. It was someone else's turn, he would protest. On one occasion the *amchi*'s son tried to throw his weight around by being physically aggressive to the schoolteacher. The latter told me that he thought the boy was trying to rely on his father's status. The *amchi*, however, disciplined his son severely for his behaviour. He was ambitious for his children, but told me that he wanted them to be well educated so that they might become *amchi*s or astrologers. These are the only forms of status to which individuals can properly aspire. Elder men are often deferred to as a source of knowledge and experience but they do not have status within the *yulpa*. One grandfather actually complained to me that he now had less influence because he was growing old.

Social merit within Photoksar thus lies in knowing one's place, acting appropriately in any social situation and in knowing the right way to perform all household and agricultural tasks. Apart from the *dral-go*, in which the statuses of the astrologer, the *amchi*, gender and age are recognized, individual status is not acknowledged. It would, in fact, destroy an individual's standing to assert unwarranted superiority. Social capital within the village is found in modesty, self-effacement and the unassuming compliance with one's social duties. This uniformity in individual status is also reflected in the moral responsibility imposed on all individuals to maintain the social order.

The Morality of Conflict

Village practices of conflict resolution are supported by a strong morality. All forms of fighting, arguing, quarrelling and the use of abusive language are disapproved of. People shake their heads over quarrels and shudder at the mention of fighting. Even the expression of anger is morally disapproved of and this was the most definite and clearly expressed moral judgment that I ever heard in the village. Disapproval is expressed of those who fail to cooperate with others, are selfish or lazy. Alcohol drinking is also much criticized, but the real object of the villagers' disapproval is the disruption to social relations caused by the quarrels and fights that follow drinking. A common feature of these moral attitudes is an orientation towards the community. To be proud or lazy or to stir up trouble tend to create tensions and disrupt social relations. The overwhelming disapproval of anger and fighting, and indeed the whole scheme of village morality, are rooted in a firm sense of the importance and integrity of the community and the absolute need for cooperation amongst the individuals who constitute it. There is a moral obligation on every individual, as part of that community, to maintain such harmonious relations.

Outsiders and those who return from trading, pilgrimage or educational excursions bring competing moral ideas into the village, particularly religious ideas. Anger is one of the 'three fundamental poisons' of Tibetan Buddhism and the religion's texts also incorporate a set of moral rules, the *mi gewa rchu* (*mi dge ba bcu*). Monks would tell me that such norms are the basis of Tibetan and Ladakhi social practices and moral attitudes.[7] However, there was never any reference to these within the frequent discussions of disputes and morality that I heard within Photoksar. My more literate informants knew of them but never elaborated on their content. In fact, people never made an explicit link between their moral judgments and any aspect of their religious or cosmological practices, Buddhist or otherwise.[8] The villagers' moral universe forms a separate sphere, firmly linked to their sense of community and the need for cooperation and peaceful relations within it. The maintenance of order within the village is a moral issue for each individual.

The Disorder of Disputes

Conflict is always a problem and always morally condemned, never justified in terms of provocation or retribution. There is no concept of legitimate revenge, for example. Nevertheless, disputes do occur: over straying animals, within marriages, or simply as a matter of poor relations between individuals. Most of these problems are resolved informally but when poor relations evolve into overt antagonism a dispute becomes a community problem and the need for reconciliation becomes imperative. The response to conflict is always to try to achieve an agreement between the two parties. News of a public quarrel spreads very quickly throughout the village, raised voices have been heard, allegations have been flung, stones have been thrown. But very soon someone will report that the *goba* has gone to sort it out. 'He will make the two of them sit down, shake hands, and promise not to throw stones any more', someone would explain.

There is a hierarchy of mediation for dealing with disputes, about which people were quite specific. First, household members will try to resolve the problem, they told me, then the neighbours will get involved, then they will go to a mediator. If he cannot resolve the problem, the headman will be called and if he cannot solve it the case will go to a meeting of the whole village. As a last resort we can go to the police, people would usually add, although in practice the involvement of the police is almost always avoided. The police just demand money and beat people up, villagers explained. Even a suspicious death in a village near Photoksar was kept from their attention.

For the villagers, disputes are events of public significance. Successful mediation generally involves the payment of a fine by the person seen to be most at fault to the other, but all parties involved in the violence will have to pay an additional fine to the village, 'because of the fight', and to sign an agreement promising to pay a much larger fine in case they get into a fight again. In one case of long standing animosity between two men, caused by the failure of a marriage, a subsequent fight did indeed occur and there was much discussion in the village about how they were going to raise the money to pay this very significant fine. As in all serious cases, they also went through a ceremony of *yal*, an offering of beer from a ceremonial brass jug. The man who had said the first harsh words had to give *yal* first, but then the other had to offer *yal* and also a ceremonial white scarf, because he had struck the first blow.

What is crucial in these cases is the re-establishment of good relations, rather than a determination of individual rights. In one case a heated argument was heard between two women in the upper fields of the village. It turned out that some yaks had got into one woman's fields and she had complained to the woman whose household had that year's obligation to protect the fields from the livestock. However, the latter was seen to be at fault for having escalated the quarrel and the *goba* went to discipline her. When she refused to apologize a whole village meeting was deemed necessary. Since she continued to refuse to apologize for her insubordination, her whole household was threatened with a social boycott. This is the ultimate sanction that can be applied within the village since it would be impossible to survive there without cooperation in agricultural, as well as social and ritual, matters. Faced with this threat, the woman backed down, apologized and the whole matter was settled. In the meantime, the other woman's crops were completely forgotten. There was no question of her asking or demanding compensation as it was the quarrel that was the problem for the village. Disputes are, thus, characterized as disturbances to the order of the community, requiring immediate reconciliation, rather than as breaches of rules requiring the determination of individual rights. Resolution involves the acceptance by individuals of their duty to cooperate and maintain peaceful social relations.

The villagers themselves do not have a concept easily translatable as 'order'. They perceive things in negative terms, as the danger of disorder and the need to restore good relations between members of the community. In the case of a resolved dispute they will say *drig song*, meaning simply 'it is OK again'. *Drig* is a very commonly heard word meaning 'all right' or 'satisfactory'. The restoration of order is simply a return to normality. There is also very little ritual in the mediation processes, only the final agreement being marked by a ceremony of reconciliation. It is the good relations between individuals, rather than the authority of the *yulpa*, that are symbolically highlighted.

Dispute settlement does not, therefore, invoke any utopian ideal of justice, nor any religious ideal of peace and harmony, Buddhist or otherwise, nor the idea of a unified state and legal system. The region abounds in such models of social order, but none has been incorporated into the local epistemologies. Rather, the implicit concept of order is that the community itself should be peaceful, united and harmonious. The community is made up of individuals between whom and between whose households there should be a network of cross-cutting, inter-linked, harmonious relations. Cooperation, sharing, hospitality and collective work are their manifestation. Two individuals exchanging harsh words or one person refusing to cooperate with another will create a rupture that the whole community must take responsibility for mending.

The Village Order

These attitudes to the resolution of disputes are intimately connected with the construction of the boundaries of the village community. The judicial authority enjoyed by the *yulpa* obviates the need for individuals to turn to external sources for conflict resolution and the idea of containment keeps disputes away from the attention of outsiders. People invariably use phrases meaning 'inside' or 'within', referring to their village, as the context in which disputes must be resolved. Processes of conflict resolution are shaped by a sense of locality. Those boundaries, like the identity of the *yulpa* and membership of the community, have to be carefully maintained, however. Outsiders with education or government positions and representatives of development organizations are incorporated into the *dral-go* in superior positions. Yet, like the monks and members of the aristocracy, they are excluded from membership of the *yulpa*. Even the resident monk, himself from a village family, plays no part in the proceedings of the *yulpa* and is never consulted with respect to conflict resolution. It is simply not his business. The villagers resist the influence of external forms of status on the internal dynamics of order and authority.[9]

Conversely, the women, although also excluded from the *yulpa*, have an important role to play in the maintenance of the moral order. Village matters, including the activities of the village meeting, are discussed in detail around the stove, at which point the women express definite preferences, clear moral judgments and forthright opinions. It is they who are often most explicit in their evaluation and moral condemnation of others. They were important exponents of local customs for me and the men rarely disagreed with their explanations. While it is the *yulpa* who take charge of settling major disputes, women's discussions and evaluations help to form the consensus of opinion that the *yulpa* will use to bring the parties to an agreement. They help to maintain the internal force of village morality.[10]

The unquestioned authority enjoyed by the *yulpa* during processes of conflict resolution represents the supremacy of the interests of the community over those of the individual within it. At the same time, however, that community is conceptualized not as some abstract entity, but as 'everyone', 'all of us'. Each individual shares in the interests of the collective and also in the duty to safeguard it. In Strathern's (1985) terms, order has to be imposed on deviant individuals, but it is an order which is internally generated by the activities of the inclusive group of *yulpa* and the moral judgments of the whole body of villagers.

Amdo

The lush grasslands of Amdo, part of China's Qinghai and Gansu provinces, support mobile groups of pastoralists who herd yaks, sheep and horses, trading their surpluses with the agricultural populations on the fringes of the plateau. The pastoralists are organized into segmentary tribes, amongst whom there are patterns of violence and feuding, mediated by high status individuals. The boundaries around the social groups are much more fluid than in Ladakh and the nomads' concerns with order are directed as much at relations between groups as relations within them.

After the collapse of the early Tibetan empire in AD 842, Amdo was not politically unified again until the Chinese occupation of 1958.[11] In the intervening centuries Mongol and Manchu forces exercised considerable power within the region, followed by the Hui Muslims in the early twentieth century. Their administrative control was concentrated in the agricultural areas of the north east, however, while local rulers in the nomadic regions further south and west retained a significant degree of autonomy (Fairbank 1978: 36–37, 94). With the increasing domination of the Dalai Lamas in central Tibet, the Buddhist Gelukpa sect became powerful in Amdo and in 1709 Jamyang Zhepa was recognised as an important Buddhist incarnation and founded the major monastery of Labrang there. This, along with other major monasteries, became an economic and political force in the region, exercising administrative control by appointing headmen to the nomadic tribes in their areas. Certain secular leaders ruled in the same way and achieved the status of minor kings, while other tribes combined to form powerful confederations under hereditary ruling families. The Golok tribes, in particular, were renowned for their violence and became a source of terror for travellers and neighbouring groups, alike (D'Ollone 1912, Hermanns 1949: 231, Rock 1956). This paper primarily concerns groups in Machu, a tribal, nomadic area, formerly on the fringes of the influence of Labrang.

Following the Chinese occupation, the power of the monasteries was destroyed, all local leaders were deposed and all pastoral activities were collectivized. Under the reforms of the early 1980s, however, the monasteries were allowed to reopen and the animals were gradually returned to the private ownership of nomad tents. The nomads very quickly reformed themselves into the groups that had existed before 1958. Chinese rule has introduced considerable changes and material benefits in the form of roads, markets, schools and healthcare, but the nomads insist that their social organization, including their patterns of feuding and mediation, follow substantially the same patterns and principles as they did previously. This is also apparent from accounts of earlier periods (Ekvall 1939, 1954, 1964, 1968, Hermanns 1949, 1959).

The Segmentary Tribal Structures

Now, as before the Chinese occupation, the nomads of Amdo are divided into tribal groups, known as *dewa*, consisting of up to several thousand people.[12] In some areas the *dewa* are referred to as *shokwa* (*phyogs ba*) and *tsowa* (*tsho ba*), suggesting unity of descent. As I have argued elsewhere (Pirie 2005), however, this descent ideology only applies to the ruling families. The *dewa* are, rather, united on the basis of territory, combining to worship local deities. The potential for movement between tribes is, therefore, high. These *dewa* are, themselves, divided into encampments or villages, known as *repkor* (*ru skor*). A *repkor* might consist of 40 tents, around 200 people, and relations between them are relatively egalitarian. Each *repkor* is under the charge of one or more headmen, *gowa* ('*go pa*),[13] selected by the people. Their duties are to coordinate pastoral movements, allocate summer grazing land, negotiate with the local authorities, organize ritual events and resolve local fighting and disputes. A council of around 40 *gowa* now takes charge of the affairs of the *dewa* in the place of the leaders formerly appointed by the monasteries or from hereditary families.

Unlike the Ladakhis, who downplay the occurrence of conflict, the Amdo nomads talk frequently and readily about both actual and potential violence. Everyone could tell me stories of fighting and killing that had occurred in the last few years and theft is a constant concern to them. When they suffer an attack, the norms of revenge demand immediate and violent retribution. Men would tell me, for example, that they 'have' to get angry if a member of their family has been killed, and when there is conflict between two encampments all the men must combine to take revenge on the other. It is the same in the case of fighting between *dewa*. A long-running dispute over pasture land between a tribe in Machu and the neighbouring Sokwo, for example, sees the outbreak of periodic hostilities, at which point the *gowa* calls one man from each tent to join the battle. One complained to me that an encampment near the border was refusing to join in the hostilities on the grounds that it had many kinship links with Sokwo. This was thoroughly disapproved of and relations between that encampment and the rest of the *dewa* had, effectively, been cut. Feuding relations should take precedence over kinship ties.[14] On the other hand, although it is given considerable prominence in conversation and the dangers of attack are constantly asserted, the enactment of violence is not apparent on a daily basis on the grasslands. The nomads talk as if both strangers and neighbours were always just about to attack or steal from them but unprovoked violence and theft, particularly against a neighbouring encampment, are strongly condemned.

Within the encampment the nomads highly disapprove of all fighting and a murder would lead to the permanent expulsion of the killer's family. It is the duty of the local *gowa*, in particular, to diffuse the potential for violence within their encampment. On one occasion thirty sheep were stolen from the family I stayed with and one son, Jamku, went with some friends to search for the thief on the basis of divination clues given by a monk. When they identified him, in another *dewa*, Jamku declared his intention to fight immediately but was restrained by his friends. He was later persuaded by his family and relatives to let the *gowa* intervene and the whole affair was settled with compensation payments over the course of the following weeks. When Jamku's brother, Jamyang, got drunk and engaged in a senseless fight with a man from a neighbouring encampment, the man's cousin came the next day to demand an explanation from the headman. This he easily secured, along with an apology. When some young men were caught stealing yaks from tents inside the encampment considerable outrage was widely expressed. They were caught and severely beaten by their uncles and the *gowa*, who also called an encampment meeting to make new rules. Thieves should always be beaten, they decided, and in the case of theft from a neighbouring encampment, the families should pay back the livestock twice over. Good relations had to be maintained with neighbours, they explained to me. The enactment of violence is thus subject to normative control and within the local group there is considerable emphasis on peaceful relations.

Once a theft or physical injury has been inflicted, however, the norms of revenge demand immediate retaliatory violence. Even under Chinese rule, when they face the threat of punishment by the police, a death must be avenged and when this arises between men of two different tribes the pressures for restraint are weak. Escalating violence can then only be averted by invoking established procedures of mediation. Injuries and death are compensated for with the value of the damage or life, *mnyörtong* (*mi stong*) (now calculated in monetary terms), and thefts by the return of the animals together with an additional apology payment. Acceptance amounts to an agreement by the victim not to take further revenge. The mediators are the *zowa* (*gzu ba*), often *gowa* from neighbouring *dewa* or senior monks from local monasteries. Their initial task is to establish a temporary truce so that mediation can take place. The object of mediation is, then, to calculate the appropriate level of compensation after the deaths of each side have been set off against each other, or to establish where boundaries should run. Crucially, the mediators have to convince the parties to accept their proposed solution. My informants referred to the *gowa*s with 'good speech' as being those who could easily resolve such problems and renowned mediators take great pride in their skills. Ekvall (1968: 79) describes the persuasive power of such external mediators, based on their status as chiefs, their (reputed) skills of oratory or their position as famous Buddhist *lamas*.

The norms of the feud are thus liable to engender escalating retributive violence, which both *gowa* and *zowa* see it as their duty to counteract. The overall order found in the balance between stability and violence within nomad society in Amdo is fragile and, to some extent, the new governmental administration has endangered this balance. Although the nomads have been allowed substantially to regroup themselves into their former *dewa*, the regime's new territorial policies involve fencing the pastureland, which creates divisions and the potential for disputes while weakening the collective unity of the encampment. Many writers, as well as the nomads themselves, blame the Chinese government for current instances of violence and instability (TIN 2002, Yeh 2003). On the other hand, the nomads' dynamics of order have shown themselves to be adaptable to the new regime. The police respond to violence according to their system of criminal sanctions, meting out harsh punishments, but the nomads continue to insist on their own forms of compensation, thus often submitting themselves to a form of double punishment. The governmental authorities now tacitly acquiesce in these processes of mediation, recognizing that they are far more effective than their own in resolving feuds. They even invite members of the old ruling families or senior lamas to get involved in the most serious cases. Rather more surprisingly, the nomads themselves sometimes turn to the government administrators to provide them with a source of authority. They see the authorities as having the ability to avert conflict by settling borders and to do the initial work of the *zowa*, and they are resentful when these officials do not use their power in this way. The government's representatives have thus been drawn into the nomads' system of conflict and order.[15]

Individuality

A form of structural balance is apparent within these dynamics, between the norms of order enforced by the *gowa* and *zowa* and those of aggression which are enacted by individuals, and sometimes undertaken by a whole group. However, this does not mean that potentially destabilizing violence does not occur. Mobility means that boundaries between groups are porous. A whole tent can easily move its position and group allegiance.

While a certain amount of stability is generated by the imposition of social norms within an individual group, many writers talk of the way in which weaker groups in Amdo historically fell prey to stronger ones, trading caravans were decimated and conflict constantly arose over pastureland (Hermanns 1949: 229, 1959: 161, Rock 1956: 124–29, Ekvall 1964: 1128, 1981, Levine 1999). Oral histories refer to movements of whole groups as a result of conflict.

The norms of retaliation, which require that violence is only inflicted in response to aggression, are, moreover, often exceeded. The intention to take revenge is always expressed as an individual one: '*I* am going to go and fight him', '*I* want to fight the police because they injured my cousin', 'Do *you* want to come with us to fight the neighbours who are using our land?' It is not, '*we* should all go and fight'. Revenge is taken on behalf of '*my* brothers', '*my* cousins', '*my dewa*'. Group opposition and loyalty are expressed in personal terms. Both Ekvall (1964: 1124–25, 1968: 76–77) and Hermanns (1949: 231–32, 1959: 302) repeatedly emphasize the autonomy and individuality of Amdo nomads and the individual and immediate nature of the response to violence. The expression of group loyalty and opposition is dominated by a consideration of the self, and the expression of the intention to fight is always made without care for the consequences for others, who will inevitably be drawn into the escalating violence. Most importantly, there is a sense that the potential for individual violence is always only barely controlled and that an individual's anger can be provoked by the slightest transgression. Certain individuals are known to have hot tempers and to be liable to lash out at the slightest incitement. The emphasis on the control of emotion found in Photoksar is striking by its absence. In the context of an unresolved boundary dispute between two *dewa*, for example, it was well known which individuals were most likely to initiate hostilities. There is a constant threat of barely provoked violence which goes beyond the strict norms of retaliation.

Rule breaking has also been noted as a feature of masculinity in other societies (Herzfeld 1985, Loizos and Papataxiarchis 1991). In Amdo, the norms of violence are norms of manhood and these require a certain disregard, even defiance, of all types of social norms and consideration of the interests of others. Such norms are characterized by a strong emphasis on individual wishes and inclinations. Within the encampment, a (male) visitor will always appropriate the best place by the fire, if he wishes it, rather than waiting to be offered. Food is picked up and rejected without formality, in contrast to the Ladakhi village, where tiny rituals of hospitality pervade every social occasion. The habitus on the male side of the stove radiates ease and relaxation as the men lie around on carpets, playing cards and demanding food and drink, while the women cater to their needs. The appearance of industry and responsibility is minimized as they ride around on their horses or motor-bikes, never looking busy or hurried.

There is a carelessness with the effects or burdens they place on their friends and relatives, especially the women, whose responsibility it is to fulfil all their demands. The public face of the male nomad is self-centred, careless and indolent.

Within the domestic sphere it is the women who undertake the bulk of the work. In contrast to the freedom and carelessness displayed by their fathers, husbands, brothers and sons, they take responsibility for the care of the children, the collection and preparation of all water, food and fuel, the construction and maintenance of the tent and its contents, the care of the livestock and its produce. Men have certain responsibilities for herding, trading, caring for sheep and processing skins, but the daily tasks and the vast bulk of the work, are the obligation of the women.[16] At the same time, the women adopt an attitude of servitude towards their men. Although it is the women, themselves, in particular the mothers-in-law, who are primarily responsible for enforcing this servant culture, it allows the men the freedom and leisure to pursue their personal inclinations.[17]

Certain pollution concerns impose further restraints on the freedom of women, particularly concerning their clothes, washing and eating bowls, which are all considered to be dirty.[18] Ekvall (1964: 1135) describes the taboo on women carrying weapons and I never saw or heard of any instance of women fighting. Anger and aggression is very much male behaviour. However, one informant did, rather reluctantly, admit that women fighting is thought to give rise to *drib*, spiritual pollution, normally associated with life-cycle events (Das 1998: 244). The norms of aggression at the heart of the pattern of feuding in Amdo are very much male norms, balanced by equally strong norms of responsibility and restraint on the part of the women, themselves backed up by pollution concerns. An ethic of individuality and irresponsibility, therefore, characterizes the behaviour of the male nomads, while it is the women who take responsibility for the order and economic productivity of the domestic sphere.

Leadership and Mediation

The male norms of individuality are not directed towards the attainment of status or power, however. The indolence and selfishness that characterize male behaviour are not markers of supremacy. Leadership is, rather, granted to the experienced, mature and industrious (Hermanns 1959: 304–5), individuals who undertake a role of responsibility. Nor is this necessarily the elder men. The *gowa* are, rather, those who are prepared to take on the onerous task of maintaining order within their encampment, imposing punishments and restraint on its members. Their attitude to violence is one of responsibility and they articulate concerns for the overall order of the encampment, in striking contrast to the anger emphasized by others. 'I worry everyday that this border dispute is going to break into violence', one *gowa* explained, while my field assistant told me that, 'we will have to get angry if they come onto our land'. Other men normally distance themselves from such responsibility: '*the gowa* are going to meet with the local officials', 'the encampment meeting is going to have to consider this problem', 'the *gowa* asked us to attend'. It is not the 'we' of the Ladakhi village. Although there is considerable involvement in these meetings on the part of other men, they expressly attribute ultimate responsibility to their selected representatives. There is no sense of collective accountability for the maintenance of order and a subtle sense of exteriority is expressed by the nomads towards those in leadership roles.

The most prominent promoters of order in Amdo are the *lamas*, who are called in to mediate the most serious feuds. Today, as previously, Jamyang Zhepa and Khongtang Rinpoche (now deceased), from Labrang monastery, are seen as able to settle conflict whose resolution is beyond the capabilities of local mediators. 'People always tell the truth in front of them', the nomads told me, and the *lamas* suggest just solutions, taking into account the history of the case. The role of religious leaders as mediators in tribal feuds, such as the Islamic 'saints' described by Gellner (1969), has been noted elsewhere (Caton 1990).[19] These external figures act as a counterpoint to the leaders of the local groups who may themselves be required to support the norms of retaliation. In Amdo the *lamas*' status as reincarnations of Buddhist deities, or other eminent historical figures, endows them with charismatic authority which makes them particularly suited to fulfill this function. *Lamas* possess special powers to assist souls in the afterlife and are the most effective intermediaries between people and their *zhabdakh*, the local deities who can grant protection and bestow strength and good fortune on the living. The *lamas* are potent figures, able to intercede with powerful local spirits as well as to overcome the nomads' norms of violence and aggression.

Nevertheless, like other mediators, it is crucial that they are not members of either of the warring groups and do not exercise too much domination. Ekvall states that the mediators, 'had to stand high in the social and power scale, according to the importance of the case', but not, 'with such direct authority with respect to those between whom they were to mediate that they would be suspected of attempting coercion' (1964: 1140–41).[20] Moreover, their mediation attempts are far from being universally successful. Ekvall (1964: 1147) vividly describes the contemptuous rejection of a settlement proposed by senior *lamas* and the grudging admiration this behaviour attracted from the onlookers. In the Sokwo-Machu feud already described, attempts by both Jamyang Zhepa and Khongtang Rinpoche to find a solution have been unsuccessful and my informants told me that one Sokwo *gowa* had actually threatened to shoot these *lamas* if they interfered again.

The Dynamics of Order

In contrast to the Ladakhi village I have described, therefore, there is no collective responsibility for the maintenance of order among these tribal groups in Amdo. Rather, the burden for this is placed on particular sections of the society – the women, the *gowa* and the *zowa* – while the majority of the men pursue norms of irresponsibility and individualism. A certain ideal of peaceful and cooperative social relations is maintained and enforced by the headmen within their groups and the fear of fighting articulated by the Amdo *gowa* is, in fact, not so different from the fear of conflict expressed in the Ladakhi village. The language used to describe the need for an end to hostilities and the achievement of agreement is similar. However, in Amdo individual men are expected to threaten these norms by careless behaviour and the barely provoked escalation of violence. These are the norms of manhood. There are, thus, tensions and contradictions between the norms of order and those which govern individual action. As Harrison comments with respect to Melanesia (1989: 584–85), the idealization of aggression often seems ambivalent. The violent, reckless man is also considered a liability in many contexts. He exemplifies their masculine values too well. I would suggest that a very similar form of ambivalence characterizes the social order of the Amdo nomads. There is a constant fear of the consequences of violence, but individuals are expected to adopt defiant attitudes towards their headmen.

The personal norms of manhood are thus socially disruptive and a certain amount of rule breaking is expected. Like the norms of the feud they affirm group loyalty and protect the tribal group against encroachment and attack. Nevertheless, they also represent a threat to the underlying order of the group, to its property and prosperity, and have to be counteracted by those who can impose the norms of restraint and compromise. Ekvall repeatedly stresses the tension between the norms of individual freedom and the community consensus necessary to generate peace (1964: 1124, 1968: 76–77). The male nomads expect to be persuaded, cajoled or forced to exercise restraint and to consent to conciliation, but order is only ever temporary and contingent. Dresch makes a similar point with regard to segmentary Yemeni groups: 'features of shared morality are generally little stressed in contexts other than contradistinction ... and political order, or indeed its mere possibility, is a contingent good that groups have from outside' (1989: 101). It could be said that among the Amdo tribes there is a meta-order, which is found in the overall pattern of feuding and mediation, in which the restraining and conciliatory activities of the mediators play a crucial role. It is an unstable order, however, characterized by the constant fear of violence.

Conclusion: Violence and Social Order

The ecological conditions found at the opposite ends of the Tibetan plateau and the different means of subsistence employed by the populations I have described here are matched by significant differences in their social structures and in the nature and intensity of relations between them. In an isolated Ladakhi village concerns with order are focused on the internal dynamics of peace and harmony, disruption and disorder. It is these that pose the greatest threat to the stability and prosperity of the community, not border conflicts with neighbours or theft of the type that occurs so frequently in Amdo. Among the nomads of Amdo, by contrast, the orientation is outward as much as inward. Threats are posed by raids and relations between groups are often antagonistic. The headmen have to maintain peace and order within their own encampments, but they also have to coordinate its members to avenge an attack from outside. While violence is unequivocally condemned in the Ladakhi village, the nomads of Amdo valorize the strong and aggressive man, ready to take revenge at the slightest provocation. Given these structural differences and radically different attitudes to violence, however, there is more similarity in the models and ideals of order found in each group than might be expected.

Both Ladakhi villagers and Amdo nomads regard conflict as ruptured social relations which need to be repaired through processes of conflict resolution and must culminate in an agreed end to hostilities. Considering the Hageners of Melanesia, amongst whom violence is also valorized under certain circumstances, Strathern (1985: 113, 122) concludes that conflict does not represent ruptured social relations. It does not entail the need for repair through processes of conflict resolution. Order is not, correspondingly, regarded as something which has to be imposed on asocial individuals. In Amdo, however, this is just the type of order which is promoted by the headmen and mediators. Harrison (1989: 584–85), for his part, also drawing on Melanesian ethnography, critiques Sahlins's model of tribal groups as moral universes, whose normative values derive from shared membership in the group. Yet, in both Amdo and Ladakh conflict is resolved through moral pressure to comply with the norms of peace and restraint. Similar models of order are found among both Tibetan groups. Moreover, such ideas do not just characterize the internal order of the smallest groups. They are also reflected in the rhetoric of the Amdo mediators called in to settle conflict between tribes. It is not merely that differences in social structure and the location of conflict give rise to different models and dynamics of order.

A more fundamental point of difference between Ladakh and Amdo, I would suggest, is to be found at the level of individual behaviour. There are certain norms in Amdo, those governing individual, masculine activities, which promote 'asocial' behaviour. These, in turn, threaten the interests of the whole encampment or tribe. This happens within the smallest groups as much as the larger. In Ladakh there is a dominant ethic of conformity with social norms and restraint from violence. Each individual is primarily a member of the community, under an obligation to participate in harmonious relations, to cooperate with others and to acquiesce in village decision making. Social capital is only acquired by playing such a role, not by exhibiting individuality. The social order is thus internally generated by the activities of these individuals within the community. In Amdo, by contrast, there is an overwhelming ethic of individualism. Male nomads are expected to adopt careless attitudes towards many social norms and to display an incipient, barely restrained anger that is liable to break out at the slightest provocation. They are expected to flout the social norms. Order has to be imposed by responsible individuals. It is a 'contingent good', in Dresch's (1989) terms, something which they receive from outside. As Harrison (1989) describes for Melanesian societies, there is an ambivalence, among the Amdo nomads, in their attitudes towards conflict and aggression. This results in tensions between the norms of peace promoted by the headmen and mediators and the norms of individual aggression and retaliation enacted by the men. It is not so much the ideals of social order that are radically different between these two societies as the ways in which individuals are expected to observe, enforce, ignore or flout them and the consequences of such behaviour for the status of the individual.

Notes

1. I use the term 'nomad' as a shorthand to refer to these nomadic pastoralists. It is the word used by the few English speakers among them but the Tibet equivalent, *drokpa* ('brog pa), means 'people of the pastures'.
2. This paper is based on 18 months fieldwork in Ladakh, undertaken between 1998 and 2003 and funded by the Economic and Social Research Council of Great Britain, and 9 months of fieldwork in Amdo undertaken between 2003 and 2004 and funded by the Max Planck Institute for Social Anthropology, Halle, Germany. I am grateful to members of the workshop on Order and Disorder for their comments on this paper and to Keebet von Benda-Beckmann who made a detailed and constructive review of the text.
3. In both areas economic development has brought about the expansion of towns and new economic opportunities. The dynamics of order in such contexts are changing and complex (Pirie 2005, 2007). This paper concentrates on rural communities, however, which are relatively distanced from such developments.
4. Ladakhi and Amdo are Tibetan languages. I transcribed words according to local pronunciation, but I add the Wylie (1959) transcription in brackets to indicate the Tibetan spelling.
5. In the villages closer to the centre and the modernizing influence of the town, factions and power struggles have emerged in recent years. I have discussed the complex issues of hierarchy and equality and the effects of modernity at length elsewhere (Pirie 2007: 170–95).
6. This form of legitimacy contrasts sharply with the political authority of the former kings (which was based on military power, social superiority and religious patronage), the

religious authority of monks (based on cosmological efficacy, scholarship and the system of reincarnation, Mills 2003), and that of modern political leaders (based on the economic power and democratic structures of the modern state).
7. These views, which characterize elite attitudes to the role of Buddhism, are repeated in French (1995).
8. The significance and impact of religious and ritual practices is, rather, confined to the dictates of the law of *karma* and the cosmologically generated problems of physical misfortune. This is a contentious issue which I have discussed at greater length elsewhere (Pirie 2007: 88–111).
9. I have discussed the relations between the village and centres of power in the region at greater length in Pirie (2006).
10. The gender differences must not be overstated, however. Now that education is widely available, girls as well as boys are encouraged to pursue their studies to the highest levels. Moreover, in many villages closer to the centre, where job opportunities take many men away to the town, the village economy is essentially run by the women and they are full participants in the village meeting.
11. This is the date always referred to locally as the time when the Chinese 'came' to the region.
12. I use the term 'tribe', following Khoury and Kostiner (1990), to refer to these distinct groups, which have relatively egalitarian internal relations and leaders who are more like chiefs than heads of a state.
13. This is the same word as the Ladakhi *goba*, but with the Amdo pronunciation.
14. Of course, the wealth of mobile pastoralists is highly mobile and difficult to guard and, as Gellner (1988) has argued, the principles of revenge and group loyalty are, in such circumstances, logical forms of defence.
15. I have discussed this dynamic further in Pirie (2005).
16. In a telling comment on the eventual 'war-weariness' that overcomes the men following extended conflict, Ekvall (1964: 1135) refers to their longing for time to pursue pleasure, trading and religious activities. Basic economic subsistence was clearly being taken care of meanwhile by the women.
17. As in other societies with strong gender divisions (e.g., Peters 1990, Simic 1983) in-marrying wives have little influence on matters beyond the tent, but mothers do exercise considerable authority over their sons. Jamku's mother put considerable pressure on him to desist from attacking the sheep thief, for example.
18. Such concerns are weakening now among town dwellers, but many men, particularly those noted for their hot tempers, still take offence at breaches of the rules within the tent.
19. The Nuer's leopard-skin chiefs are an African equivalent (Evans-Pritchard 1940).
20. Dresch likewise describes the Yemeni Shaykhs as powerful figures who were needed to impose a measure of order, but whose power could also be found irksome. The ideal was someone who could, 'take responsibility for the safety of others without presuming on those others' prerogatives' (1984: 45–46).

References

Caton, S. 1990. 'Anthropological Theories of Tribe and State Formation in the Middle East: Ideology and the Semiotics of Power' in *Tribes and State Formation in the Middle East*, eds P. Khoury and J. Kostiner, Berkeley and Los Angeles: University of California Press, 74–108.
Das, S.C. 1998 [1902]. *A Tibetan-English Dictionary*. Delhi: Book Faith India.
D'Ollone, H.M, Vicomte. 1912. *In Forbidden China: the D'Ollone Mission 1906–1909*, trans. B. Miall. London: T. Fisher Unwin.

Dresch, P. 1984. 'The Position of Shaykhs among the Northern Tribes of Yemen', *Man*, 19(1), 31–49.
——— 1989. *Tribes, Government and History in Yemen*. Oxford: Oxford University Press.
Ekvall, R. 1939. *Cultural Relations on the Kansu-Tibetan Border*. Chicago: University of Chicago Press.
——— 1954. 'Mi sTong: the Tibetan Custom of Life Indemnity', *Sociologus*, 2, 136–45.
——— 1964. 'Peace and War among the Tibetan Nomads', *American Anthropologist*, 66(5), 1119–48.
——— 1968. *Fields on the Hoof*. Prospect Heights: Waveland.
——— 1981. *The Lama Knows: a Tibetan Legend is Born*. New Delhi: Oxford & IBH Publishing Co.
Evans-Pritchard, E.E. 1940. *The Nuer*. Oxford: Oxford University Press.
Fairbank, J. ed. 1978. *Cambridge History of China*, Vol. 10: *Late Ch'ing, 1800–1911*, Part II, Cambridge: Cambridge University Press.
French, R. 1995. *The Golden Yoke: the Legal Cosmology of Buddhist Tibet*. Ithaca: Cornell University Press.
Gellner, E. 1969. *Saints of the Atlas*. Chicago: University of Chicago Press.
——— 1988. 'Trust, Cohesion and the Social Order' in *Trust: Making and Breaking Cooperative Relations*, ed. D. Gambetta, Oxford: Blackwell, 142–57.
Harrison, S. 1989. 'The Symbolic Construction of Aggression and War in a Sepik River Society', *Man*, 24(4), 583–99.
Hermanns, M. 1949. *Die Nomaden von Tibet*. Vienna: Verlag Herold.
——— 1959. *Die Familie der Amdo-Tibeter*. Freiburg and Munich: Verlag Karl Alber.
Herzfeld, M. 1985. *The Poetics of Manhood: Contest and Identity in a Cretan Mountain Village*. Princeton: Princeton University Press.
Khoury, P. and Kostiner, J. eds 1990. *Tribes and State Formation in the Middle East*. Berkeley and Los Angeles: University of California Press.
Levine, N. 1999. 'Cattle and the Cash Economy: Responses to Change among Tibetan Nomadic Pastoralists in Sichuan, China', *Human Organisation*, 58(2), 161–72.
Loizos, P. and Papataxiarchis, E. eds 1991. *Contested Identities: Gender and Kinship in Modern Greece*. Princeton: Princeton University Press.
Mills, M. 2003. *Identity, Ritual and State in Tibetan Buddhism*. London: Routledge Curzon.
Peters, E. 1990. 'The Status of Women' in *The Bedouin of Cyrenaica*, eds J. Goody and E. Marx, Cambridge: Cambridge University Press, 243–77.
Pirie, F. 2005. *Feuding, Mediation and the Negotiation of Authority among the Nomads of Eastern Tibet*. Max Planck Institute for Social Anthropology, Working Paper No. 72, Halle/Saale.
——— 2006. 'Legal Autonomy as Political Engagement: the Ladakhi Village in the Wider World', *Law and Society Review*, 40(1), 77–103.
——— 2007. *Peace and Conflict in Ladakh: the Construction of a Fragile Web of Order*. Leiden: Brill.
Rock, J.F. 1956. *The Amnye Machen Range and Adjacent Regions: a Monographic Study*. Roma: Instituto Italiano per il Medio ed Estremo Oriente.
Sahlins, M. 1968. *Tribesmen*. Englewood Cliffs: Prentice-Hall.
Simic, A. 1983. 'Machismo and Cryptomatriarchy: Power, Affect and Authority in the Contemporary Yugoslav Family', *Ethos*, 11(2), 66–86.
Strathern, M. 1985. 'Discovering Social Control', *Journal of Law and Society*, 12, 111–34.
Tibet Information Network (TIN) 'Nomads Killed in Pasture Fights'. http://www.tibetinfo.org (accessed 21 June 2002).
Wylie, T.V. 1959. 'A Standard System of Tibetan Transcription', *Harvard Journal of Asiatic Studies*, 22, 261–76.
Yeh, E. 2003. 'Tibetan Range Wars: Spatial Politics and Authority on the Grasslands of Amdo', *Development and Change*, 34(3), 499–523.

Chapter 5

VIGILANTE GROUPS AND THE STATE IN WEST AFRICA

Tilo Grätz

Introduction

Many contemporary African states are weak states in the Weberian sense of the term because they lack full control of their territories, an absolute monopoly of violence and feature ineffective institutions (Jackson and Rosberg 1982, Roitman 1999, von Trotha 2000). The existence of local powers, authorities and independent political arrangements, as well as legal structures and modes of resource appropriation, further accentuates this picture. Parallel power structures and practices range from corporate groups which organize tax evasion, corruption, smuggling and informal production, to autonomous realms of local jurisprudence, including adjudication, sanctioning and taxation, to opposing political movements, quasi-independent regions and warlords. There are many 'intermediary' forms of local political control beyond the reach of the state which may draw upon both local modes of political action and new institutions (Alber 2000, 2001, Schlee 2001). Among these are vigilante groups[1] and local militias, which have recently increased in importance in many African countries. Vigilante groups are often able to generate specific regimes of public order (Abrahams 1998), dominate legal processes and control economic subsystems, at least in a certain region. They often operate in marginal or peripherical regions of African states – for instance in the area of Lake Chad and Sudan (Perouse de Montclos 1998, Roitman 2000) – although not exclusively, as many examples from urban areas in South Africa and Kenya reveal. In any event, they are often more than simple organizations of self-defence; they give rise to local movements, create multiple social ties and ritual relationships among their members and are shaped by pertinent moral discourses. Regardless of their local legitimacy, they may share similar features with sectarian groups, bandits and secret associations. Their rootedness in local societies may, nevertheless, be very different, as may their relationship to local elites and the central state.

This essay[2] introduces two such vigilante groups, one from Mali and the other from Benin. I discuss whether these groups contribute to a reordering of local society or create instability. They both represent a creative adaptation to local conditions, while they avoid infringing on the state's hegemony. The aim of this contribution is to consider the conditions of existence of these groups, to discuss whether they operate against or within the regional and national political framework. These phenomena arise in the context of political changes in contemporary West Africa which are redefining the relationship between citizens and the central state in its various manifestations. At the same time, they revitalize certain local modes of politics and legal authority by giving them a new meaning in changing contexts, combined with innovations resulting from postcolonial experiences. I shall point to two important dimensions of these phenomena: that of political legitimacy and the opportunity it offers for the rise of new ordering institutions.

Gold Mining Communities in Mali and the Rise of a Vigilante Group

In many West African countries, including south-western Mali, small-scale gold mining has seen a boom in the last decade. The Mandé region of Mali has been known as a gold producing area since medieval times. In the recent past, however, due to many factors such as the crisis in cash-crop production, droughts, currency devaluation and civil wars, there has been a considerable increase in artisanal gold production.[3] Migrants from all over West Africa have been seeking gold, opening new pits and establishing huge camps close to the mines. Thus the region is characterized by massive immigration, the presence of people of heterogeneous social and ethnic origins and an increased circulation of money.[4]

I studied such a mining camp close to the village of Kobadan, south of Samaya, not far from the Mali-Guinean border. In this mining camp, which is far from any regional centres with police stations, mayors and other officials, the local population has managed to control the influx, activities and the public behaviour of the newcomers. Local inhabitants, mostly ethnic Soninké, have been able to set rules of access to resources and to establish a system of jurisdiction and control.

The central institution which achieves this is the *tomboloma*, a sort of vigilante group. This group is composed of young men and some elders from the local village, and includes among its number the *damantigi*, the local 'master of gold'. The *damantigi* is elected by the village council and acts on behalf of the first settler-clans of the village. He officially assumes control of all gold-mining activities. He decides where to open a new pit, how to organize the work, assigning particular periods of the year for mining activities (in the past limited to the dry season, but with the influx of migrant miners, now extended throughout the year). The *damantigi* is expected to conduct special rituals related to the prosperity of the mines, the health of the miners and aimed at minimizing the spiritual 'dangers' of gold. According to my research, access to this office is handled quite differently in each village. A *damantigi* is always male and at the same time a clan elder and head of a farming or gold-mining household. In some cases, the *damantigi* is only elected for a certain period of time and may hand this office over to a successor at later date. In other cases it is a lifelong job for a member of the same clan. There is also a degree of variation when it comes to the actual power, mining capacities and prestige of a *damantigi* in any one village. The *tomboloma* are more than an assistant group serving the *damantigi*. According to my observations, especially in the region of Samaya on the Nouga plains, *tomboloma* enjoy considerable autonomy, self-determination and, in same cases, they control the *damantigi* more than he does them.

Each *tomboloma* group – often called the 'mining police' – is associated with the area controlled by a particular village. These territories largely correspond to historical Mandé agricultural areas, usually confined by rivers, which serve to define borders between *tomboloma* groups. They are paralleled by the hunter's association, *don-zon*,[5] which is exclusively responsible for the forest parts of the village. The *tomboloma*, together with the *damantigi*, determine how to compensate the local landlords (often elders representing the resident clan) affected by gold mining and how to organize important ceremonies and rituals.[6] They observe the activities of local as well as immigrant miners to ensure both continuing profits from mining and that local taboos are not infringed. The *tomboloma* supervize the observance of norms and public order in the mining camps, such as the avoidance of any mining activities on Mondays, the acceptance of certain rules for sharing, negotiated prices, good behaviour and so on.

For a long time, the roles of the *tomboloma* were only relevant at a particular time of the year and for the few local miners. Since the advent of the gold boom in the early 1990s, however, the *tomboloma* have acquired a new importance. Their duties have been expanded with respect to the immigrant mining communities and the newly established mining fields and camps. Before the new gold boom they acted more as a village defence group against thieves. Today, they are recognized by locals as a legislating, arbitrating and sanctioning body for almost all affairs concerning the extraction of gold, life in the new mining camps and the parts of the local economy related to the camps. Some *tomboloma* groups in the Nouga area even established a land tenure system called *niaro*.[7]

Their role differs, of course, from one village to another, but in most cases *tombolama* collect contributions and taxes and supervize all mining activities. The *tomboloma* assume the role of sanctioning everyday transgressions and quarrels, but also deal with cases of theft and murder. Officially, they should hand over those they seize to the police, who are often physically far away. However, cases of vigilante justice, from beatings to the poisoning of delinquents, have been reported, though they are seldom. A more frequent form of sanction is to demand compensation or fines; a more dramatic option is the expulsion of delinquents from the mining region.

The *tomboloma* hold regular and ad hoc meetings. In these meetings, recent affairs are debated and sanctions against those who have broken rules and norms are decided and thieves are tried. In some camps, *tomboloma* work together with elected representatives of immigrant mining groups. In many cases, they have also appropriated a wide range of juridical powers in their villages and also intervene in matters that are not related to gold mining or the mining camps, such as family affairs.

In some villages, the village head (*dugutigi*) cannot operate without them. Their power and legitimacy is based on autochthony claims connected to the attempts of locals to control the influx of strangers. Further power stems from their financial resources, derived from the many taxes and duties they levy. However, it would be too simple to characterize their activities in purely economic terms. As their membership is composed of many young men and those of the middle generation, they represent a counterbalance to the elders who have conventionally enjoyed more power in village affairs. The *tomboloma* give the young more social power and prestige in a region which has been marked by emigration and the loss of economic and social options for this generation.

In this way, with the help of the *tomboloma* the local population of the Samaya area has, in contrast to other West African mining regions,[8] not only been able to control the influx of migrants,[9] but has also established an important bargaining position vis-à-vis the state's agents, who are often unwilling to intervene in these areas, both with respect to the creation of infrastructure and the mediation of conflict. The *tomboloma*[10] do not fill a particular gap between the state and local societies. They still operate on the fringes of state interest, and their role is very much confined to the local context. They claim moral continuity in a rapidly shifting economic context and discursively refer to ancient institutions. I would argue that despite their many powers, the *tomboloma* embody neither an alternative institution nor a challenge to the state. They do not interfere in matters of the state that the latter claims overtly. They are localized and do not operate outside their respective region. Many recent interventions by the Malian state have actually strengthened the position and role of *tomboloma*. For example, joint efforts to reduce child labour, prospecting work, and the introduction of new pumps by specialized development agencies like PAMPE[11] have only been possible with the cooperation of the *tomboloma*. At least in the region where I did fieldwork, they are much stronger than the above mentioned (and much studied) hunters' association, the *don-zon*.

The Group of Colonel Dévi in Benin

The vigilante group of Colonel Dévi only existed for some years in the Mono region of south-western Benin and apparently came to an end with the arrest of its leader by military forces in January 2002. This group was formed in 1999 as a response to the growing insecurity and criminality attributed to the activities of armed gangs operating in the border region between Benin and Togo. Economic and social life was very much endangered, as market activities decreased and public life was influenced by increased cases of violent rape and murder. The state's agents were, despite some arrests, unable to reduce these criminal activities and were accused of being ineffective, fearful and of lacking strategy.

During this period, a group of youths clustered around the former soldier nicknamed Colonel Dévi (they were always called 'Dévi's men', and did not have a formal name) and formed a self-help group. Initially conceived as a defence unit, they soon started to chase and try robbers and gangsters throughout the region. They organized regular patrols, set up night watches, established road blocks, encouraged people to report any suspicious movements and organized punitive assemblies.[12]

Dévi's actions thus comprised many typical elements of militia activity, but he also borrowed, at least performatively, from some practices of official institutions. One noteworthy example is the way tribunals were held. According to my informants, they began as court trials do, by calling everybody to stand up when the judges entered, calling upon the accused to give his name and so on.

At a later stage, however, the group tortured delinquents and most of those arrested were put to death, being buried alive. State agents were unable to stop these actions and seemed, in a way, content to let them continue. Things changed, however, at the end of 2001. More and more cases of arbitrary arrest were reported, and even minor crimes were punished with the death penalty. Witchcraft accusations were also investigated by them and the mutilated bodies of women accused of being witches were found. The group had transformed into a mafia-like group or militia, refusing all collaboration with state security forces, which they did not tolerate in the area, threatening them when they attempted to intervene. They started to challenge the state, not only in its monopoly of violence but also in its endeavours to control public services, taxes and roads, which were important means for its agents to generate resources.

State agents now started to move more effectively against this group, which had established a veritable territorial hegemony in the Mono region. In January 2002, government forces, including the army and police, moved into the area in a joint action, arrested many of the group, including Colonel Dévi. Today, the group is insignificant.

Comparative Aspects

If we compare both groups, we may first of all detect their very different social roots and modes of internal organization. Unlike the *tomboloma*, Dévi's men represented a paramilitary group, operating in a larger territory, which tried to appropriate power over all types of criminal activity, finally being able to control a wide range of activities in the region. Despite being tolerated, the group was regarded by the state authorities with suspicion and declared illegal from the very beginning. The social roots of the members of these groups are quite different as well. In both cases we are dealing with youth, operating within a generation set, but the starting point and ritual culture of these age sets are very different. The armed vigilante groups, such as Dévi's men, are more heterogeneous with regard to age and local origins of their members, but are nevertheless tied to a particular ethnic group. The *tomboloma* in Mali integrate members of different ages, but of the same ethnic and regional origin. They are all united by common interests and a discourse on local identity or autochthony. The new vigilante groups often play with local symbols, but do not present themselves as direct descendants of an ancient tradition, whereas the *tomboloma* claim to act in straightforward continuity with old institutions, founding quite a substantial part of their legitimacy on such a discourse of local tradition.

The group of Colonel Dévi derived its internal cohesion largely from the personal capacities of its leader, including prestige and charisma. An indicator of this fact was its weakening after the arrest of Dévi in January 2002.

Furthermore, both groups differ considerably with respect to the degree of wider regional political integration and the respective range of local control. The *tomboloma* often operate in a regionally confined area. As their members are recruited on the basis of territoriality and kinship (members of the first-settling clans), they hardly integrate into larger power groups or militia such as Dévi's group. Currently, they do not organize themselves into larger networks or form sub-regional associations, as do some hunter organizations in Mali and especially Côte d'Ivoire (Bassett 2003). Their political power is also limited by the fact that they have only limited links with political elites. On the other hand, their members are very much integrated in their respective villages and include local youth, peasants and often gold miners themselves or small-scale traders. Where they work in collaboration with the 'master of the gold', with other village authorities or dominant clans and castes, they may establish a sort of village elite, thus profiting both economically and politically from the gold boom. Militant groups such as Dévi's men are organized much more like sectarian or secret associations. Apparently, they recruit their members less on the basis of territory than according to personal capacities. These members are gradually detached from local communities.

Both groups operate at the margins of the state, but have different relationships with central power. The *tomboloma* of Mali operate largely in connivance of state agents. The latter deliberately leave much room for manoeuvre to these groups. This could be explained by the fact that they do not represent a real threat to the state, nor do they strive for economic accumulation or challenge central state power. Thus it rarely comes to situations of conflict. In the case of Dévi, the vigilante group gradually entered into direct conflict and competition for judicial power with the state, so finally their members were persecuted and punished.

Thus, the relationship between vigilante groups and the state is far from being stable. Colonel Dévi, although officially regarded as an outlaw, was able to operate for a long time without effectively being touched. Unofficially, he was welcomed by many to do 'the dirty work of the state'. He only became dangerous when he began to establish territorial hegemony, becoming unpredictable and threatening even government officers and police forces.

Vigilante Groups and Militias in a Wider Perspective

What makes these groups successful or explains their failure? In the following, I shall discuss this issue from different perspectives.

Vigilante groups have emerged at various times in different parts of Africa. Ray Abrahams (1987) gives an intriguing account of *sungu sungu* groups in Tanzania in the 1980s that still exist today.[13] *Sungu sungu* groups are communal defence groups operating in rural areas. Also supported by the state, they were founded by village committees in an attempt to end the banditry that was widespread in times of economic crisis and also connected to many forced migration movements in that period (see also Campbell 1989, Fleisher 2000). Whereas the *sungu sungu* are more a rural phenomena, the South African vigilante groups described by Barbara Oomen (1999, 2004) operated in both towns and villages, sharing with the *sungu sungu* the aim of fighting criminality.[14] A similar trend can be seen in the proliferation of private guards and militias to protect companies and businessmen as well as the creation of gated communities for the wealthy. The case of the rise and fall of the Bakassi boys in Nigeria has seen a similar scholarly debate (Harnischfeger 2001, Baker 2002, Gore and Pratten 2003, Smith 2004).[15] In the case of *tomboloma*, some local commentators claim that they feature a strong continuity with pre-colonial times, but were also able to deal with the considerable social changes introduced by the gold booms. The importance of this institution is certainly connected to the necessity to manage communal relations between immigrant miners and local operators and to regulate economic relations in an area far from any political centres. My research suggests, however, that it is difficult to conceive of *tomboloma* today simply as a stable institution, even though it draws from local cultural registers and routines. They are influenced considerably by new village council procedures established in recent decades and managerial systems introduced by young literate returning migrants from the towns. In all cases discussed so far, the role of the central state, its institutions and procedures appears to be an important reference point.

Local systems of governance in Africa always consist of a high degree of 'informal politics' (Bierschenk and Mongbo 1995, Bierschenk and Olivier de Sardan 1997). Whether these local forms of power and control represent 'traditional', 'African' or 'local' forms of governance or not, whether they could be considered alternative modes of political integration, at least locally, is still matter of debate in African studies.[16] The degree of autonomy of local judicial[17] and defence groups has never been absolute and always changed over time. One should rather speak of a pendulum movement between stronger state interventions and withdrawal of the central state.

On the one hand, these institutions and movements are often interpreted as being a part of a general political change in Africa connected to a new liberalism, structural adjustment and the decline of statehood. This line of debate centres on weakening state sovereignty in the process of democratization after the end of the cold war and the general withdrawal of the state (Lauth and Liebert 1999). The rise of vigilante groups and militias is often portrayed as a reaction to decentralization processes, the growing illegitimacy of the state and increasing insecurity and violence.[18] The same commentators link the ethnic base of many such groups to the growing interethnic clashes, which give legitimacy to those trying to protect 'their' population (e.g., Anikulapo 2000). Beatrice Hibou (1999: 12) attributes the growing number of private mercenaries to the demise of state power and a general tendency to privatize public services (see also Elwert 1997, Perouse de Montclos 1998). The rise of private militias is often seen as a consequence of social decay, a vision also shared by other commentators for other parts of the world (Elliesen 2002). It is certainly true that many actors creatively profit from a situation of transition, for example with reference to new discourses of decentralization and the promotion of local initiatives. The discourse on autochthony, in particular, deriving from various debates and discourses, is one important aspect of such developments observable in many parts of Africa in recent times (Geschiere 2001).

It should also has to be mentioned that, from a sociological point of view, participation in these groups enables young, deprived male members of local societies to gain entry into the core of local affairs, usually dominated by elders.

On the other hand, these structural explanations do not clarify why these vigilante groups arise in some regions more than in others. Thus, it is necessary to consider additional aspects, to take into consideration the respective regional political arenas, with their institutional arrangements, the need for what is locally conceived as public order[19] and the quest for legitimacy, as well as the salience of political discourses, such as those on decentralization.

Institutional Insecurity and the Quest for Legitimacy

Let us consider the relationship between the public perception of order and the activities of vigilante groups. As has been explained above, the rise of local institutions appropriating legal authority should be seen in the context of political change in West Africa. The central state is retreating more and more, and local actors such as vigilante groups, village councils and committees are gaining much political weight. In parallel to this, the discourse and political practices of decentralization and local empowerment, also promoted by foreign donors, gives local actors more legitimacy, and this often covers acts of communal self justice, which are already spreading in various parts of West Africa (Alber and Sommer 1999, Paulenz 1999). Furthermore, there is a general tendency for local groups to try to exclude strangers such as settlers, pointing to their rights as first comers, and establishing local hegemony by referring to discourses of autochthony prevailing in most West African countries. The withdrawal of the state, unable to guarantee viable solutions to conflict, and the informality and weakness of local bodies leads to institutional insecurity, as Le Meur (1999) puts it, which creates new demands related to public order (Baker 2004), especially the viability of arbitrating and sanctioning powers.[20]

The groups we are discussing here could be seen as successful in that they seize a particular opportunity: that is, the need for protection and punishment independently of the state. Their success depends on their interpretation of the situation, the creation of apt regimes of control and, above all, the establishment of legitimacy. The course of action adopted in both cases illustrates the way in which legitimacy is discursively sought in particular ways by these groups and is also attributed to them by the local community.

One important aspect of the popular discourse on order in all the mentioned cases is the need for retribution, in the case of a transgression, as a precondition to re-establishing social relations between those affected by the breach of norms. Whenever somebody does something wrong, whenever social and moral norms are broken, there should be compensation or retribution. The guilty party should be shamed or punished indirectly through bad luck or a disease within the family, or by the direct act of the authorities. The state, even when asked to intervene, does not act immediately and effectively. Nor does not provide enough retribution in the eyes of many, which explains why there is generally little confidence in the state, as Alber and Sommer (1999) also show.

If official institutions no longer guarantee such retribution, people look for alternatives in, for example, a vigilante committee that forces the person to pay compensation. This may explain the rise of popular vengeance as it has been observed in Benin, especially in urban centres, where they even go so far as burning believed delinquents alive.[21] Whether or not this is a sufficient explanation for such phenomena, we should notice that a state of insecurity arises when neither the state nor local institutions satisfy the popular need for the justice of sanctions.

Common modes of retaliation, or forms of negative sanction, which form part of the 'corrective exchange', as Goffman (1971) puts it, such as shaming the person or appropriating some of their wealth as compensation, or making them work or organize expensive ceremonies, are not, however, possible in the case of foreign criminals who may not easily be identified or persecuted. In these cases, classic communal sanctions (Roberts 1979) do not work because there is no question of their being part of the local society or of maintaining this position. They are outlaws and have nothing to lose. In the same way, threats of magic or witchcraft are ineffective, as are village councils, especially when the phenomenon of trans-border crime grows and gains a new dimension. In this context, vigilante groups as self-declared guarantors of order may gain a particular legitimacy, despite the fact that they also use violence. This is, to a certain extent, locally accepted as a means of establishing order and the discourse of 'filling a gap' creates a particular space for their actions[22]. As mentioned above, not all of these vigilante groups were able to stabilize their success, however. They are more successful the more they are able to play simultaneously on both registers: of local modes of communal justice as well as those usually offered by the state; and the more they are able to maintain their position between both realms without trying to substitute one for the other. Effective or not, both case studies teach us that a situation of flux, conflict or disorder in the sense of institutional insecurity, may create an arena of new micro-politics, offering the potential for new groups to appropriate legislative powers and even the use of violence. These groups need to obtain popular legitimacy but must not challenge the hegemony of the state. They must respect local ideas of justice without ignoring those offered by the state.

Vigilante Groups Shaping the Communal Order

In both the cases I have discussed, the local communities were facing many challenges, stemming both from general political changes as well as particular regional developments. In the Malian case, the gold boom brought not only new resources to manage but also huge waves of immigrants. In the Benin case, it was above all the high crime rates that caused general public insecurity in daily life. In both cases, a demand for institutions to manage these issues arose. This could also be seen as part of a more general quest for the redefinition of the responsibilities of public control. This opened the way for a certain institutional creativity. In this respect, the problems that arose had the positive effect of bringing order back onto the agenda for the local communities. In this way, a state of disorder was useful in reshaping the local political arena, by forcing the adaptation of local politics to new circumstances. Furthermore, both cases reveal that local notions of order do not exclude violence, as long as it serves to re-establish security and is not exercised to excess. People do approve of violent practices, such as the vigilante groups that 'correct thieves', to deter such acts in future. But it is a matter of degree: when Dévi's men started to burn almost every presumed crook alive, this degree of violence became arbitrary and even terror-like. It created fear instead of peace and security and was thus no longer acceptable.

Another central aspect of these cases is predictability. A local power regime may gain acceptance, even if it is oppressive or disadvantageous for some actors, as long it is predictable and people can adapt to it. As soon as it loses this predictability, it may also lose its legitimacy, including for those profiting from it. In the Malian case, the gold mining immigrants from Guinea were obliged to pay high fees for opening new pits and for rituals, but accepted the *niaro* regime, as long as it facilitated their continuing work and engagement. The same applied to the market traders who used to collect money for the protection offered by Dévi's men: as long as the group's activities were predictable, to support them represented a kind of investment in stability.

Summary: Vigilante Groups at the Margins or the Core of Political Creativity?

In this paper I have discussed the role of vigilante groups in some parts of Africa today, based on empirical material from Mali and Benin. I have suggested that their popular legitimacy is linked to the demand for legal institutions that publicly punish those who breach local norms, but also create a sense of general predictability. This is related to the specific local situation, in which the state is not able to handle massive migratory movements, growing crimes rates and insecurity. The groups in question certainly differ in their mode of operation, as well as the regional context to which they are responding. A simple structural model is thus difficult to develop. They could be said to fill an institutional gap but do not act completely against the state system (being ignored when doing the 'dirty jobs').[23] Nor do they entirely reinvent the juridical processes, at least at the performative level, as the references to official tribunal standards by those established by Dévi may indicate.

We should not, therefore, confuse the discourse these groups themselves create to gain legitimacy with the actual course of their actions, which we have to assess in order to understand their rise and fall. Dévi's group developed into a more state-challenging social actor, which ultimately led to its demise. Before this occurred, however, it filled a space that had arisen out of many contradictions in the process of state devolution. In both cases, although their political culture is shaped by elements stemming from local traditions, the groups discussed became part of the general national political field during a period of change. They were, however, established in the context of the state, often borrowing from official norms or, at least, trying to adapt to them. Thus, they cannot be considered as completely extra-legal or non-juridical entities, as many superficial observers would suggest. Local actors may develop their own power regimes which, from the point of view of the population, may work and even gain legitimacy, at least for a certain period of time (see also von Trotha 2000). They are part of an ongoing process in Africa in which the institutional landscape beyond the state, while sharing many of its features and tasks, becomes more adapted to and viable with regard to changing demographic and economic issues, as well as local normative systems.

Notes

1. Although vigilante groups emerged at various historical moments and localities, the term derives from communal self-defence units that were set up in the nineteenth-century United States (Abrahams 1998).
2. Research was possible due to grants from the Max Planck Institute for Social Anthropology, Halle/Saale. Earlier versions of the text benefited from valuable comments by participants of the Africanist network session at the EASA meeting, Vienna, September 2004, at a workshop on 'Order and disorder', Halle/Saale, November 2004, and by Fernanda Pirie in particular. Responsibility for the views expressed here is mine exclusively.
3. The social conditions of small-scale gold miners are portrayed in Grätz (2003, 2004).
4. For the time being, the Malian state only intervenes partially in this sector. The government mining board is trying to establish a system of official licences and to promote foreign investment, with limited success.
5. The *don-zon* hunters' association of people 'protecting the woods' from thieves and others share symbolic and political ideals across ethnic groups in the Mande area and display a particular code of behaviour and morals (Diallo 2001, Hagberg 2004). In northern

Côte d'Ivoire, especially, they also became vigilante groups and intervened in political turmoil (Bassett 2003, Hellweg 2004).
6. In April 2003, I witnessed a ceremony of blessing at a newly-opened mining area close to Numusulku close to Kobadan and the subsequent distribution of pits to interested miners by a kind of 'commission' of members of the *tomboloma*. All pit owners were registered and had to pay a fee, which was protocolled by a young educated member of the *tomboloma*.
7. The *niaro* system prescribes that local miners should become owners of pits, hire workers and cater for their requirements and receive a considerable part of the yield, irrespective of whether they have worked themselves or not. Some *tomboloma* explained that the *niaro* system was a reaction to the uncontrolled influx of strangers that 'took more than they gave'. Compared to other camps, they declared, the taxes were 'rather moderate'.
8. Compared to other gold mining sites, the Malian case proves to be an exception because in most cases the immigrant gold miners set up their own rules and continued to impose their internal power structures upon the local settings (Grätz 2002).
9. The ways in which local populations react to the influx of migrant miners in boom regions of West Africa is quite diverse. In some cases, villagers not interested in gold mining at all were able to defend their territories and simply expel miners. In other cases, the immigrants were able to appropriate resources without any concessions. In other villages, multiple arrangements establish a balance between locals and immigrants miners, although conflicts over land, settlement and water resources are frequent.
10. The members of the *tomboloma* in this region originate both from the villages of Niaouleni and Samaya. Niaouleni was a new settlement, emerging in the 1980s after previous gold booms. Now, many new migrants live there, and local families have at least a second homestead there. This can be considered a conscious social strategy to sustain their claims.
11. Project: Promotion de l'Artisanat Minier et Protection de l'Environnement, Bamako.
12. During the proceedings they also invoked many legal terms such as 'court', 'judge', 'jury' and so on, although they did not allow defence lawyers.
13. Visiting the area south of Mwanza in April 2002, I still found many such vigilante groups, some of them also operating as local defence groups in gold-boom areas.
14. Oomen places the rise of vigilante groups in South Africa in the context of local political actors and their relationship to the state. Informal justice is legitimized by reference to the inability of the state to guarantee security. They also operate more in concordance with local state agents than other vigilante groups. Some of them act today within the framework of religious movements, including Islam (Le Roux 1997, Fauvelle and Renou 1999). Other vigilante groups in South Africa grew out of ethnic organizations and gangs within the compound system into which the black migrant labour force of the mining schemes was ordered during the apartheid system (Breckenridge 1990, Kynoch 2000). See also Charney (1991), Keiser (1991), Taylor (2002), Buur and Jensen (2004). For vigilante groups in Kenya, see Anderson (2002).
15. Daniel Smith (2004) argues that the Bakassi boys are not against the state: they partly imitate the predatory practices of state agents and are to some extent integrated into the state, serving local politicians. The popular perception of their activities is widely shaped by the political climate in Nigeria, the experiences of long-term military rule and the ubiquity of violence. People have developed ambiguous perceptions, that violence is both necessary to maintain order and arbitrary in its application by state agents. Carina Tertsakian (2002) notes that the uses of Bakassi boys by influential and wealthy politicians against their opponents could be even considered as state-sponsored terrorism.
16. Some political scientists even speak of a current 'africanization' of politics (Chabal and Daloz 1999). Institutions that are flexible and adaptable to new contexts demonstrate, it is argued, the potential of local African political systems to cope with new circumstances.

Beside the danger of a hidden exoticization, on the methodological level it is often difficult to decide what is 'local' and what is 'external', what is 'adaptation' and what is part of very complex historical developments. The most important danger is that what may be portrayed locally as tradition may be a complete innovation or importation. External influences may outweigh local 'roots'.

17. Local mediating committees, village councils and ward tribunals (in Benin called *tribunal de reconciliation*), were often established with the help of the state. At times abolished, they have recently been revitalised in many African countries.
18. The debate over the rise of violent self-help actions is reminiscent of the recent increase in cases of collective self-justice in Benin, linked with the public killing of thieves in the capital Cotonou (Paulenz 1999).
19. Order and disorder are not absolute conditions, nor measurable independently of the local context.
20. Potentially, the central state may also make use of a situation of insecurity to justify authoritarian political practices, as has been argued by Chabal and Daloz (1999); see also Bangura and Gibbon (1993).
21. Paulenz (1999) discusses several of these, without giving priority to one or other explanation.
22. A similar interpretation of the use of violence to control violence by vigilante groups in Uganda is given by Suzette Heald (1989). We should thus avoid a methodological trap, construing too sharp a distinction between state (as an abstract entity) and 'society', between formal institutions, so-called 'informal' structures and modes of political action. Many 'informal' political and local institutions have, since colonial times, been part of the larger political process, even part of the state, and not opposed to it. Actors and institutions outside official state politics may be linked in many ways – including patron-client relations – with the state, often playing the role of intermediaries. We also cannot set local law against state law, but should speak of interrelated legal systems, marked by many transitions and semi-autonomous structures. References to official laws are constantly made by all actors, for example mining rights in the case of gold miners and the *tomboloma*, either to affirm or to oppose such legislation.
23. This account adds to the critical points in Abrahams' seminal comparative socio-historical study on vigilantism (1998). Abrahams argues that these actors dwell on a criticism of the central state, but often try to defend rather conservative ideas, and reveals their ambivalent practices in both protecting and oppressing those from whom they seek legitimacy.

References

Abrahams, R. 1987. 'Sungusungu: Village Vigilante Groups in Tanzania', *African Affairs* 86: 179–96.
——— 1998. *Vigilant Citizens: Vigilantism and the State*. Cambridge: Polity Press.
Alber, E. 2000. *Im Gewand von Herrschaft: Modalitäten der Macht bei den Baatombu (1895–1995)*. Köln: Rüdiger Köppe Verlag.
——— 2001. 'Hexerei, Selbstjustiz und Rechtspluralismus in Benin', *Afrika Spectrum* 36(2): 145–67.
Alber, E. and Sommer. J. 1999. 'Grenzen der Implementierung staatlichen Rechts im dörflichen Kontext: Eine Analyse der Rechtswirklichkeit in einem Baatombu-Dorf in Benin', *Afrika Spectrum* 34(1): 85–111.
Anderson, D. 2002. 'Vigilantes, Violence and the Politics of Public Order in Kenya', *African Affairs* 101(405): 531–55.
Anikulapo, J. 2000. 'Nigerias Bürger schützen sich selbst', *taz*, 6216 (11.8.2000), 10.

Baker, B. 2002. 'When the Bakassi Boys Came: Eastern Nigeria Confronts Vigilantism', *Journal of Contemporary African Studies* 20(2): 1–22.
────── 2004. 'Protection from Crime: What is on Offer for Africans?' *Journal of Contemporary African Studies* 22(2): 165–88.
Bangura, Y. and Gibbon. P. 1993. 'Adjustment, Authoritarianism and Democracy: An Introduction to Some Conceptual and Empirical Issues', in Y. Bangura, P. Gibbon and A. Ofstad (eds), *Authoritarianism, Democracy and Adjustment*. Uppsala: Nordiska, pp. 7–38.
Bassett, T. 2003. 'Dangerous Pursuits: Hunter Associations (donzo ton) and National Politics in Côte d'Ivoire', *Africa* 73(1): 1–30.
Bierschenk, T. and Mongbo. R. 1995. 'Le Terroir en Quête de Démocratie', *Politique Africaine* 59: 2–6.
Bierschenk, T. and de Sardan J.-P. Olivier. 1997. 'Local Powers and a Distant State in Rural Central African Republic', *Journal of Modern African Studies* 35(3): 441–68.
Buur, L. and Jensen. S. 2004. 'Vigilantism and the Policing of Everyday Life in South Africa', *African Studies* 63(2): 139–52.
Breckenridge, K. 1990. 'Migrancy, Crime and Faction Fighting: The Role of the Isitshozi in the Development of Ethnic Organisations in the Compounds', *Journal of Southern African Studies* 16(1): 55–78.
Campbell, H. 1989. 'Popular Resistance in Tanzania: Lessons from the Sungu Sungu', *Africa Development* 14(4): 5–43.
Chabal, P. and Daloz. J.-P. 1999. *Africa Works: Disorder as Political Instrument*. London: James Currey.
Charney, C. 1991. 'Vigilantes, Clientelism, and the South African State', *Transformation* 16: 1–28.
Diallo, Y. 2001. *Conflict, Cooperation and Integration: A West African Example (Côte d'Ivoire)*. Max Planck Institute for Social Anthropology, Working Paper No. 22, Halle/Saale.
Elliesen, T. 2002. 'Polizeihilfe – mit welchem Ziel?', *Entwicklung und Zusammenarbeit* 2: 39.
Elwert, G. 1997. 'Gewaltmärkte. Beobachtungen zur Zweckrationalität der Gewalt' in T. von Trotha (ed.) *Soziologie der Gewalt*. Opladen: Westdeutscher Verlag, pp. 86–101.
Fauvelle, F.-X. and Renou. X. 1999. 'L'Islam contre le Crime? Les Ambiguïtés du "Vigilantisme" Islamique en Afrique du Sud', *Afrique Contemporaine* 192: 40–56.
Fleisher, M. 2000. '"Sungusungu": State-sponsored Village Vigilante Groups among the Kuria of Tanzania', *Africa* 70(2): 209–28.
Geschiere, P. 2001. 'Issues of Citizenship and Belonging in Present-day Africa', in L. Kropaček and P. Skalnik (eds), *Africa 2000*. Prague: Roman Misek Publisher, pp. 93–108.
Goffman, E. 1971. *Relations in Public: Microstudies of the Public Order*. New York: Sage.
Gore, C. and Pratten. D. 2003. 'The Politics of Plunder: The Rhetorics of Order and Disorder in Nigeria', *African Affairs* 102(407): 211–40.
Grätz, T. 2002. *Gold Mining Communities in Northern Benin as Semi-autonomous Social Fields*. Max Planck Institute for Social Anthropology, Working Paper No. 36, Halle/Saale.
────── 2003. 'Les Chercheurs d'Or et la Construction d'Identités de Migrants en Afrique de l'Ouest', *Politique Africaine* 91: 155–69.
────── 2004. 'Friendship Ties among Young Artisanal Gold Miners in Northern Bénin (West Africa)', *Afrika Spectrum* 39(1): 95–117.
Hagberg, S. 2004. 'Political Decentralisation and Traditional Leadership in the Bekandi Hunters' Association in Western Burkina Faso', *Africa Today* 50(4): 51–70.
Harnischfeger, J. 2001. 'Die Bakassi-Boys in Nigeria. Vom Aufstieg der Milizen und dem Niedergang des Staates', *Konrad-Adenauer Stiftung – Auslandsinformation* 12(1): 13–46.
Heald, S. 1989. *Controlling Anger: The Sociology of Gisu Violence*. Manchester: Manchester University Press.
Hellweg, J. 2004. 'Encompassing the State: Sacrifice and Security in the Hunters' Movement of Cote d'Ivoire', *Africa Today* 50(4): 3–28.

Hibou, B. 1999. 'De la Privatisation des Economies à la Privatisation des Etats: Une Analyse de la Formation Continue de l'Etat' in B. Hibou (ed.) *La Privatisation des Etats*. Paris: Karthala, pp. 11–67.

Jackson, R. and Rosberg. C. 1982. 'Why Africa's Weak States Persist', *World Politics* 35(1): 1–24.

Keiser, L. 1991. *Friend by Day Enemy by Night: Organized Vengeance in a Kohistani Community*. Fort Worth: Harcourt Brace.

Kynoch, G. 2000. '"Marashea" on the Mines: Economic, Social and Criminal Networks on the South African Gold Fields, 1947–1999', *Journal of Southern African Studies* 26(1): 79–103.

Lauth, H.-J. and Liebert U. (eds). 1999. *Im Schatten demokratischer Legitimität: informelle Institutionen und politische Partizipation im interkulturellen Demokratievergleich*. Opladen: Westdeutscher Verlag.

Le Meur, P.-Y. 1999. 'Coping with Institutional Uncertainty: Contested Local Public Spaces and Power in Rural Benin', *Afrika Spectrum* 34(2): 187–211.

Le Roux, C. 1997. 'People against Gangsterism and Drugs', *Journal of Contemporary History* 22(1): 51–80.

Oomen, B. 1999. 'Vigilante Justice in Perspective: The Case of Mapogo at Mathamaga', *Acta Criminologica* 12(3): 45–53.

——— 2004. 'Vigilantism or Alternative Citizenship? The Rise of Mapogo at Mathamaga', *African Studies* 63(2): 153–71.

Paulenz, S. 1999. 'Selbstjustiz in Benin', *Afrika Spectrum* 34(1): 59–83.

Perouse de Montclos, M.-A. 1998. 'La Privatisation de la Sécurité en Afrique Subsaharienne: Le Phénomène Milicien dans le Sud du Soudan', *Politique Africaine* 72: 203–11.

Roberts, S. 1979. *Order and Dispute*. Harmondsworth: Penguin.

Roitman, J. 1999. 'Le Pouvoir n'est pas Souverain: Nouvelles Autorités Régulatrices et Transformation de l'Etat dans le Bassin du Lac Tchad (les Marges Transfrontalières dans la Zone du Lac)' in B. Hibou (ed.) *La Privatisation des Etats*. Paris: Karthala, pp. 163–96.

——— 2000. 'New Sovereigns? The Frontiers of Wealth Creation and Regulatory Authority in the Chad Basin', in T. Callaghy, R. Kassimir and R. Letham (eds) *Transboundry Formations: Global/Local Constructions of Authority and Violence in Africa*. Cambridge: Cambridge University Press, pp. 190–215.

Schlee, G. 2001. 'Regularity in Chaos: The Politics of Difference in the Recent History of Somalia' in G. Schlee (ed.) *Imagined Differences: Hatred and the Construction of Identity*. Hamburg: Lit, pp. 251–80.

Smith, D. 2004. 'The Bakassi-Boys: Vigilantism, Violence, and Political Imagination in Nigeria', *Cultural Anthropology* 19(3): 429–455.

Taylor, R. 2002. 'Justice Denied: Political Violence in Kwa-Zulu Natal after 1994', *African Affairs* 101(405): 473–508.

Tertsakian, C. 2002. 'State-sponsored Terrorism: The Bakassi-Boys; the Legitimization of Murder and Torture', *Human Rights Watch* 14(5): 856–59.

von Trotha, T. 2000. 'Die Zukunft liegt in Afrika. Vom Zerfall des Staates, von der Vorherrschaft der konzentrischen Ordnung und vom Aufstieg der Parastaatlichkeit', *Leviathan* 28(2): 253–79.

Chapter 6

IMPOSING NEW CONCEPTS OF ORDER IN RURAL MOROCCO: VIOLENCE AND TRANSNATIONAL CHALLENGES TO LOCAL ORDER

Bertram Turner

Introduction

In this paper the maintenance of local order in south-west Morocco is analysed as the interaction between different models of order informed by different but interrelated legal spheres. These models are based on different legal repertoires which incorporate different notions and ideals of what order actually is, according to various moral codes and philosophies. These concepts of order partially overlap but may be mutually exclusive or contradictory in certain circumstances. Thus, the paper concerns a plurality of concepts of order and their respective relations to practices of regulating disorder. The focus is on the connection between concepts of local order and ideas about what are permissible or necessary instances of violence. In certain circumstances in rural Morocco violence is perceived as a necessary contribution to the rearrangement of order.

Models of order are situational and relate to specific social contexts such as descent, the constraints of agrarian and pastoral life conditions, alliance and the requirements of Islam. Some subunits in social formations claim to provide and control a model of order which applies to the whole community and predominates over others. Individual actors, such as state representatives and religious experts also do so in some cases. The negotiation of local order is also affected by power relations and the pursuit of domination and influence (Nader 1990, 1991). This is considered here by analysing the relationship between institutionalized forms of conflict settlement and ad hoc arrangements. This does not mean, however, that the maintenance of order in rural communities, whether social, political, economic or religious, is equivalent to the management of conflict. This approach is inadequate to understand the discourse on order in a local context. Rather, the purpose is to highlight the underlying contours of order.

A simplistic distinction between so-called harmonious and so-called feuding societies – outmoded in legal anthropological theory today – tends to equate the issue of order with one of conflict (see Otterbein 1993, Cooney 2001). However, promoting consensus may lead to a suppression of conflict but also result in its cyclical eruption. Idealizing violence, by contrast, may be a successful strategy for restricting its use.[1] A re-evaluation of the concepts and rhetorics of consensus and confrontation and their relations with practices of conflict and violence, an exercise to which this paper contributes, is needed to eliminate the artificial distinction between societies dominated either by a permanent state of tension, called feud, and those dominated by harmony and conciliation.[2] What is required is a reconsideration of the conjunctions between ideal order and local practice. But is it sufficient just to deconstruct categories of order once more? When reconsidering the issue of order from a legal anthropological perspective we can benefit from the development of theory in the social sciences in general. Discourses on representation and habitus, local knowledge and agency may help to exonerate the notion of order from its past circumscription for 'primitive' or 'informal' law.[3]

In this paper order is examined as a set of ideas about human interaction inspired and framed by law, moral codes, and religion in their wider social context. Order is perceived as an ideal model of how people should live together or organize social life in a community. In a narrower sense, order is understood to involve the application of sets of moral standards and collective values, the allocation of responsibility and social commitment.

Before referring to ethnographic data, the social and legal local environment is briefly sketched. In a second step the underlying ideas of order and the different social relations in south-west Morocco are outlined. Major local debates are referred to and analysed to allow a more coherent presentation of the empirical data. Key notions illustrating the way in which order is perceived are discussed. In order to do this I discuss the effects of certain transnational impacts which are not objects of analysis per se but serve as diagnostic instruments which permit a better analysis of local notions of order. They allow an analysis which distinguishes the models from their social frames of reference and for critical reflection on concepts used in legal anthropology. In a conclusion, order and disorder are related to the questions of violence, security and justice, morality and law and the social spaces, frames and dynamics concerned.

The Local Setting

The Souss is a plain surrounded by the mountains of the Atlas and Anti-Atlas in south-west Morocco.[4] It is the area of the Argan forest, a unique ecosystem and object of transnational development intervention. Most of the Souassa are *fellahin*, farmers, although Sahraoui nomads from the west Sahara invade the region regularly with their large herds of camels and goats. During the dry season nomad encampments are numerous in the Argan forest, even in the vicinity of the villages. Local forms of agriculture, combined with small livestock raising, are diverse. There are zones of conventional and zones of hyper-modern agrarian production, irrigated zones as well as rain fed cultivation. Apart from agriculture, the exploitation of the Argan forest provides an essential means of livelihood for large parts of the local population. The range of products includes the staples of barley and oil from Argan fruits as well as citrus fruits and early vegetables, grown as cash crops.

The majority of the Souassa are Berber speaking, whose self-designation is *Ishilhayen*. However, there is a high proportion of Arab speaking people in the plain particularly concentrated in the urban centres and some enclaves in the countryside.

Souassa clan affiliation, the patrilineage system and segmentation, as well as alliance relations have given rise to extensive debates in anthropology (see Berque 1978, Montagne 1989, Hatt 1996). However, descent criteria do not dominate social relations today and increasing mobility and longdistance marriage arrangements have affected the spatial distribution of the members of a descent group. Nevertheless, in times of crisis they may be reactivated. Other social criteria of inclusion and exclusion, such as territorial bonds and neighbourhood solidarity, contribute to the composition of the principal unit with which local concepts of order are associated. This is the *taqbilt* (Berber) or *qabīla* (Arabic) and it represents the basic frame of reference for local identity. It is a named territorial group that understands itself as a social unit, in which solidarity obligations transcend the descent group. The *taqbilt* is sometimes referred to as a 'tribe', sometimes as a 'tribal fraction', and sometimes as a completely different type of social unit. These groups persist as the social basis of rural districts and have thus been integrated into the Moroccan state administration. Rural districts are generally divided into a number of villages and hamlets. There is no one dominant pattern of social organization in the villages. Some are composed of or dominated by members of one lineage; others consist of members of a number of quite equal lineages.

Political organization in these rural districts oscillates, in practice, between tendencies towards centralization and the decentralization of power. This affects official as well as informal institutions: in some villages prominent figures or elitist oligarchies of wealthy landholders dominate the political sphere. In others informal collective organisations take responsibility for leading and organizing the community.

State influence in the Souss has always been significant. The area was for centuries connected with the outside world through trade and migration. Agrarian activities and irrigation remain important points of transnational connection today. The Souss is also a centre of peaceful scholarlySufism (ṣūfī) represented by venerated and erudite specialists (fuqahā'). However, the religious history of the region has been violent. The local Islamic Sufi movements were involved in military activities and the region was a centre for both religious and political movements which were decisive for the political history of the whole of Morocco (cf. Jacques-Meunié 1982, Montagne 1989). Given this history, external influence from development organizations and religious groups is not something completely unfamiliar to the Souss.

The Legal Arena

A number of legal regimes interact in the Souss. There is, firstly, the legal system of the Moroccan state. Secondly, there is the official Islamic legal regime of *Maliki* orientation, along with unofficial and local versions of Islamic legal order. Thirdly, there is a variety of local legal practices, locally known as '*urf*.

Local tradition, '*urf*, is a flexible and dynamic legal framework which has the capacity to integrate aspects of state and religious law but also to take into account rural conditions on the periphery of the state's legal influence. This assures its function as the legal matrix and point of departure for local legal reasoning. The state's concept of normative order has little flexibility to cope with local problems but considerable space is left for the development of local order arrangements and corresponding institutions.[5] As long as local order is maintained, external state officials avoid becoming too much involved in local affairs. The state's legal processes explicitly allow local models of order to apply in many fields, such as the regulation of access to collective natural resources and the organization of religious life. This includes criteria of order expressed in terms of '*urf*.

Official Islamic doctrine has only limited influence in the countryside, being more closely associated with urban Arabic life. Nevertheless, in almost all fields of dispute conflicts are regulated, if not fully in accordance with, then at least to some degree with reference to, Islamic ideas. To a certain extent Sufi experts act as brokers between the judicial orthodoxy of Islam and local practices. Popularized Islam however is essential for local order. Islamic brotherhoods, religious events on the local and regional level, such as festivals and the annual celebrations of venerated religious figures, are very important for the local regulation of social tensions.

The impact of transnational forces on local order is a new phenomenon, but has become significant since 1999 with the establishment of a UNESCO biosphere reserve within the Souss and since then increased activity of development agencies.

Local Concepts of Order

The Souassa express their views on local order in a variety of proverbs and narratives about concrete cases of conflict or breaches of order. These reveal a plurality of notions and an ambivalence which is typical of local thinking about order. However, one category of order is described as being more inclusive than others: the religious order, which is often presented as the ideological foundation of all other concepts. This, at least, is the opinion of local experts who declare that the one order that is perfect is the order that God Himself imposed on the creation of the universe. It includes the whole universe, the cosmos, the realm of spirits and all sentient beings. Connected with this is a rather diffuse idea that order on earth, including local forms of order, are a reflection, a micro-version, of the overarching divine scheme.

There is also a plurality of moral codes which influence the negotiation of local order and the operation of *'urf*, state law and the legal aspects of Islam, of which there are several varieties. In the local trading codes, for instance, which are dominated by *'urf*, moral standards of correct behaviour form the basis of the trust which is essential to the orderly exchange of goods. Official Islamic morality is, on the other hand, perceived as an ideal type with little relevance to the problems of daily life. It is more suited to an urban trading economy and its associated property relations than the conditions of an agricultural economy.

There are several different principles of order and different social frames in which they are expressed. Religion, morality and *'urf* are the ideologies most frequently emphasized as the bases of the local principles of order. But these are framed in the context of kinship, descent, segmentation and territoriality. The focus in this paper is on the local sphere of order which incorporates but is not defined by all of these factors. Religion adds to the picture by connecting local order with the supernatural sphere. The secular state, on the other hand, is regarded as imposing external ideas which do not reflect local notions of order. To this extent order is relative (cf. Rosen 2000: 170–75).

Disorder by contrast is often described as a state of internal discord or chaos (*fitna*), equated with temptation and schism in both a social and religious sense. Within the public discourse at village level the idea is that disorder and order are distinct qualities of the same social phenomenon created by the continuous balancing of divergent interests. The line separating order from disorder is not clear but the object of constant negotiation and depends on context. However, there are expressions of different and inconsistent ideas about the relation between orders and disorders. On the one hand, most of the Souassa I asked repeated the proverb that there is no order realized on earth, there are just different stages of disorder and order remains an ideal unachievable in practice. On the other hand, some make a distinction between stages of disorder.

The idea of an institutionalized central authority which can guarantee order is present in the minds of the Souassa, but is rarely invoked as an ideal. More local ideals of collectivity and collective action are, rather, emphasized. The Islamic imperative of 'commanding the good/right and forbidding the evil/wrong' is mostly regarded as a community task and links the notion of order with a collective body. However, local intellectuals recognize that it retains a marked potential for violence, subversion and egalitarianism, as Cook (2000) has pointed out. Concepts of shared responsibility also generate institutions of order, but the social composition of the collective always depends on context. The organized defence of village interests is one example, as are the arrangements that farming neighbours make for their mutual assurance. But the resulting forms of order are dynamic, requiring different institutions and social mechanisms to maintain and ideals of order must remain flexible.

Models of Order as they Appear in Practice

In the following I focus on some of the most frequently discussed principles of local order in Morocco.[6] For analytic reasons they are first presented separately.

Reciprocity and Retaliation

The principle of reciprocity is fundamental to the operation of local order in the Souss. It also dominates the everyday notion of order, as elsewhere in Morocco. Reciprocity is the relationship that exists between clearly distinguishable legal persons or groups on the basis that all kind of action demands the appropriate reaction. Differences and disagreements are conceptualized and enacted in terms of opposed social interaction. If a balancing out of differences cannot be achieved then the relationship is disordered and may even lead to the creation of permanent distance.

Social stratification, divorce, physical separation, migration, and the establishment of unequal power relations may result.

When conflict arises between members of any type of distinct group the notion of reciprocity is fundamental. Behaviour which is locally characterized as deviant and which negatively affects another party is perceived to be a social challenge, which activates a relationship of reciprocity. If a party is thought to have obtained an advantage through social transgression this has to be balanced out through retaliation or by achieving a compromise based on compensation. These are two poles of behaviour, which are not mutually exclusive. Reciprocity can be expressed as a moral requirement without referring to any emotional desire for revenge or gratification. It is those who take advantage of their social transgression by avoiding the consequences of reciprocity who pose the real threat to local order.

In cases of violent action, the principle of reciprocity is not an instruction for the automatic exercise of counter-violence. In Mediterranean and Islamic contexts the concept has often been reduced to a concept of retaliation, implying the use of violence, connected to a rhetoric of 'honour'.[7] The emphasis in this literature on retaliation in reciprocal relationships suggests a social state of permanent disorder. The skewed reference to selected sequences of complex and longstanding social processes in narratives and memories is largely responsible for this image. However, the logic of retaliation is not a logic of violence. Central to the retaliatory component of reciprocity is the idea of prevention. When prevention fails and events take another step towards the escalation of conflict, the principle of reciprocity still offers the option to come to an arrangement.

The ability to defend one's interests and display a disposition to violence is primarily necessary in order to establish social relations between groups and can be characterized as social capital. What is claimed to be acceptable violence in the context of retaliation may, in practice, be subject to protracted negotiations and pressure is usually applied to the parties by the wider community to accept compensation in lieu of taking violent retribution.[8] The social challenge for a community is to ensure that the retaliation does not go too far, crossing a line between acceptable reciprocity and disorder. Retaliation is thus one element of the ambivalent concept of reciprocity, which implies both complementary and antagonistic relations between groups and can include compensation. This is what the Souassa say and it is inconsistent with certain theoretical conceptualizations in legal anthropology.[9]

The 'flavour of justice' ('*adl*) is integral to the notion of reciprocity. Justice, particularly its secular version, is close to the notion of appropriateness and implies the maintenance of mutual rights and obligations, as well as the transfer of material and social capital based on reciprocity. It implies a relationship of either social equality, mutual legal capacity or respectfulness (*iḥtirām*).

Order as Harmony

In the Moroccan context harmony (*muā'ama*) has emotional connotations[10] and must be distinguished from the Islamic notion of harmony which instead suggests equality. Consensus (*itafāq*) dominates for more practical purposes but it also has a religious connotation: decisions should be reached by consensus. The notion of conformity is, rather, a secular value and is not always a positive virtue. Solidarity (*tadhāmun*) as a principle requires active support. They form part of a local code based on ideas of belonging, identity and group cohesion. In practice, in the local context, all these different and often inconsistent notions might be used to emphasize different, but hardly distinguishable, aspects of one complex that is summarized as local order. However, the dominant notion is that of consensus-oriented conformity and this is what underlies a network of social solidarity. This defines what I will refer to as the 'order of harmony'.

This order has an outward oriented message. It defines a certain type of relationship, which excludes those outside the network who may, nevertheless, have other descent or territorial ties. This order expresses identity against the external environment, thus reflecting social distance and proximity. It defines a sphere of harmony, a social space without reference to the social imperative of reciprocity. The allocation of mutual obligations and (re)distribution of symbolic and material goods is instead emphasized. In the absence of reciprocity, this form of order is not associated with social justice, which involves adjustment between social equals. It is thus limited to a group with defined ties of belonging which are not characterized by balanced social accounts. Accordingly, the size and type of such social groups is limited.

The idea of order as harmony is an ideal model not realized in everyday life and it is also viewed with some ambivalence. Internal consensus is sometimes enforced through extreme social pressure, such as the threat of exclusion, and can thus be perceived as the terror of harmony. Internal relations are dominated by conflict avoidance and the suppression of differences, which may aggravate tensions and lead to escalation if they are not resolved in other ways. The ideals of harmony thus deny differences in wealth, skills and influence, which have to be ignored or downplayed as potential sources of conflict. The price is a considerable amount of social control since harmony does not rely on trust.[11]

Recourse to violence represents a breach of the rules of the harmony sphere. However, this does not mean that there is no violence. Local informants often describe the ideals of harmony with exasperation because they prevent reciprocity. Herein lies the dilemma of the harmony sphere. The social space it defines is loaded with the potential for conflict because there are numerous conflicting interests, but instead of relations of reciprocity, through which such conflict could be managed, a form of coercive loyalty is prevalent, which disallows reciprocity. This leads to a constant reconsideration of membership of the harmony sphere. Descent groups may split off, territorial units may be divided into several parts, friendship abandoned and so on, so that the former members of a harmony sphere enter a relationship ordered by reciprocity and retaliation.[12]

Reciprocity and Retaliation: Consensus and Harmony

The ideals of consensus and reciprocity are thus linked to particular social frames which are mostly, but not always, respectively described in terms of territorial belonging and descent. However, such groups may overlap and individual actors may thus experience conflicting loyalties between these different units. Under these circumstances, the notion of reciprocity has limited instrumental and operational value because, depending on the constellation of conflicting individuals, the giving and receiving parties of material compensation may be identical. Where harmony is found there cannot be retaliation.

The concept which unites these different spheres and models of order is that of respect or respectfulness (*iḥtirām*). This term is used to characterize the relationship between married persons, parents and children; between brothers, elderly and younger people; and between friends or people cooperating as sharecroppers or traders. It transcends the boundaries of social stratification and agonistic social groups. When consensus is achieved outside the harmony sphere it is attributed to respectful behaviour. In this way, consensus can be achieved, even in a social environment in which a permanent state of tension prevails, as occurs in some relations of reciprocity. Within the harmony sphere, on the other hand, relations of reciprocity may be established and this is also attributed to respectful behaviour.

External Interventions and Their Impact on Local Order

External intervention in the Souss comes from two primary sources, international development agencies and Islamic activism. The implementation of international standards of environmental protection and sustainable development in the Argan forest is the main focus of development agencies and international donor organizations in south-west Morocco. Their concepts of sustainable development involve regulating access to scarce natural resources as well as alleviating the increase in rural poverty. The incorporation of international conventions on sustainable resource management into national law is widely perceived as having failed in Morocco and legal reform has not reached the rural areas so transnational actors try to implement these standards in the local field by bypassing the state. A reorganization of regulations of access to scarce natural resources on the local level is one consequence. This has had a considerable impact on the organization and negotiation of local order, with results that illustrate the social significance of the concepts discussed above.

Domestic Violence, New Forms of Resource Exploitation and Local Order

Within the framework of development initiatives, transnational actors have introduced new forms of resource exploitation in the Argan forest. One was the establishment of oil producing cooperatives for women. However, such initiatives led to an unintended overexploitation of scarce resources rather than to sustainable resource management (see Turner 2005b). Moreover, the introduction of these cooperatives resulted in a massive disruption to the local social order, despite the fact that collective labour activities by women were not unfamiliar to the Souassa. The result of these new opportunities for income generation has been that women have been expected to contribute more to the household budget than men. But, even more significantly, married women were forced into regular contact with men unrelated to them. One consequence was the increase in violence by husbands against their wives. At one point it appeared as if beating women had become part of a campaign against the perceived threat to the local order provoked by such cooperatives.

A series of divorces resulted, however, and in this way domestic violence came to be viewed as a threat to the local order. Local institutions, in particular committees and councils composed of old men and other village dignitaries, intervened and mediated several cases with success. Descent groups, from within the village, and matrilineal alliances, from the wife's natal village, would normally be expected to take the sides of the husband and wife respectively. However, in these cases they combined to support these traditional institutions of conflict management in their attempt to resolve the problems. In this way these institutions, which had largely lost their reputations as guarantors of local order in the era after independence in 1956, were reinstated and reinvigorated.

Gender inequalities are an integral part of local order and there is no strict interdiction of male violence against wives. In the course of this process, therefore, the conventional explanations for gender violence, such as the correction of wrong behaviour or the legitimate expression of matrimonial disapproval, had to be disregarded and the men's behaviour characterized as 'blameworthy'. However, spouses do not necessarily belong to the same descent or territorial groups, within which the interests of consensus require the renouncement of violence. In this new situation, therefore, the husbands' violence was characterized as being against principles of local order. The committees referred to principles with which the husbands had to agree: the appropriateness of action and the need to adapt distributive obligations in order secure the economic survival of the family. Furthermore, they were able to demonstrate that these new forms of violence exhibited obvious contradictions: the husbands were not willing to accept the new economic positions of their wives but were also profiting from them. Some husbands argued that the social circumstances of working in a cooperative contradicted local codes of moral conduct. However, the mediators were able to resolve the apparent contradictions and a public consensus emerged that people should be careful with external relations because of their unforeseen consequences, but that domestic violence also had to be restrained. Such violence represented a threat to local order and could not be justified in accordance with local notions of morality and appropriateness.

In these ways local institutions were responding to new challenges to the local order by transforming and adapting local concepts of order and morality. This example also indicates that individual behaviour not in itself normally considered to be deviant (husbands beating their wives) accumulated, in the circumstances of this case, to such a degree where it threatened the local order, that is it passed the implicit threshold between order and disorder.

Inheritance and the Emergence of Violence in the Sphere of Harmony

Another consequence of the overexploitation of the Argan forest has been conflict in cases of inheritance of usufruct rights among local farmers. It had formerly been expected that heirs would not insist on sharing the parcels over which usufruct rights were exercised in favour of the eldest member of the family and as a sign of respect for him. Exercising 'low-level' violence is generally accepted as the appropriate way to claim access rights. The act of bringing the plough to a halt can be a symbolic act of violence in this regard, according to the local code of *'urf,* and is interpreted as an assertion of inheritance rights with legal consequences. However, this is not permissible between brothers or members of the same solidarity network. The members of such groups are obliged to reach agreement without employing violence because their relationship excludes the relations of reciprocity that would legitimate such action. When conflict arises in such situations the need to maintain harmony is sometimes cynically referred to by the people involved as harmony-terror.

However, the increasing value of exploitation rights in the forest which have resulted from development initiatives, coupled with increasing poverty in the countryside, has led to an acceptance of low level violence, even within solidarity groups. Conflicts have been decided by violence. Competing heirs have attacked one another when trying to exercise usufruct rights in the forest. Even violence between brothers is now regarded as inevitable under certain circumstances, although it is still publicly disapproved of. However, in some circumstances, the combination of inheritance disputes and fights between brothers has been interpreted as a serious threat to the local order.

External intervention is not expected within solidarity networks and an appeal to the state for intervention was rejected because of the unpredictability of the outcome. Nevertheless, the village public expressed the need to intervene and the cases were discussed in the informal village council where all households are represented. After long discussion some activities, including certain clearly specified forms of low-level violence, were declared to be locally acceptable forms of conflict between spouses or co-heirs. However, what was perceived to be a disturbance to local order through violence was regarded as unacceptable. The council confirmed the principle that there cannot be any solution while one party is exercising contested exploitation rights. However, this generally did no more than establish a truce and a considerable number of inheritance cases remain to be settled. The principles of reciprocity were imported into the social frame of consensus because it was obvious that the conflict could not be settled without compromise. The members of the village council described this situation as defective order lacking a moral justification and not directed towards social justice ('*adl*).

Order and Retaliation

While both in the case of the Argan oil producing cooperatives and in the case of contested inheritance rights litigants act in a relationship of social proximity based on affinal and agnatic relations, in the following case of contested access rights such social conditions are not implied. In this case the social background to the conflict lies in the longstanding relations between mobile pastoralists and local agriculturalists, which oscillate between economic and social complementarity and antagonism. Haouari farmers traditionally practised seasonal cultivation in the Argan forest while the Sahraoui camel-herding nomads used it for pasture after the harvest. In the past, their usage claims only overlapped to a certain degree and both parties felt bound by a common local order. Both sides still describe themselves as being in a relationship of reciprocity, based on their shared use of the forest despite the tremendous transformations in exploitation patters in the last decades. New front lines have, however, emerged as a result of the emphasis placed on environmental protection and sustainability by transnational agencies, and this has accelerated competition over access to scarce resources. While both Haouari and Sahraoui regard certain forms of aggression and low intensity violence as being typical of their relations, in one case conflict became more violent and a farmer was killed.

The two parties involved could have been regarded as representing segments from different tribal settings. According to segmentary logic, this should have lead to a conflict between 'tribes'. According to the principles of retaliation one might have expected that the five or six agnates closest to the perpetrator and the victim would oppose each other as accountable and injured parties respectively. However, this did not happen, largely because of long-established relations between the groups. The victim was regarded as having been killed in violence between interest groups, not between segments.

Although the Haouari's exploitation rights in the forest originally derived from their lineage affiliation, in recent years usage rights have been transmitted by sale. Thus, the people interested in the outcome of the conflict were not identical with a descent-based solidarity network, which would normally become involved in the repercussions of a homicide. Only a couple of the agnates were even on the spot and able to take on responsibility. Nevertheless, front lines between opposing parties were quickly drawn. Apart from some agnates, the members of the victim's village council and his major partner in a sharecropping arrangement became active as the injured party.[13] The victim had been a member of the council, which today unofficially represents the territorial unity of the village and is organized as an NGO.

On the other hand, the nomads supported one another and enjoyed active sympathy from other Sahraouis, who had been resident in the Souss for 30 years. They felt themselves to be the stronger group since the owners of the camel herds were powerful members of the political elite.

Despite the involvement of many different actors on both sides, including state representatives (who preferred to observe the case without intervening because of its political dimensions) and local environmental NGOs (which were supported by transnational development organisations) the parties discussed the conflict in terms of retaliation strategies and their actions followed that logic. This was the line adopted by all parties in the expectation that, by channelling violence in the terms of the logic of retaliation, an escalation of the conflict would be avoided. However, in the course of the negotiations, threats of retaliatory violence and claims for compensation were augmented with new arguments taken from the rhetoric of human rights and civil society discourses – such as protection for displaced and unprivileged people, a typical Sahraoui argument, or the duty of resident citizens to take care of their environment for future generations.[14] Finally, the negotiations moved beyond the death to include the controversial questions which had led to the violent conflict, that is the contested access rights to forest resources. The discussion did not produce any new arrangements, however, but confirmed the status quo. Finally the Sahraouis had to agree to pay compensation, despite their affiliation with politically powerful actors, because they had surpassed the acceptable degree of violence. They accepted the loss of livestock inflicted on them by the farmers in the meantime as an indication of their determination to obtain compensation, and they also accepted that they should leave the region for the rest of the season. Although these events had started with an individually deviant act, the killing of the farmer, the subsequent course of events was interpreted by the villagers as ordered. It was just one episode in established retaliatory relations, albeit one whose course was affected by the changing social frames of reference.

Local and Religious Order

The second intervention in local affairs has been by the Islamic movement of the Salafiyya between 1999 and 2003. This transnationally active movement has a history as a reform oriented force in the Islamic world and was involved in struggles for independence against colonial power in North Africa. It has no close connections with Moroccan Islam and does not recognize practices of piety which are integral to Moroccan Islamic practice. It started its intervention in Morocco with non-Moroccan missionaries from Middle Eastern countries. The Salafiyya attempted to promote a return to the roots of legal Islam and to reorganize social life according to its core principles. They challenged the capacity of other actors, particularly those connected with local Islamic practice, to maintain local order and to promote the conditions under which social life could be conducted according to Islamic rules. They constantly talked about law and order. Their primary missionary method was an incessant indoctrination about 'the correct way' according to the Wahhabi interpretation of Islam. They gave their advice everywhere and to everybody, for instance pursuing people on the street, explaining to men that smoking is unacceptable, or telling women that wearing the veil and not looking at men would help them find salvation. They intervened in all spheres of everyday life. Not only hegemony within the social sphere but absolute control over it was the declared goal of their strategy.

The Salafiyya's attempts to undermine local order were relatively successful when the alternative they offered corresponded, at least ostensibly, with the local sense of justice. Breaking the established local rules in subtle ways was also part of their agenda. However, through their interventions the Salafiyya introduced new dimensions of violence, which had hitherto been unknown and were incompatible with the locally accepted sense of order and justice.

One such event involved confrontation between two brothers on the occasion of the burial of their father. One of the two was attracted by Salafiyya ideology. When the burial procession to the cemetery began he insisted on the introduction of orthodox practices unknown to the rural community and in contradiction with local ideals of piety. It was customary to hold prayers in the cemetery after the burial. This brother, however, insisted on praying beforehand in the mosque and leaving the cemetery immediately after burial without uttering a word. His brother objected to this proposal as a desecration of their deceased father. Immediately an opposition emerged, the mourners split off into two parties, and a fight started. In the end the Islamists were defeated and local peace was restored. Never had a burial been the occasion for violent action, however, and the incident was highly disapproved of. The event was interpreted as a threat to local cohesion and the brutalization of human relations. Subsequently, fights between youths of both factions became more frequent. A certain inhibition threshold seemed to have been crossed (cf. Turner 2005c).

There is a strong memory amongst the local community of external attempts to exercise control over the region made successively by the Portuguese, the Spanish, the Sultan and the Makhzen (the political elite of the Moroccan state) and the French Protectorate.[15] In the recent past new attempts have been made by various development agencies. Recollections of these interventions have been quoted when the Salafiyya activities have been discussed. However, the Salafiyya are seen to have challenged the most revered notion of order, that of religion. Furthermore, while pretending to put Islamic ideals into practice they have interpreted them in such a way as to put them into competition with secular notions of order based on descent, social, rural, legal, and state relations (including the harmony and reciprocity models discussed here). As a result, they are regarded as having forfeited the legitimacy of their interpretation of Islam through profanization.

Violence and Conflict Management

In the first three examples a certain amount of low-level violence emerged as a result of new social configurations concerning gender relations and access to scarce resources. Such forms of violence are regarded as more or less legally justified even though they have undesirable economic consequences. On the other hand, the violence associated with the imposition of a new order by the Salafiyya activists has provoked opposition, resistance and counter-violence. The Salafiyya practices were regarded as provoking an unacceptable level of violence.

Local actors typically operate with two perspectives in mind. Within the harmony sphere conflict management does not involve satisfying legitimate claims on the basis of reciprocity. Therefore, emerging conflicts are sometimes suppressed. From an outward oriented perspective, however, single instances of conflict are normally seen as being embedded in long lasting relationships which demand appropriate responses. The nature of such relationships of reciprocity entails that final solutions are inappropriate and illusory. Violence is regarded as being integral to such relations, which can be described as being in a permanent state of tension. A 'solution' only allows the temporary cessation of violence. This is true even when the period of non-violence lasts several decades. This is because violence is often as much a means of maintaining or re-establishing order as it is a disruption to that order. Violence is also associated with the religious order, which never claimed to exclude violence. However, it is inimical to the sacred order, which embodies a distinct set of principles, including that of non-violence. This probably lay behind the local attitudes to Salafiyya violence.

Certain dimensions of calculated violent intervention are thus considered to be legitimate and integral to local order in south-west Morocco. To claim usufruct rights, for instance, one must demonstrate the capacity to defend such rights. To be always prepared is a social expectation. However, such violence is strictly limited in its intensity and scope. Furthermore, there is a corresponding set of corrective institutions for channelling and suppressing violence. Violence may also be an indication of an ongoing exchange of challenges and responses between solidarity groups. Certain kinds of violence are thus considered to be legitimate and integral to the local order. However, other forms of violence may also be regarded as a breach of norms and presage an escalation of conflict. This was the case with the domestic violence as well as with the Salafiyya interventions aimed at inciting local tensions.

The examples have shown that violence has also afforded the opportunity for the local community to reconsider its order. In local village councils, informal meetings or during Friday prayers in the mosque, for example, it is often discussed why some sorts of violence are favourable to the local order while others are not. Such debates often revolve around questions of social distance, proximity, and solidarity. Such debates have arisen particularly in the context of external interventions in the local order.

Order, the Political and Social Stratification

In the Moroccan case, access to institutions of conflict management is not independent of power relationships. Members of the post-independence political elite control access to state institutions to a certain extent. The political actors who replaced the former political elite after independence tried to take over legal responsibility for maintaining order. From their perspective maintaining order means regulating and controlling access to state institutions involved in conflict.

Fomenting disorder is still an instrument used in political competitions. Violent confrontations between different loyalty groups are only one example. According to traditional political thinking particular versions of 'ordered disorder' are a precondition for order. At times of political instability, a phase of disorder in the form of ritual anarchy producing an inverted world (order) is a condition for transformation, which allows claimants to power the chance to prove their supernatural ordering capacities. This particular idea of disorder is not regarded as chaos but is characterized by local intellectuals as the inversion and ritual mirroring of a social order which corresponds with social stratification and the legitimation of power. This background was discussed intensively in the rural Souss once again during the very short period between the death of Hassan II and his successor Mohammed VI's ascent to the throne in 1999. Narratives circulated concerning a competition between the two royal brothers and informal attempts to convince one brother to oppose to the designated king, who refused to intrigue. Such narratives express local considerations on how political ideas dealing with order at the state level are related to the supernatural sphere.

The same principles are apparent within the social life of the village, albeit here realized in different ways. At this level ritual techniques of trance dancing during annual festivals celebrate social chaos – or rather inversion – and are perceived as a supernatural affirmation of local order. On these occasions exposed or prominent figures are socially made equal and reintegrated into the local order.

Conclusion: Order, Violence, Security and Justice

The aim of this paper has been to analyse local reasoning and practices of order in south-west Morocco as a contribution to the development of a comparative perspective on order in legal anthropology.[16] This means not neglecting internal contradictions. In the Souss, disorder is a real life experience and not an unacceptable situation which requires immediate reaction and resolution. Conflict is not necessarily regarded as a disruption to order, whereas the inadequate handling of conflict is. When things go well disputes lead to the confirmation of order through collective efforts taken to manage it. In the process, different models of order are set off against each other and priorities are formulated. The goal is to overcome legal insecurity in a new context and constellation. Disorder is perceived as legal insecurity and order in the strict sense as perfect legal security which will never be realized on earth. Furthermore, the contradictions between consensus and reciprocity as principles of individual action means that under some conditions order is locally regarded as providing room for manoeuvre while in others it is a coercive constraint.

The Moroccan example shows that the use of violence is morally evaluated on a scale between acceptable and unacceptable. At one end it is necessary, unavoidable and positive in its results or consequences and at the other it represents overreaction, an escalation of conflict with negative results. Peaceful behaviour, where this entails subordination, is not seen as a virtue.[17] Peace as a temporary phase of non-violence outside the consensus circle can only be provided by the threat of potentially violent retaliation. The option of resorting to violence is occasionally realized – otherwise non-violence would mean weakness. But it is imperative that the reaction is morally appropriate. As a consequence, violent intervention in order to prevent a violent confrontation is considered the legal duty of every adult male. Low level violence, or better still, proving the ability to defend one's rights with reasonable force, is the major instrument for maintaining order. It is also the means of modifying existing rules and maintaining legal relations between different interest groups. In harmony-oriented settings the actual use of violence is, in some cases, relatively high compared with people bound in retaliatory relationships in which a rhetoric of violence is ubiquitous but the exercise of violence is restricted.

Order has been described as a set of relationships and mutual rights and duties which are often given moral interpretations. Such order requires a common knowledge of the perpetual modification of the social networks of all members of a community. The contrary is state order, which has an impact on local relations of order but is not associated with justice, or even with predictability. The state order is about power relations and instrumentalized as a political tool. Concentrations of power backed by the national legal system complicate reciprocal relations and may contradict basic ideas of local order.

It should have become clear that order and justice ('adl) cannot be seen as synonymous.[18] However, there must also be a level of justice. This is particularly associated with sacred times and places. The ideal is for the principle of reciprocal order, its actions and consequences, to be realized without destroying the possibility of realizing order as consensus. However, this ideal is not fully compatible with the complex of often conflicting principles mentioned here. The realization of justice merely creates islands of order in the ocean of human struggle. Two main components of order, consensus and reciprocity, predominate and have been analysed separately. However, as I have also described, they exist in an osmotic relationship which can only be understood by considering the notion of respectfulness.

Disorder has been presented here as the passing of the threshold towards a precarious and critical stage of legal insecurity. However, individually deviant behaviour does not necessarily entail a state of disorder. Moreover, the threshold is variable, depending on the individuals involved and on the social network and context, descent ties and many other smoothing factors. Disorder means that a certain threshold-limit value has been surpassed in that particular case and by that particular action. This implies that the same or identical action may be seen as not threatening order in other circumstances or when other individual actors are involved. To this extent disorder is anticipated long before the transgression of the threshold and the line is always shifting. The distinction between order and disorder should accordingly be conceived as a transition zone.

The plurality of concepts of order and their connections with distinct legal realms results in a local legal sphere in which processes of order are constantly being undertaken. Local actors have room for manoeuvre in the context of a relatively stable institutional set-up and procedures. This does not mean, however, that the Souassa are not acutely aware that they are embedded in a wider social and political environment. This is the social context in which it was suggested that there is no consistent concept of one local order in Morocco but distinct, partly parallel, partly overlapping, and partly contradicting features describing local order, in practice, as a process. Order is produced and socially constructed in a discourse in which several concepts of order are used and adapted to local conditions in a creative way. Recently imposed external orders have made these processes more obvious.

Acknowledgements

Many thanks to Andreas Hemming and Eva Diehl for proofreading and stimulating suggestions to earlier versions of this paper and to Fernanda Pirie for intensive discussion and revision of the final text.

Notes

1. See, e.g., Strathern (1985); Caton (1987) on the rhetoric of violence in segmentary societies; and in particular the recent literature on violence: Stewart and Strathern (2002), Scheper-Hughes (2004).
2. This re-evaluation questions the epistemological value of all simple dichotomies relevant in this context which have been postulated not exclusively but particularly with regard to Islamic and Mediterranean societies. Some seem to be ineradicable such as violence/non-violence; right/wrong; guilty/innocent, etc.
3. This is frequently done by referring to Evans-Pritchard (1940: 162, 168). See also Diamond (1980) and Ellickson (1991).
4. The data on which this chapter is based have been anonymized. Fieldwork on transnational impacts by development agencies and the Salafiyya movement has been carried out for several weeks annually between 1999 and 2004. Data from different villages of the Souss plain are included in the analysis. Since 2001 the fieldwork has been conducted as part of the Legal Pluralism Project Group at the Max Planck Institute for Social Anthro-

pology in Halle. The current research project is entitled Sustainable Development and Exploitation of Natural Resources: Legal Pluralism and Trans-National Law in the 'Arganeraie' Biosphere Reserve.
5. Since local orders are dynamic and adaptive, it is not possible, except in a very limited way, to analyse recent conditions on the basis of older sources, although these can provide an excellent basis if they are regarded with the proper critical distance; cf. Ben Daoud (1924, 1927), Surdon (1928), Lafond (1948), Marcy (1954) and Montagne (1989).
6. For a different approach to order in Morocco see Geertz, Geertz and Rosen (1979). The empirical data presented in this paper are no less situational and selective than those used in the cited literature and do not allow to develop an exhaustive typology which is applicable to a wider context than the research area. The analysis is based on proceedings in village councils and the accounts of various informants, among them legal and/or religious experts, interested intellectuals and disputing people on the street. Accordingly, there is a considerable variety of opinions in local responses.
7. See for literature Turner (2005a). Stewart (2000) identifies honour as a right (ḥaqq) which should not be confused with categories of emotions. Dominant dichotomies of order criteria such as the 'honour and shame model' have, nevertheless, proved tenacious: See, e.g., Giordano (2001).
8. This is an empirical fact. It is in contrast to the model often referred to in anthropological literature according to which order can be equated with an absence of violence and that the use and threat of force always represents disorder. These ideas must come from somewhere else but are absent in the Maghreb. Nevertheless, the maintenance of tension and hostile relations has been explained from Ibn Khaldun to Ernest Gellner (1969) as typical for segmentary societies in North Africa; see Turner (2005a).
9. For Morocco see Turner (2005a: 416–49); in general see Cooney (2001).
10. Harmony is the established term in legal anthropology, see, e.g., Nader (1991). The Moroccan idea of harmony, however, hardly fits the predominant model in legal anthropology.
11. For a more detailed analysis, see Schulze (2004).
12. Friendship, for instance, may establish descent-like relationships as found between brothers. Such established relationships, however, have a contractual aspect which may be annihilated. Friendship can be broken off whereas brotherhood can not.
13. On the mutual rights and obligations of sharecropping partners, see Turner (2003).
14. See Roque (2004) on civil society activism in the Souss.
15. See Montagne (1989) and Pennell (2000) for the historical background.
16. On comparison see Appadurai (1986), Gingrich (2002), Turner (2005a: 31–44); on the theory-in-place-dilemma see Fardon (1990); for different approaches in legal anthropology see e.g., Diamond (1951), Barkun (1968), Colson (1974), Roberts (1979).
17. On 'peaceful' societies, see e.g., Sponsel and Gregor (1994).
18. On the idea of justice and its connection with order in Morocco, see also Rosen (2000: 153–75, esp. 164), who offers a highly essentialized version of 'Islamic concepts of justice' based on Moroccan data and with respect to notions of reciprocity.

References

Appadurai, A. 1986. 'Theory in Anthropology: Center and Periphery', *Comparative Studies in Society and History*, 28(2), 356–61.
Barkun, M. 1968. *Law without Sanctions: Order in Primitive Societies and in the World Community*. New Haven: Yale University Press.
Ben Daoud, M. 1924. 'Receuil du Droit Coutumier de Massat', *Hespéris*, 4(3), 405–39.

―――― 1927. 'Documents pour Servir à l'Etude du Droit Coutumier Sud-Marocain', *Hespéris*, 7, 401–45.
Berque, J. 1978 [1955]. *Structures Sociales du Haut-Atlas*. Paris: Presses Universitaire de France.
Caton, S. 1987. 'Power, Persuasion, and Language: A Critique of the Segmentary Model in the Middle East', *International Journal of Middle Eastern Studies*, 19(1), 77–101.
Colson, E. 1974. *Tradition and Contract: The Problem of Order*. Chicago: Aldine.
Cook, M. 2000. *Commanding Right and Forbidding Wrong in Islamic Thought*. Cambridge: Cambridge University Press.
Cooney, M. 2001. 'Feud and Internal War: Legal Aspects', *International Encyclopedia of Social and Behavioral Sciences*, 8, 5605–8.
Diamond, A.S. 1951. *The Evolution of Law and Order*. London: Watts & Co.
―――― 1980. 'The Rule of Law Versus the Order of Custom' in *The Social Organisation of Law*, ed. D. Black, New York: Seminar Press, 318–43.
Ellickson, R.C. 1991. *Order without Law: How Neighbors Settle Disputes*. Cambridge, Mass.: Harvard University Press.
Evans-Pritchard, E. 1940. *The Nuer: A Description of the Modes of Livelihood and Political Institutions of a Nilotic People*. Oxford: Oxford University Press.
Fardon, R. 1990. 'Localizing Strategies: The Regionalization of Ethnographic Accounts' in *Localizing Strategies: Regional Traditions of Ethnographic Writing*, ed. R. Fardon, Edinburgh: Scottish Academic Press, 1–35.
Geertz, C., Geertz, H. and Rosen, L. 1979. *Meaning and Order in Moroccan Society*. Cambridge: Cambridge University Press.
Gellner, E. 1969. *Saints of the Atlas*. London: Weidenfeld and Nicolson.
Gingrich, A. 2002. *Anthropology, by Comparison*. London: Routledge.
Giordano, C. 2001. 'Mediterranean Honour Reconsidered: Anthropological Fiction or Actual Action Strategy?', *Anthropological Journal on European Cultures*, 10, 39–58.
Hatt, D. 1996. 'Establishing Tradition: The Development of Chiefly Authority in the Western High Atlas', *Journal of Legal Pluralism and Unofficial Law*, 37/38, 123–53.
Jacques-Meunié, D. 1982. *Le Maroc Saharien des Origines à 1670*, 2 vols. Paris: Klincksieck.
Lafond, J. 1948. *Les Sources du Droit Coutumier dans le Souss*. Agadir: Imprimerie du Souss.
Marcy, G. 1954 [1939]. 'Le Problème du Droit Coutumier', *Revue Algérienne, Tunisienne et Marocaine de Législation et de Jurisprudence*, 69, 1–44.
Montagne, R. 1989 [1930]. *Les Berbères et le Makhzen dans le Sud du Maroc*. Casablanca: Editions Afrique Orient.
Nader, L. 1990. *Harmony Ideology: Justice and Control in a Zapotec Mountain Village*. Stanford: Stanford University Press.
―――― 1991. 'Harmony Models and the Constuction of Law' in *Conflict Resolution: Cross-cultural Perspectives*, ed. K. Avruch, New York: Greenwood Press, 41–60.
Otterbein, K.F. 1993. *Feuding and Warfare: Selected Works of Keith F. Otterbein*. Langhorne, PA: Gordon and Breach.
Pennell, C.R. 2000. *Morocco since 1830: A History*. London: Hurst & Company.
Roberts, S. 1979. *Order and Dispute: An Introduction to Legal Anthropology*. Harmondsworth: Penguin.
Roque, M.-A. 2004. *La Société Civile au Maroc*. Paris: Publisud.
Rosen, L. 2000. *The Justice of Islam: Comparative Perspectives on Islamic Law and Society*. Oxford: Oxford University Press.
Scheper-Hughes, N. 2004. *Violence in War and Peace*. Oxford: Blackwell.
Schulze, R. 2004. 'Islamische Solidaritätsnetzwerke. Auswege aus den verlorenen Versprechen des modernen Staates' in *Transnationale Solidarität. Chancen und Grenzen*, eds J. Beckert et al., Frankfurt and New York: Campus, 195–218.
Sponsel, L. and Gregor, T. 1994. *The Anthropology of Peace and Non-Violence*. Boulder: Lynne Rienner.
Stewart, F. 2000. 'What is Honor?', *Acta Histriae*, 8(1), 13–28.

Stewart, P.J. and Strathern, A. 2002. *Violence: Theory and Ethnography.* London: Continuum.
Strathern, M. 1985. 'Discovering Social Control', *Journal of Law and Society,* 12(2), 111–34.
Surdon, G. 1928. *Esquisses du Droit Coutumier Berbère Marocain.* Rabat: Moncho.
Turner, B. 2003. '*Chr'ka* in Southwest Morocco: Forms of Agrarian Cooperation between *Khammessat* System and Legal Pluralism' in *Legal Pluralism and Unofficial Law in Social, Economic and Political Development.* Vol. 3., ed. R. Pradhan, Kathmandu: The International Centre for the Study of Nature, Environment and Culture, 227–55.
——— 2005a. *Asyl und Konflikt – von der Antike bis heute. Rechtsethnologische Untersuchungen.* Berlin: Dietrich Reimer.
——— 2005b. 'Der Wald im Dickicht der Gesetze: Transnationales Recht und lokale Rechtspraxis im Arganwald (Marokko)', *Zeitschrift für Entwicklungsethnologie,* 14(1), 97–117.
——— 2005c. 'The Legal Arena as a Battlefield: Salafiyya Legal Intervention and Local Response in Rural Morocco' in *Conflicts and Conflict Resolution in Middle Eastern Societies: Between Tradition and Modernity,* eds H.-J. Albrecht et al. Berlin: Duncker and Humblot, 169–85.

Chapter 7

LAW, RITUAL AND ORDER

Peter Just

Virtually all human action depends on order, creates order, defends order, contests order. One hardly needs to be a cognitive scientist to recognize that human mental activity is, fundamentally, a process of conferring categorical order on a universe in which phenomena and processes are unique and continuous (Lakoff 1990). And, whether one prefers the earlier formulations of Sapir (1986) and Whorf (1964) or the more recent and fashionable ones of Michel Foucault (1982, 1994), it seems that few fail to take for granted the crucial and determinative role that natural language plays in ordering one's perception of reality. So any consideration of order and disorder necessarily opens an immensely wide field of inquiry. What, one might reasonably ask, doesn't have at least *something* to do with order and disorder?

At the same time, however, some varieties of human behaviour fetishize order. At times, the way in which a social goal is accomplished is deliberately and precisely ordered in ways that exceed what is technically required, ways in which the social legitimacy of creating or sustaining social order depends on the ordering taking place in a prescribed orderly fashion. In other words, in an important sense these are prescribed ways of acting in which the process of imposing order takes place through an ordering of things, whether in the sense of elements which are in a set temporal sequence or in a set hierarchy. Among institutions law, however broadly defined, is surely concerned with order in this way; while we can imagine 'law without precedent' (Fallers 1969) it is much harder to imagine law without procedure.

But where else might we look? Etiquette might be one such place in social behaviour where proper ordering is both highly visible and inseparable from the legitimacy and efficacy of the act accomplished. Legal proceedings and forms of dispute settlement may take on aspects of etiquette as integral elements of procedure. Clifford Geertz, for example, once characterized Indonesian customary law as 'what one can only call high etiquette' (1983: 32). Later in this essay I will explore some of the ways etiquette is mobilized in legal proceedings to enhance their legitimacy by creating an aura of formality and authority.

I am also very much struck by the ways in which law and ritual resemble one another, struck by their shared tendency to fetishize order. I was put in mind of this more or less serendipitously by a concatenation of meanings from a lexicon well outside my chosen ethnological area: the word for 'order' in Hebrew is *seder*. Now *seder* is a pretty straightforward translation for 'order'; *haKol beseder*, for instance, would be a perfectly unremarkable translation of 'everything is in order' or, if you like, *Alles ist in Ordnung*. But *seder* is also the name of a central ritual, the ritual meal celebrating the feast of Passover. The term was originally meant to apply to the prescribed order in which the symbolic foods of the meal are blessed and consumed in conjunction with the recitation of a narrative, but the word has come to stand for the whole ritual itself. When this occurred to me, I was struck that many if not all of the properties regarding law and its articulation with order and disorder seem to apply as well to ritual in general. As with law and etiquette, ritual also depends deeply on regularity and predictability. Law and ritual also both depend on there being an order in the world and they both act to articulate that order, dispense it, recreate it and, of course, impose and enforce it. In what follows I adhere to the premise that law and ritual share a common deep structure derived from serving the shared task of articulating a vision of a world that is ordered, both ontologically and morally, 'a sense', as Clifford Geertz put it, 'without which human beings can hardly live at all, much less adjudicate anything, that truth, vice, falsehood, and virtue are real, distinguishable, and appropriately aligned' (1983: 231). We express this as much in our rituals, both sacred and secular, as we do in our law courts. Moreover, it seems possible that as societies increase in scale of size and organizational complexity they tend to rely less on legalizing ritual and more on ritualized law. Let me now turn to some of the ways in which this happens.

Ritual as Law

I cannot claim to be the first anthropologist to note a connection between law and ritual. Indeed, the evolutionists of the nineteenth and early twentieth centuries took it rather for granted that law had its origins in the sacred (Yelle 2001: 627–29). Take, for example, Sir Henry Maine's (1901: 26) proposition:

> The most ancient of the books containing the sacred laws of the Hindus appear to me to throw little light on the absolute origin of law. Some system

of actual observance, some system of custom or usage, must lie behind them; and it is very plausible conjecture that it was not unlike the existing very imperfectly sacerdotalised customary law of the Hindus in the Punjab. But what they do show is, if not the beginning of law, the beginning of lawyers. They enable us to see how law was first regarded, as a definite subject of thought, by a special learned class; and this class consisted of lawyers who were first of all priests (1901: 26).

Similarly, in *The Elementary Forms of the Religious Life* Emile Durkheim asserts that 'we are beginning to realize that law, morals and even scientific thought itself were born of religion, were for a long time confounded with it, and have remained penetrated with its spirit' (1965: 87, see also Yelle 2001: 628 from which this quote is cribbed). More latterly, Max Gluckman felt that law and ritual in tribal societies were part and parcel of the same dynamics, although he also seemed to feel that ritual was more about expressing conflict and perhaps glossing over it than about really resolving conflict:

> We can understand the beliefs and rituals of tribal society by relating them to the same conditions that explain the course of economic activity and political struggle, as well as the structure of law and order in the widest sense. These conditions are the relatively undifferentiated nature of social relations. … Ritual cloaks the fundamental disharmonies of social structure by affirming major loyalties to be beyond question (1965: 265).

Notice that these connections between ritual and law are largely seen as peculiar to the small and relatively homogeneous communities characteristic of so-called 'tribal' societies. A little later I will try to see if we can look at some of the abstract properties of ritual and see if they do not pertain as well to law in the context of the complex nation-state. But for the moment, I will simply take the position that, in societies of the kind it once pleased us to call 'primitive' or 'tribal', the analytic distinctions we are inclined to make between institutions like 'law' and 'religion' are more likely to be a reflection of Western institutions, or even the disciplinary and sub-disciplinary boundaries of Western academia, than they are an accurate portrayal of institutionalized distinctions in small-scale societies. In my own characterization of Dou Donggo dispute settlement (Just 2001) I have repeatedly asserted the integration of law with other aspects of social life, contending that there are a variety of 'public evaluative forums' in which the society's moral business is conducted. As anthropologists of law we should regard law not as a discrete domain with a set of specific institutional features – courts, judges, jails, police, etc. – but as a set of social processes engaged to settle disputes, resolve conflicts, and impose order on behaviour. And there is no reason that some of those processes cannot be ones we are inclined to characterize as 'ritual', particularly when those involved are apparently indifferent to such distinctions. In Donggo those individuals we would be inclined to regard as 'judges', because the social processes most closely resembling trials are entrusted to their hands, are for the most part the same individuals to whom is entrusted the conduct of rituals. In this society, as in many similar societies, the objective of both law and ritual is healing and repair, whether it be the repair of broken social relations, broken norms, or broken bodies. Nor are the Dou Donggo unique in this regard; 'harmony ideology' (Nader 1990), law that is designed 'to get people back into a situation where they can successfully (re)negotiate their relationships', as Michael Peletz (2002: 85–86) and others (e.g., Rosen 1989) have described the work of Muslim *kadis*, is if anything the norm, not the exception, outside the industrialized West. Indeed, there may even now be said to be an increasing movement in the West away from adversarial win/lose adjudication and towards what may be called the social healing of 'the therapeutic state' (e.g., Nolan 1998, 2001).

Let me give an example, described more completely elsewhere (Just 2001: 123–24), of a Dou Donggo dispute settled by means of ritual. The Dou Donggo are a group of subsistence swidden farmers who occupy the highlands to the east of Bima Bay on the island of Sumbawa in Indonesia. For several centuries they resisted conversion to Islam, the faith of their sovereign and more numerous neighbours, retaining an autochthonous religion, but by the end of the last century most had converted to Islam or Christianity. Socially egalitarian, they prefer to settle disputes consensually and within the confines of the village community.

> Basé and Halisa fell in love and wished to get married. Basé went through the proper procedures, engaging a marriage broker and observing all the formalities. But Halisa's parents rejected the suit out of hand, despite Halisa's protestations of love for Basé and her impassioned pleadings. Frustrated, Halisa and Basé ran off and married without payment of a brideprice and without her parent's blessing.
>
> Such elopements are relatively unusual, but they are not unknown and when they do happen they virtually always force the acquiescence of recalcitrant parents. Halisa's parents, however, were adamant. They refused to accept this fait accompli and greeted the return of the newly-weds with fits of shouting. In an act of deep symbolic resonance, Halisa's mother ran to the newly-weds' house and began to chop at the houseposts with a hatchet until she was restrained by onlookers and escorted away, weeping and screaming.
>
> Provoked beyond all bounds, Basé cursed his unwilling in-laws, bidding the 'sun to rise in the west', saying, in effect, that Halisa's parents were as unnatural to their daughter as would be the sun rising in the west. Even Halisa responded with the symbolic act of cutting to pieces clothes given to her by her mother, literally cutting the ties that bind and in effect 'disowning' her parents. All the cursing and bad words and bad feelings were seen to have rapid and devastating effect. The first of Basé and Halisa's children died soon after birth and the second was taken very ill, almost to the point of

death. This softened the hard hearts of Halisa's parents. Everyone decided that enough was enough and that things had to be put to rights again.

Basé turned to ama Tifé and ama Balo for help, two of the preeminent ritual and legal specialists of the community. Interestingly, Basé regarded his guilt as paramount. For a reconciliation to take place, younger must defer to elder, and Basé, who had uttered the fateful curse, was sure that a matter of this gravity required the sacrifice of a buffalo, the most expensive and lavish sacrifice in the ritual repertoire. Ama Tifé, however, also recognized equity in the situation. After all, Basé had tried to contract the marriage openly and with the permission of Halisa's parents, and while he ought to have deferred to their wishes and he certainly ought not to have uttered so deadly a curse at the parents of his wife and the grandparents of his unborn child, there was fault enough to go around. Ama Tifé, as he so often did, found a solution and told Basé, 'God doesn't want your buffalo. He already owns it'. As ama Balo put it, chuckling, 'Ama Tifé had sufficient esoteric knowledge [*rahasia*] to make two chickens enough for the job'. Such was 'the price of bad talk', and with the performance of an elaborate ceremony, presided over by ama Tifé, ama Balo and another village elder, ompu Ni, peace was restored to the family and things were allowed to return to an even keel. In addition to the sacrifice of a pair of chickens (male and female, of course) the *Nompa Lo'i Sake* ritual involved the creation of a ball of rice flour half again as large as a basketball which at the climactic moment was smashed to pieces, representing, I think, the dissolution of all the bad feelings that had snowballed into an indigestible lump. 'The badness', said ama Balo, 'was gathered up and taken by the Angel of God to God'.

There are a number of ways in which this case and its (ritual) resolution were law-like, especially in the juridical vernacular of Donggo. First, the entire thrust of the process was devoted to *kataho eli ro nggahi* to the 'repair of [bad] sounds and speech'. That is to say, there were ruptured social relations and the effect of the process was to restore them to their accepted valences. Second, the normative order, both cosmic and social, was articulated and reinforced. All of the parties involved had violated the social order in some way: the young people by failing to defer to their parents; the parents by unreasonably withholding their permission. The natural order had also been violated: Basé's curse invoking the sun to rise in the west was most palpable, but there had also been the unnatural reversal of children predeceasing their parents that had precipitated the resolution. And order that was both natural and social had been violated: Halisa cutting up the clothes her mother had given her, Halisa's mother attacking the newly-wed's houseposts, were violations of the natural sentiments of affection that should pervade relations between parents and children. All these violations constituted not chaos, not an absence of order, but anti-order, a reversal of order. By engaging in a ritual that gathered everything up into a great ball and smashing that ball, the *Nompa Lo'i Sake* symbolically reversed these reversals, reinstating the natural and social order.

Third, the *Nompa Lo'i Sake* required the intervention of officiands, men who are publicly legitimized as representing the social and natural order. By lending their authority and charisma to the ceremony, they made the resolution possible, visible, and lasting. And fourth, we see as well that the resolution was a public one – and indeed, the *Nompa Lo'i Sake* was well attended by many neighbors and relatives, perhaps as many as a hundred. Although those involved were willing to be reconciled well in advance of the ritual, a private reconciliation would not have been adequate; the participation of both the human and the supernatural community were necessary if the reconciliation was to be effective. Efficacy depends not only on the intervention of legitimating authority, but also on the witnessing of the event by the public at large. This, too, helps to make the resolution a lasting one, for it has been validated by the participation of many hands and voices.

In all four of these ways, then, this ritual operated in the same way that more intuitively 'legal' processes, such as the trial-like *paresa*, work in Donggo. Note that, like law, this ritual action is predicated on an understood sense of the natural and social order of the world. Relations between parents and children, elder and younger affines, are understood and are understood as natural, constituting a part of what I call the 'moral ontology' of the society. Basé's symbolic assertion that his parents-in-law were as unnatural to their daughter as the sun rising in the west was a powerful and crucial element in the rift, and perhaps the reason a ritual resolution was called for. But other disputes in this community, those solved by means of a *paresa*, are also dependent on the invocation of a sense that someone's behaviour has run counter to the natural order of things, that the moral ontology of the society has been ignored or violated. In a case in which a young man is accused of assaulting an older woman, he is told 'You can't behave this way, even if you *were* slandered. [The assaulted woman] is your sister. She's your mother. She is *vei dou*, a man's wife. You can't just do as you please; you are owned by your parents, you are owned by your siblings, you are owned by your cousins, you are owned by God' (Just 2001: 172). In a great many ways this trial was about rearticulating the structure of the social order, rehearsing the lineaments of that order for the miscreant.

Now it is one thing to assert that ritual operates like law in a place like Donggo. After all, as Marshall Sahlins noted long ago, while materialist theory envisions society 'divided into "component purposive systems" – each organised by specialised institutions (market, state, church, etc.)' it is 'the absence of just that differentiation between base and superstructure [that is] the hallmark of the "primitive" in the array of human cultures' (1976: 6). But we must also be very careful and remember, as Geoffrey White reminds us, that 'one of the difficulties with the opposition of "law" and "ritual" is that lurking just behind the scenes is the evolutionary claim that "we" have rational law, whereas "they" have emotive ritual' (1991:

189). It is another thing, therefore, to look for ritual as law in societies like our own, that circumscribe a domain of law, institutionalize it and expend a good deal of power – some of it violently coercive – defending the state's monopoly over that domain.

One pretty obvious place to look is in the realm of what Moore and Myerhoff (1977) called 'secular ritual'. Rituals of the state come to mind at once: coronations, inaugurations, openings of parliaments, the taking of oaths of office, as well as a variety of ceremonies honoring war dead, and so on (see Bell 1997: 83–88). We academics enjoy our own secular rituals, too, of course, especially surrounding the conferral of degrees. Are such rituals law? Well, they certainly have legal effects. It can certainly be argued that one does not hold a political office until one has taken the appropriate oath, and that is done as much ritually as it is done legally. Such secular rituals have a strongly performative character (Austin 1975), a characteristic they share with a good deal of legal activity. Eve Darian-Smith (1999: 175–80) provides us with a fascinating example of a quasi-legal secular ritual from Kent, England, in the recent revival of the ceremonial 'beating of the bounds', a practice thought to have its origins in Roman times. The practice traditionally consisted of assembling a group of clergy and village worthies on an appointed day, who would then process to the village's boundary stones and, accompanied by appropriate litanies, beat the stones with willow wands. According to Darian-Smith the practice 'reinforced a sense of justice and local authority by marking property rights and the property owner's responsibilities to the parish poor' and also acted to affirm 'a lord's duties to his poor tenants as well as the peasants' rights to bring their lord to trial through an established system of manorial courts' (1999: 175–76). What seems to be at stake here is a need to give expression to a social order that is also a political order, emphasizing both the rights and duties of classes of individuals and the territorial boundaries enclosing that order. Darian-Smith feels that the contemporary revival of the custom cannot be dismissed as mere 'sentimental yearnings for a past golden age', but rather sees it as a response to anxieties over the sublimation of local identities in the face of immigrating urbanites and Britain's increasing political and cultural incorporation in Europe. In this secular ritual the people of Kent are using the ordered behaviour of 'beating the bounds' to reassert a socio-jural order they feel to be under attack (1999: 180).

In addition to such secular rituals, we must not forget those religious rituals that have extraordinary legal effect: marriages are principal among them. Western marriages, whether religious or secular, are famously sites of the classic 'performative' (Austin 1975) utterance 'I now pronounce you husband and wife', and our lavish elaboration of weddings as social events and occasions for conspicuous consumption is something broadly shared among the societies of the world. Marriages, like oath-takings, inaugurations, and other rituals with legal effect, share a common articulation with social and natural order: they are about creating and constituting that order. By validating and facilitating legal and political status changes these rituals create the order they preserve. In the United States, at least, clergy are licensed to perform marriages that the state is obliged to recognize and to which attach many rights and duties that the state's legal apparatus is enjoined to protect and enforce. As Western states have become more secularized, the ritual process of marriage has been taken over by the state, sometimes with confusing effect. Because marriages most clearly create new order, new structure, much of the virulent and septic opposition to same-sex marriage abroad today in the United States and Europe derives from what its opponents see as the 'unnatural' nature of homosexual relations. The opposition is so bitter because the challenge to a fundamentalist sense of order is so great and because it falls at precisely the juncture of the 'natural' order and the social order and, as we all know, culture is working hardest when it presents the cultural as the natural.

In Donggo the past several decades have seen a shift in the order-making rituals surrounding marriage from ceremonies formalizing betrothal and bridewealth payments to *resepsi*, wedding receptions that borrow their form as well as their name from metropolitan, Western models (Just 1997). While the older rituals persist, there is clearly much greater emphasis, especially among young people, on the newer form. I argue that these ceremonies, conducted in the national language (Bahasa Indonesia) rather than in the indigenous language (Nggahi Mbojo), using Western-style attire for the bride and groom, are a way for the Dou Donggo to align their rituals for creating new order with their entry into a globalized world economy. It is interesting to note that in their rituals for restoring order the Dou Donggo rely on traditional forms like the *Nompa Lo'i Sake*, but are adopting new, borrowed forms for rituals creating new order. Similarly, the people of Kent need to reach far back to pre-modern ritual forms to reassert a threatened civil order, while gay couples in Britain are busily inventing new ways of celebrating civil unions, a novel form of civil order.

Law as Ritual

I have up to this point made some preliminary observations on some of the ways ritual may be law-like. Let me now explore the converse, and examine some of the ways in which law is ritualistic. I propose to do this by taking some of what may be generally assumed to be properties of ritual and searching for their presence in law. Catherine Bell (1997: 138–69) identifies formalism, traditionalism, invariance, rule-governance, sacred symbolism, and performance as characteristics of 'ritual-like activities'. These will do for starters.

Let me begin with symbolism, sacred and otherwise. It seems unremarkable to observe that legal proceedings engage in symbolic communication. I am immediately reminded that the case of assault tried in the Dou Donggo *paresa* I mentioned earlier was not allowed to conclude until the convicted assailant had knelt before his victim and begged her forgiveness, nor yet until she had administered a symbolic blow to his head. Both acts re-established the asymmetric order of their relationship, with the victim's blow acting as a metaphoric enactment of the law of talion (see Robert Yelle's [2001] fascinating discussion of the connections between the law of talion and sympathetic magic). I have seen legal symbolism operate metonymically in Donggo as well: Dou Donggo farmers who cut swiddens forbidden by law would nominate one of their number to stand trial for the crime, be duly convicted in the regency court, and serve a sentence in jail. This (along with a substantial bribe) would satisfy the government's

Plate 7.1: *United States Supreme Court*

claims to sovereignty and the rule of (their) law. The convicted man would have his swidden farmed for him by his neighbors while he served the sentence on their behalf. As for symbolism invoking the sacred, one need look no further than the typical architecture of our own courthouses. In America, at least, the modal courthouse replicates a Greek temple, replete with an idol of the blind Goddess of Justice seated in front:

Plate 7.2: *Courtroom, Otter-Tail County Minnesota*

The interior architecture, too, with its formal, imposing proportions, elevated judge's bench and costly materials, is designed to produce an atmosphere of awe, reverence and majesty, in other words the atmosphere of a house of worship. Note, in the image below from a court in Otter-Tail County, Minnesota, the partially obscured fresco of Moses as Lawgiver over the judge's bench, as an invocation of the divine.

The attempt in 2004 of the Chief Justice of the Alabama Supreme Court to install a two-and-a-half ton monument to the Ten Commandments in his courthouse failed on constitutional grounds, but met with the approval of three-quarters of Americans polled on the subject. I am reasonably sure, by the way, that virtually all of those polled also subscribe in principle to the American constitutional separation of church and state. The iconography of the Ten Commandments is to most of them, I feel, less a reference to specific religious beliefs than a reassurance that the impenetrability of a complex legal system is in some way responsive to and governed by simpler principles that they can grasp and of which they approve. Their sentiments, I believe, reflect a deep-seated desire to see the legal, civil order correspond to a cosmic order and respond to a diffuse and deeply-seated cognitive frame conceptualizing an integrated model ordering the family, community and state (Lakoff 2002).

Nowhere does the behaviour of our courts become more ritualistic than in the area of formalism and traditionalism. Formality was to Roy Rappaport the first among the more 'obvious aspects of ritual', and he specifically mentions 'the rather invariant procedures of ... the courtroom within which the variant substance of litigation is contained and through which it is presented in an ordered fashion' (1979: 175–76) as an example midway along a cline of invariability in ritual-like events. Bell (1997: 139) observes that 'in general, the more formal a series of movements and activities, the more ritual-like they are apt to appear'. Take, for example, some of the rules for behaviour in the Chancery Court of the State of Tennessee (Memphis Bar Association 2004):

> (b) The Chancellors shall wear judicial robes at all sessions of the Court, except the requirement may be waived by the Chancellor at any informal hearing.

Plate 7.3: *Justice Moore and His Monument*

(c) All persons in the Courtroom shall stand at the opening and closing of Court.
(d) All papers shall be handed to the Chancellor by the Sheriff, and no attorney shall approach the bench or witness stand from the bar except when directed by the Chancellor.
(e) There shall be no smoking in the Courtroom, nor shall food or drink be brought into the Courtroom.
(f) All attorneys and Court attendants shall be appropriately dressed during Court sessions; male attorneys shall wear coats and ties.
(g) All litigants and witnesses shall wear appropriate attire and make a clean and neat appearance.
(h) Upon the Chancellor entering the Courtroom preparatory to the formal opening of Court, the Sheriff shall call the Courtroom to order, directing all in attendance in Court to stand, and upon being so instructed by the Court, shall open Court in substantially the following manner: 'Hear Ye! Hear Ye! This Honorable Chancery Court of Tennessee is now open for the transaction of business pursuant to adjournment; all persons having business with the Court draw near and you shall be heard. The Honorable _____, Chancellor presiding. God Preserve these United States and this Honorable Court. Be seated, please.' Thereupon the Chancellor and those in the Courtroom shall be seated.
(i) Whenever anyone addresses the Court or is addressed by the Court, they shall rise and remain standing. Attorneys are not required to stand while interrogating witnesses.
(j) Whenever the Chancellor is ruling, all persons in the Courtroom shall remain seated and, if entering the Courtroom, shall be seated until the Chancellor has finished ruling.

Note how the rules work at creating a situation of regularity and predictability, properties I mentioned at the outset of this paper that law and ritual share with etiquette. Indeed, the rules of decorum of the kind cited above are generally referred to as 'courtroom etiquette' (Clarke 1991). The restricted behaviour of courtroom participants sets the business of the court apart from everyday affairs in precisely the same way that ritual sets apart the sacred and the profane.

The language of the courtroom, too, is a 'restricted code', a use of ordinary language in a rigid fashion, as well as the use of archaic language, both of which are properties of liturgy. Note, for example, the restrictiveness and predictability produced in this admonition to Australian law students as to how to cite cases in court:

> When citing cases to the court – the full reference to the case should be quoted, not the abbreviation, unless the Court has given you permission to dispense with the full cite. For example, the correct way of citing the case *Bloggs v Bloggs* [1989] 2 All ER 324, is as follows: 'Bloggs and Bloggs, 1989 volume 2 All England Reports at page 324'. You should check the complete

citation of cases to which you intend referring before coming to court. *Note*: in civil matters the 'v' is referred to as 'and' while in criminal cases, 'v' is referred to as 'against'. Never use the Americanism 'versus'. (Bond University Law School 2004)

'The rigidity of liturgical discourse', argues Rappaport, 'is such that it can represent whatever is conceived to be never-changing' (1979: 203). The archaisms of courtroom language – 'Hear Ye! Hear Ye!'; the arcane forms of address – 'my learned friend'; and the detailed, intricate differences, for example, in the way a barrister addresses an English appellate judge who is a Peer of the Realm as against one who is a Lord of Appeal in Ordinary (Bond University Law School 2004), create both a sense of ancient tradition and intricate esotericism. These, too, are properties of liturgy and, as Rappaport put it, 'liturgies are restrictive orders standing against the possibility of unrestricted disorder' (1979: 203).

Special clothing, too, adds a ritualistic aura to courtroom procedures for both litigants and officiands. It is not coincidental that the two professions in the modern world that continue to wear the gown everyday are the ministry and the law. In both instances, the robes mark the special status of the wearer, emphasizing the authority of the office as independent of, and superior to, the fallible personal qualities of the office-holder. As intercessors between citizens and the ordering principles of the world, it is desirable that both the priest and the judge be set apart from the ordinary and that attention be drawn away from them as individuals and toward the mediating offices they occupy. Judicial robes are the sartorial equivalent of liturgy.

According to Catherine Clarke: 'a familiar justification for the codification of etiquette standards is that rules preserve professionalism and the power structure. In other words, courts are respected in that they are respectable. Society allocates decisional authority and its functions to the authorities that it accepts. Etiquette is the bridge to acceptance' (1991: 962). Indeed, a good deal of courtroom ceremonialism is designed to invest the judge with dignity, legitimacy and authority. The elevated bench separates the judge from lawyers and litigants; he or she is given papers indirectly, by means of an armed law officer in the Tennessee instance; all stand for the judge's entrance and exit; and so on.

It seems odd that all this ceremonialism should be necessary. Though possessed of far greater power, the modern nation-state seems to rely much more heavily on ritualism in its legal proceedings than do small-scale societies. The proceedings in a Dou Donggo *paresa* are informal, sometimes chaotic. Peletz (2002: 68–73) describes the Malaysian *kadi*'s courthouse as a 'nondescript' building. Although litigants are expected to dress appropriately (meaning women must wear headscarves), the *kadi* himself never wears his robes and conducts hearings with his three-year-old son wandering in and out of chambers. Why should Dou Donggo judges be able to conduct their business in drab and tattered clothes while the late William Rehnquist felt ordinary judicial robes so inadequate he had to add four gold stripes to the sleeves of his robes to mark his status as Chief Justice? (The new Chief Justice, a more prepossessing man, has reverted to plainer robes.)

The difference, I believe, is a matter of charisma, something that might even be apparent by comparing the pictures above of ama Balo and William Rehnquist. The Dou Donggo judge derives his authority from consensus and charisma. He is a judge because his fellow citizens have chosen him to be such and they have done so because his personal qual-

Plate 7.4: *British Colonial Judge*

ities make him an effective representative of both the social and the cosmic order. He knows that order, he commands that order, he is proof against disorder, be it civil or supernatural. 'In primitive circumstances' that quality of charisma, as Max Weber imagined it, rested on the deference 'paid to prophets, to people with a reputation for legal or therapeutic wisdom, to leaders in the hunt and heroes in war. It is very often thought of as resting on magical powers' (1947: 356–57), all of which might be said to pertain to ama Balo. Unlike ama Balo, the Malaysian *kadi* does not have an authority derived by the consensual election of his community, but also unlike ama Balo, he does possess a bespoke building, an office, a staff, a title, and a salary to buttress his authority and to attest to his command of his knowledge of canon, that is, sacred law. William Rehnquist, who commanded great influence over the lives of millions,

Plate 7.5: *Ama Balo*

has the least charisma of the three. A man of singularly unimpressive personal presence, he had to derive his authority, legitimacy and majesty from the office to which he was appointed. Hence the impressive building, the elaborate courtroom etiquette and the robes with gold stripes on the sleeves. Comparing ama Balo to William Rehnquist we may say that it is characteristic of the differences between the two societies that the one uses ritual to restore and interleave the cosmic and social orders, while the other uses ritual to buttress the means at its disposal to create and enforce a civil order. Perhaps the Dou Donggo have so little need for ritual in their legal proceedings because they have retained enough law in their ritual proceedings.

One might go a bit further in looking comparatively at formalism and ritualism in the courts. The tenor of the magistrates' courts described by Peletz (2002: 68–73), Rosen (1989), and Bowen (2003: 72–73) might, as Michael Peletz (personal communication) suggests, stand at an intermediate position between the informality of Dou Donggo proceedings and the hyper-formality of High Court proceedings in the industrialized state. Two dimensions of variation suggest themselves. One is that as the complexity of the society increases, so does the ritualization of its legal proceedings. The other is that as the range and power of the court's

Plate 7.6: *Chief Justice Rehnquist*

jurisdiction expand, so does the need for ritualization. The courts described by Peletz, Rosen, Bowen and others are courts at the lowest levels of their respective legal systems. If one were to compare them to Malaysian or Indonesian appellate or high courts, one would find an increasing degree of architectural splendour, linguistic archaism, sartorial formality, and procedural ritualization. A similar dynamic applies in Western courts as well: not surprisingly, the American magistrate's courts, described by Barbara Yngvesson (1993) and Sally Merry (1990), are similarly less formalized and ritualized than that of higher American courts. We might conclude that greater judicial scope and power are seen quite generally as requiring greater legitimation by ritual means, or that, perhaps, greater power is seen to be in need of greater restrictions on spontaneity and innovation imposed by the formality and ritualization we have observed.

At first it seems strange, even paradoxical, that we should find greater ritualization, more elaborate and refined restricted codes of dress, language and etiquette in societies or at levels of legal systems that would seem already to have at their command the greatest degree of brute power, the broadest range of authority. Ama Balo commands no police force, much less an army, and his writ runs no further than the little stream at the bottom of the hill that separates his village from the next. Yet he needs no special clothing and those whose disputes he settles address him with no more formality or deference than they use on other occasions. The authority of the Chief Justice of the United States is backed by forces of unimaginable power and violence and so he sits enthroned in marble and mahogany. The difference may be as simple as great power seeking to display itself. Nonetheless, it seems odd that the society with the greater degree of Weberian rationalization should also be the one exhibiting the greater degree of supposedly irrational ritualization. After all, what purpose is served by the lavish expense and effort of these symbolic displays? Perhaps they are there because producing social solidarity in complex societies is hard work. Durkheim regarded law and morals as having 'remained penetrated' with the spirit of religion. But if we can find aspects of ritual in the law of modern, secular nation-states, perhaps it is not because it was once there, and hangs atavistically on as a 'survival', but because it continues to be produced that way. Societies need all the order they can get. They depend on formulations of order to give meaning to social life and they require mechanisms for advertising, disseminating and compelling order. If we see ritual and law as technologies for doing that, we should not be surprised to see them both at work in any sort of society and the greater the scope of the order to be produced, the greater the need for its ritualized symbolic expression.

This leaves us with a deeper question as well: why fetishize order at all? Here we may depart the sociological and enter the psychological.

Freud noted the 'resemblance between what are called obsessive actions in sufferers from nervous afflictions and the observances by means of which believers give expression to their piety' (1963: 17). He called both 'ceremonials'. In typical fashion, Freud attributed the ritualistic behaviour of the neurotic to the displacement of forbidden sexual thoughts and the ritualistic behaviour of the pious to the renunciation of egoistic pleasure. Thus, he opined, 'one might venture to regard obsessional neurosis as a pathological counterpart of the formation of a religion, and to describe that neurosis as an individual religiosity and religion as a universal obsessional neurosis' (Freud 1963: 26, see also Dulaney and Fiske 1994). This diagnosis is unlikely to please the religious; nor is it likely that judges and barristers will be pleased at having courtroom ceremonial regarded as a collective obsessional neurosis. But Freud's speculations draw our attention to the notion that ritualized behaviour, order that is fetishized, can be deeply comforting at the individual, psychological level. Perhaps, then, the greater ritualization of modern law helps to assuage the alienation of the individual from the impersonality of law dispensed by those who are both unknown to him and immensely more powerful. And knowing what to do, what to say and how to dress, can all help to remove anxiety from a situation of grave consequence, like the courtroom, where one would want as little as possible to be left to chance.

Finally, it can be said that there is a good deal of symbolic power in acts that are 'performatives', something encountered in both ritual and law. Both are conspicuous for doing what they say and relying on specifiable 'felicity conditions' in order to be efficacious (Austin 1975). There is more than a passing similarity between a priest saying 'I baptize thee ...' and a judge saying 'I sentence you ...'. These acts create and impose order in doing what they say, whether it is ama Balo smashing the great ball of discontent in *Nompa Lo'i Sake* or a magistrate or a priest saying 'I now pronounce you husband and wife'. By surrounding actions that create, restore or impose order with behaviour that itself is highly attentive to its own ordering, ritual and legal acts become what we might call 'super-performatives': they draw attention to order by being orderly, supersaturated, as it were, with an abundance of order. This abundance of order is then available to be dispensed by authority, doing the work of ordering it wishes to do.

References

Austin, J.L. 1975. *How to Do Things with Words*, 2nd edn. Cambridge: Harvard University Press.
Bell, C. 1997. *Ritual: Perspectives and Dimensions*. Oxford: Oxford University Press.
Bond University Law School. http://www.bond.edu.au/law/mootcomp/etiquette.htm. (accessed November 2004).

Bowen, J.R. 2003. *Islam, Law, and Equality in Indonesia: an Anthropology of Public Reasoning.* Cambridge: Cambridge University Press.

Clarke, C.T. 1991. 'Missed Manners in Courtroom Decorum', *Maryland Law Review*, 50(4), 945–1026.

Darian-Smith, E. 1999. *Bridging Divides: the Channel Tunnel and English Legal Identity in the New Europe.* Berkeley: University of California Press.

Dulaney, S. and Fiske, A.P. 1994. 'Cultural Rituals and Obsessive-Compulsive Disorder: Is There a Common Psychological Mechanism?', *Ethos*, 22(3), 243–83.

Durkheim, E. 1965 [1915]. *The Elementary Forms of the Religious Life.* New York: Free Press.

Fallers, L.A. 1969. *Law without Precedent: Legal Ideas in Action in the Colonial Courts of Busoga.* Chicago: University of Chicago Press.

Foucault, M. 1982. *The Archaeology of Knowledge and the Discourse on Language.* New York: Pantheon.

—— 1994. *The Order of Things: an Archaeology of the Human Sciences.* New York: Vintage.

Freud, S. 1963 [1907]. 'Obsessive Acts and Religious Practices', in *Sigmund Freud: Character and Culture*, ed. P. Rieff, New York: Collier Books, 17–26.

Geertz, C. 1983. 'Local Knowledge: Fact and Law in Comparative Perspective' in *Local Knowledge: Further Essays in Interpretive Anthropology.* New York: Basic Books, 167–234.

Gluckman, M. 1965. *Politics, Law and Ritual in Tribal Society.* Oxford: Blackwell.

Just, P. 1997. '*Resepsis*: Dou Donggo Wedding Receptions as Cultural Critique' in *Social Organization and Cultural Aesthetics: Essays in Honor of William H. Davenport*, eds W.J. Donner and J.G. Flanagan, Lanham: University Press of America, 95–112.

—— 2001. *Dou Donggo Justice: Conflict and Morality in an Indonesian Society.* Lanham: Rowman and Littlefield.

Lakoff, G. 1990. *Women, Fire, and Dangerous Things: What Categories Reveal about the Mind.* Chicago: University of Chicago Press.

—— 2002. *Moral Politics: How Liberals and Conservatives Think*, 2nd edn. Chicago: University of Chicago Press.

Maine, H. 1901. *Early Law and Custom.* London: John Murray.

Memphis Bar Association. 2004. Rule 1. Sessions and Courtroom Procedure http://www.memphisbar.org/courts/chancerycourtrules/r01.html (accessed November2004).

Merry, S.E. 1990. *Getting Justice and Getting Even: the Legal Consciousness of Working Class Americans.* Chicago: University of Chicago Press.

Moore, S.F. and Myerhoff, B.A. 1977. 'Secular Ritual: Forms and Meanings' in *Secular Ritual*, eds S.F. Moore and B.A. Myerhoff, Amsterdam: van Gorcum, 3–24.

Nader, L. 1990. *Harmony Ideology: Justice and Control in a Zapotec Mountain Village.* Stanford: Stanford University Press.

Nolan, J.L., Jr. 1998. *The Therapeutic State: Justifying Government at Century's End.* New York: New York University Press.

—— 2001. *Reinventing Justice: the American Drug Court Movement.* Princeton: Princeton University Press.

Peletz, M.G. 2002. *Islamic Modern: Religious Courts and Cultural Politics in Malaysia.* Princeton: Princeton University Press.

Rappaport, R.A. 1979. 'Some Obvious Aspects of Ritual' in *Ecology, Meaning, and Religion*, Richmond: North Atlantic Books, 173–221.

Rosen, L. 1989. *The Anthropology of Justice: Law as Culture in Islamic Society.* Cambridge: Cambridge University Press.

Sahlins, M. 1976. *Culture and Practical Reason.* Chicago: University of Chicago Press.

Sapir, E.L. 1986. *Selected Writings of Edward Sapir on Language, Culture, and Personality.* Berkeley: University of California Press.

Weber, M. 1947. *The Theory of Social and Economic Organization.* New York: Free Press.

White, G.M. 1991. 'Rhetoric, Reality, and Resolving Conflicts: Disentangling in a Solomon Islands Society' in *Conflict Resolution: Cross-Cultural Perspectives*, eds K. Avruch, P. Black and J. Scimecca, New York: Greenwood, 165–86.

Whorf, B.L. 1964. *Language, Thought, and Reality: Selected Writings*. Cambridge: MIT Press.

Yelle, R.A. 2001. 'Rhetorics of Law and Ritual: a Semiotic Comparison of the Law of Talion and Sympathetic Magic', *Journal of the American Academy of Religion*, 69(3), 627–47.

Yngvesson, B. 1993. *Virtuous Citizens, Disruptive Subjects: Order and Complaint in a New England Court*. New York: Routledge.

Chapter 8

THE DISORDERS OF AN ORDER: STATE AND SOCIETY IN OTTOMAN AND TURKISH TRABZON

Michael E. Meeker

Introduction

How should we understand the relationship of a state order and a social order?[1] Is it possible to theorize the state apart from society, and society apart from the state? For example, would it be possible to institute a state as a kind of protective umbrella for a collection of societies, as in the instance of a collection of tribes, peasantries and citizens, speaking different languages and ascribing to different religions? And might such a state, in its role as a protective umbrella, take a variety of forms, including the form of a liberal and democratic state as anticipated by some for the new Iraq? Or should we consider instead another hypothesis? The politics of a state might always be inseparable from a politics of society. This would mean that the order of the state and the order of society would react one upon the other, and so always be mutually implicated, one with the other.

With this last possibility in mind, how might a state order and a social order be intertwined one with the other? Some states, more than others, might have the capacity to overwhelm subject societies, transforming them into their own unique social order. Or instead, some societies, more than others, might have the potential to transform or even to generate a unique state order. Perhaps the relationship of state and society might resemble the relationship of hunter and hunted, that is to say of a predator searching for a prey. Some states might have the potential to reduce and weaken social structures, so that they pose virtually no challenge to centralized authority. Correspondingly, some societies might have a special potential to penetrate and colonize official classes and institutions, undermining and corrupting them.

These various hypotheses suggest that the relationship of state and society is often, if not normally, a disorderly conjunction. Indeed, studies of the eclipse of empires and the rise of nations in the Euro-American sphere have portrayed the relationship of state and society as a disorderly conjunction from different angles. Simmel's (1978) account of the evolution of monetary institutions and Anderson's (1991) account of the dissemination of vernacular printing are just two of many examples. In different ways, and by different rhythms, money and books fostered new individual psychologies and new social structures that eventually resulted in new governmental arrangements as a consequence of political crises. From the early modern period, the interaction of state and society in Europe moved irregularly, even violently, from an Age of Empires to an Age of Nations. Sometimes the passage from empires to nations is summed up by the term 'modernization', as though political history was leading inexorably in a certain direction and exhibited regularities despite incidental catastrophes along the way. But the arrival of the Age of Nations did not bring a new equilibrium to the relationship of state and society, but rather new kinds of crises: political revolution, financial booms and busts and total war.

Studies of the relationship of state and society outside the Euro-American sphere have also focused on their disorderly conjunction, especially during the colonial or post-colonial period. This last preoccupation may have encouraged the assumption that it is westernization that uniquely destabilizes the relationship of state and society. The concept of 'tradition' is commonly applied to states and societies outside the Euro-American sphere but more rarely to the Euro-American sphere itself. This suggests the existence of a world without change, perhaps even a world without time before the advent of westernization. In some accounts of the Ottoman Empire, the Mughal Empire, the Middle Kingdom and Tokugawa Japan, the possibility of change, and so also the possibility of time, is reduced to the degeneration of tradition, that is, to 'decline'. It is as though the relationship of state and society did not have a history before the onset of modernization operating through westernisation.

A dominant theme in the historiography of the Ottoman Empire illustrates such a presumption. The Ottomans ruled over a collection of tribes, peasants and townspeople who spoke a variety of languages and ascribed to a variety of religions. The exercise of centralized sovereign power hinged on preserving the integrity of the state against the decentralizing tendencies inherent in this motley collection of subject peoples dispersed over a vast and varied landscape. When this principle was compromised during the late seventeenth or early eighteenth century – by governmental corruption, military defeat and economic depression – the result was institutional decline. During the nineteenth century, however, the adoption of Western governmental institutions and technologies resulted in a process of reform and renewal. For a while, the Ottomans were able to reverse the course of decline and re-establish state domination of subject societies. Eventually, increasing contacts with the Euro-American sphere resulted in the transformation of the social order as well as the state order. Overwhelmed by the centrifugal forces of nationalism, the imperial regime began to lose its legitimacy as a protective umbrella. The disaster of the First World War provided the occasion for its final demise, and in time its subject societies became nation states. By this account, the history of state and society in the Ottoman Empire is entirely degenerative. The transition from empire to nation is entirely a result of modernization operating through westernization.

In what follows, I shall argue that the history of state and society in the Ottoman Empire is closer to the history of state and society in the Euro-American sphere than has previously been estimated. In doing so, I shall provide indications that the disorders of state and society characteristic of the Age of Nations in Europe occurred earlier rather than later in certain parts of the Ottoman Empire. This suggests that the Ottoman/Turkish relationship of state and society has its own special history before (as well as after) modernization through westernization.

To make this case, I shall first consider two recent theories of the relationship of state and society in Europe. Each theory can then be used as a measure of the extent to which the relationship of state and society in the Ottoman Empire was either different or similar.

Recent Theories of State and Society in Europe

The first theory views the state as a machine designed for a single purpose. A corps of functionaries collects taxes and assembles conscripts by means of polices and institutions. Their objective is to make war, in order to reinforce commercial prerogatives and extend territorial reach, so as to make more war. Competition among states leads to the rationalization of official policies and institutions. While not every state survives, the system of states evolves with the perfection of their operation of war machines.

We find such a theory in Charles Tilly's (1990) analysis of the evolution of the state system in Europe over the course of a millennium. In his study, Tilly divides states into two groups: (1) those that ruled over large populations and extensive lands, and (2) those that had prosperous commercial economies but lacked large numbers of subjects and extensive territorial domains. The first type of state, as exemplified by the Kingdom of France during the seventeenth century, enjoyed a surplus of lands and peasants. State functionaries were therefore in a position to raise armies and finance military expansion by conscription and taxation of a subject population. The second type, as exemplified by the Low Countries during the same period, enjoyed a surplus of money. State functionaries could rent armies and buy arms with which to enforce commercial prerogatives. In this fashion, Tilly demonstrates that there were two paths by which states became formidable war machines. By his account, official classes and institutions dominate and exploit subject populations in a game of military competition that heads toward the end point of total war. The theory is ingenious, but it is a history of the state without a history of society.

This judgment, however, is a bit severe. Tilly does address the relationship of state and society in at least two ways. In an article published before his book appeared and entitled 'War-Making and State Making as Organized Crime', Tilly (1985) likened the elites of a state to a form of criminal organization. From this irreverent – but not altogether false – perspective, Tilly proposes that every state is also a zero-degree society. That is to say, state functionaries are Mafiosi with political legitimacy. They exploit populations and dominate markets by the calculated exercise of violence against any potential competitor. In other words, Tilly implicitly recognizes that the official state always comes in the company of an official society, even if he does not examine the implications of this association. I shall return to this point later in the chapter.

Tilly addresses the issue of state and society more broadly in his later study of the evolution of the state system of Europe. He does so as his account moves forward toward the Age of Nations, that is to say, when he is unable to avoid the issue. From the time of Napoleon, war-making was less and less an aristocratic pastime. With the possibility of mass mobilization, the size of military forces and the breadth of military operations expanded. The state systems of Europe were moving toward total war. It would not be enough to conscript and train ever more soldiers. To survive in this military environment, each state would have to rely more and more on popular support for the war effort. The state system of Europe would therefore begin to exhibit institutions of representative government. Broadening the scope of popular participation in governing institutions would be the price paid for insuring popular support for total war.

By this argument, the emergence of bourgeois democracies during the nineteenth century was the direct consequence of a *raison d'état*. The crises of state and society that arose with the Age of Nations, including class revolution and radical reform, were provoked by military competition among states. The analysis is ingenious, but it is entirely state-centric. States are active victimizers. Societies are passive victims. The changes in social beliefs and practices that led to the Age of Nations are largely out of sight.

The second theory that I shall consider explicitly addresses the disorderly conjunction of state and society. We find such a theory in the works of Michel Foucault. In *Discipline and Punish* (1977), for example, he insists on the close relationship of sovereign power and social disciplines. For Foucault, a government that depends on force alone is excessively expensive and inefficient. The effective management of a population must rely on propagating a constellation of beliefs and practices. This would mean that every regime is associated with supervisory and indoctrinating techniques. Turning to the question of the rise of bourgeois democracies in the Euro-American sphere during the nineteenth century, Foucault looks for the earliest instances of 'tactics of power' whose deployment resulted in the remaking of the relationship of state and society.

By Foucault's account, the new tactics of power first appeared at the level of society, not of the state, the initial example being workhouses for the poor in Protestant Europe. Almost immediately, however, the supervisory and indoctrinating techniques of these charity foundations began to be applied to other contexts for other purposes: prisons, hospitals, barracks, schools and factories. The proliferation and diversification of the new supervisory and indoctrinating techniques were a direct consequence of their socio-political utility. It was possible to carry out correctional, medical, educational, military or productive tasks by inculcating certain kinds of behaviours in individuals who could then be organized in certain ways.

To expose the character of the new supervisory and indoctrinating techniques, Foucault turns to Jeremy Bentham's (1791) treatise on the 'panopticon'. Bentham explains how an architectural design can achieve psychological effects. (1) Individuals are placed in cells so that they are deprived of contact with one another. (2) Each isolated individual is exposed to an invisible observer located at a central point. (3) Under perpetual observation, the individuals in their separate cells are subjected to the same set of behavioural regulations. (4) All the individuals acquire a personal conscience that conforms to behavioural regulations. (5) As a result, the individuals can be deployed in disciplined groups to accomplish certain tasks.

For Foucault, Bentham was the theoretician of already existent institutional practices. He explained their mechanisms and effects only after, rather than before, the fact of their application. As a theoretician, however, Bentham was able to pinpoint the essence of the new institutional practices. Referring to the panopticon, Foucault demonstrates how practices of isolation, individuation, regulation and self-control played a role in the founding of new kinds of prisons, hospitals, barracks, schools and factories during the nineteenth century.

Foucault located the origins of revolutionary change in the state system of Europe at the level of the 'micro-physics' of daily social life. The Reformation had led to new ideas about the individual's relationship to God. These ideas inspired new kinds of charitable foundations that were the seeds of a new kind of socio-political utility. Eventually this new socio-political utility favoured the emergence of bourgeois democracies; however, they also threatened bourgeois democracies, since they led to an expansion of the role and scope of government. For Foucault, the passage from the Age of Empires to the Age of Nations turns upon a disorderly conjunction of state and society.[2]

State and Society in the Ottoman Empire

Let us now consider the Ottoman Empire from the perspectives of Tilly and Foucault. Their theories direct our attention to remarkable characteristics of the Ottoman regime during the so-called 'classical' period, that is, from the late fifteenth to the late sixteenth century.[3] The result could be described as déjà vu. In accordance with Tilly's thesis, the sultan's government did take the form of a corps of functionaries who extracted taxes from a subject population and deployed military forces to extend imperial domains. Indeed, one historian has recently described the Ottoman Empire as one of the most militarized states of the early modern period (Aksan 1999a, 1999b). And in accordance with the thesis of Foucault, the sultan's government also put into play tactics of power that instilled habits of solidarity and obedience, first among functionaries but then later among elements of the subject population. This is an argument that I have recently developed elsewhere (Meeker 2002). But in citing Foucault, I insisted on a difference, which I shall now outline.

The Ottoman Empire of the classical period featured the same functional requirements as the states of early modern Europe. At the same time, the satisfaction of these functional requirements was achieved in a different way. Ottoman tactics of power originally had no affinities with a Benthamite panopticon, until the onset of modernization through westernization during the nineteenth century. To demonstrate the plausibility of these claims, I shall cite a famous description of the Ottoman palace. I am referring to an analysis of the so-called 'palace system' that appears in Machiavelli's *The Prince*.

In a brief passage, Machiavelli compares the Kingdom of France and the Ottoman Empire. In the text, which dates from 1515, the essential characteristic of the sultan's authority is reliance on a corps of slave officials:

> The entire monarchy of the Turk is governed by one lord, the others are his servants [slaves]; and, dividing his kingdom into sanjaks [sub-provinces], he sends there different administrators, and shifts and changes them as he chooses. But the King of France is placed in the midst of an ancient body of lords, acknowledged by their own subjects, and beloved by them; they have their own prerogatives, nor can the king take these away except at his peril. Therefore, he who considers both of these states will recognize great difficulties in seizing the state of the Turk, but, once it is conquered, great ease in holding it.

> The causes of the difficulties in seizing the kingdom of the Turk are that the usurper cannot be called in by the princes of the kingdom, nor can he hope to be assisted in his designs by the revolt of those whom the lord has around him. This arises from the reasons given above; for his ministers, being all slaves and bondmen, can only be corrupted with great difficulty, and one can expect little advantage from them when they have been corrupted, as they cannot carry the people with them, for the reasons assigned. (Machiavelli 1992: 17–18)

In sketching the palace system of the Ottomans, Machiavelli relies on certain doubtful suppositions regarding the master/slave relationship. But before examining this issue, consider the logic of his analysis, which is still today a common European analysis of the classical Ottoman regime.

In the text just cited, Machiavelli was thinking of a notorious institution of the Ottomans: the *devşirme*. This was the levy of children, normally from among the Christian population, for training as military officers and government functionaries. Some of these children – the most gifted – were chosen to enter into the palace service where they were trained at the residence of the sultan by predecessors who had themselves been recruited as youths. By such measures, the so-called slave official reached maturity by a path that entailed the loss of any loyalty toward his family, his ethnicity, his relatives or his country of origin.

As a corollary, the sultan's government lacked any profound relationship with its subject populations and so staked no claim on their loyalty. Ottoman rule was constituted in minimizing, or even in suppressing, the relationship between the governing and the governed classes. This was done for very good reasons. The Ottomans faced a large and dispersed population of variable social qualities. Their government was therefore threatened by centrifugal forces of ethnic, religious, linguistic and regional affiliation.

However, this classical analysis of the palace system neglects an important, even a fundamental, dimension of the recruitment and training of the servants of the sultan. The loyalty of palace officials cannot be explained by the simple fact of their enslavement. Their loyalty was the positive result of an instilled discipline of association, as well as a negative result of their removal from their original families and communities. That is to say, the state order came in the company of a social order. Tactics of power were linked with beliefs and practices of association by which a new social relationship could be constructed. These beliefs and practices were adapted from Islamic disciplines whose objective was self-control and social reciprocity.

For example, the daily rites and prayers turn upon themes of obedience and solidarity. By means of these themes, the Ottomans fashioned a discipline for the personal and group formation of functionaries. This discipline, moreover, was transmitted and celebrated by a coordination of structures and institutions, including architectural designs, educational programmes, methods of supervision and inspection, and official ceremonies.

There was then an Ottoman panopticon but it was completely different from the Benthamite panopticon in its conception, design and operation. The Ottoman panopticon depended on the psychological control of the subject by a mechanism of group association and inspection rather than a mechanism of isolating individuals in separate cells placed under perpetual surveillance.

I have described the palace system as a sort of utilitarian political machine. But the Ottomans of the classical period were proud of it and devoted to it. They saw the palace system as the expression of an ethical ideal. It was the basis of centralized sovereign power that was both true and just. They displayed sultanic rule by means of great imperial centres designed to demonstrate and celebrate this tactics of power (Necipoğlu 1991). Consequently, the design and use of these imperial centres can be examined in order to understand the operations of the Ottoman panopticon (Meeker 2002: 118–44).

Consider the overall layout of the imperial palace. It was a walled fortress situated on a hilltop that overlooked the imperial domains of two continents. At the same time, specific features of this edifice – its massive portals and walls, its observation towers and kitchen chimneys – indicate that the sovereign has many eyes and many hands to assist him. The walled fortress was also a residence of a sovereign surrounded by thousands of loyal retainers. Within the walls of the palace, a ceremonial court formed the axis of the layout of the grounds. Here the functionaries of the imperial regime, numbering in the thousands, periodically assembled to display themselves for the edification of foreign ambassadors. On these occasions, they appeared as a disciplined association under the watchful eye of the sultan. A choreography of bodily movements performed in silence became a representation of invincible sovereign power.

While the central ceremonial court was the stage set for the display of a mechanism of gaze, discipline and rule, other architectural features of the palace indicate the practical deployment of this tactics of power. However, we do not have the time to examine this matter here. Rather, I want to insist that the state order was linked with a social order. The classical imperial regime can certainly be viewed as a war machine, but it was also a machine for inculcating solidarity and obedience. The recruitment and training of slave officials were linked with a discipline of association that was part of a tactics of power. Furthermore, this discipline (and so also its socio-political utility as a tactics of power) was not necessarily limited to the men and women of the palace. Since it consisted of a kind of social ethic, nothing prevented its exportation, or for that matter its appropriation, beyond the walls of the palace. That is to say, the tactical combination of a state order with a social order featured an inherent disorder.

During the classical period, no power holder in the provinces was able to duplicate the splendor, the glory and the extravagance of the ceremonies of the imperial palace (Meeker 2002). In effect, the very purpose of these ceremonies was to demonstrate that the sultan's government was without rivals or peers. Nonetheless, it was very easy to adapt the social ethic of the palace to the external Ottoman world. Its essential elements were as follows:

1. A leading individual who exercised sovereign power
2. A body of armed followers composed of friends, allies, and relatives
3. Islamic beliefs and practices oriented toward obedience and solidarity
4. A corps of religious experts acting as councilors and teachers

The result was a form of sovereign leadership and grouping without any connection to any particular ethnicity, language, country of origin or any particular family. That is to say, the elements of this social ethic would provide the basis for a cosmopolitan, rather than a primordial, construction of solidarity and obedience. In other words, the discipline of association at the foundation of the palace system could travel. It could potentially leave the palace and move far and wide through the imperial domains, transcending and confounding primordial loyalties.

In the Ottoman provinces, two kinds of personalities and two kinds of structures attest to the dissemination of this discipline of association in the later Empire: The agha (*ağa*) was a leading individual supported by friends and followers, like the sultan himself. His residence was a great mansion (*konak*) situated on a hilltop and overlooking the surrounding population, like the palace in Istanbul. The hodja (*hoca*) was a religious teacher and advisor who represented Sunni Islam. He was associated with a religious academy (*medrese*) where sometimes very large numbers of students were instructed in an official Sunni Islam (Meeker 2004, 2005a, 2005b, 2005c).

Machiavelli was wrong, or at least he would soon be wrong, when he contended that there was no relationship between the palace system and the people. The Ottomans always had the choice of exporting a discipline of association from the palace to the provinces. By such a politics, they were able to fashion partisans – and might one even dare to say to fashion citizens – in the villages and towns of the Ottoman domains. But at the same time, the Ottomans did not have a sure means of controlling or limiting the appropriation of this discipline of association. As a result, there was a double possibility. The temptation to recruit partisans among the population came in the company of the problem of decentralization of sovereign power. The result was a running crisis of state and society.

The Formation of an Ottomanist Provincial Society in Trabzon

I shall now travel – in time – from the sixteenth to the eighteenth century and – in space – from the palace in Istanbul to the old province of Trabzon on the southern Black Sea coast. This shift in perspective brings into view the dissemination of the social ethic of the palace system, and as a consequence, the remaking of a provincial society.

The province of Trabzon was one of the last parts of Byzantine Anatolia to fall to the Ottomans (in 1461, eight years after the fall of Constantinople). The century before and the century after Ottoman annexation, only limited numbers of Turkic people entered the eastern coastal region. As a consequence, the large majority of the population in the eastern province of Trabzon consisted of Christians who spoke the languages of the Byzantine period, that is to say, Greek, Armenian and Lazi (Meeker 2002: 94–98).[4] During the seventeenth century, however, the character of the people inhabiting the coastal region was transformed, partly as a result of increasing immigration of Turkic Muslim peoples but also by the increasing conversion of Byzantine Christians. By the beginning of the eighteenth century, the large majority of the inhabitants in the eastern section of the province were Muslim.

The Islamization of eastern Trabzon was not a simple matter of the assimilation of the resident Byzantine peoples to the religion of the immigrant Turkic peoples. The Turkic peoples who had entered Trabzon were often heterodox Muslims, more Shi'ite than Sunnite in their beliefs and practices. By the eighteenth century, however, the large Muslim majority of eastern Trabzon was strongly oriented towards an official Islam, rather than any form of heterodox Islam. Indeed, the inhabitants of the eastern rural areas had become one of the most homogeneous Muslim populations in all of Anatolia, as well as the most firmly oriented toward a state Islam.

This creation of a new Muslim majority in Trabzon was the direct result of local participation in imperial military and religious institutions. Elsewhere in Anatolia, Islamic beliefs and practices are closely associated with *tarikat* Islam; that is to say, with religious lodges and brotherhoods, such as the Nakşibendi and the Kadiri. But eastern Trabzon during the eighteenth century was exceptional precisely for the lack of religious lodges and brotherhoods. Islamization had worked directly through the official military and religious establishments rather than through unofficial channels (Meeker 2002: 273, 273n42).[5]

By participation in official imperial institutions, a collection of diverse peoples – Greek, Turkic, Lazi, Armenian, Kurdish and Georgian – had become an 'ottomanist provincial society' (Meeker 2002, Meeker 2004). Such a society was characterized by an oligarchy of local elites embedded in networks of interpersonal relationships that extended from the bottom to the top of the imperial regime. Each set of local elites represented an interpersonal network in a particular district of the province. The sets of local elites in different districts had interpersonal relationships with one another. The more prominent of the local elites in the region had interpersonal relationships with higher provincial officials or higher palace officials. In effect, the ottomanist provincial society of Trabzon was not strictly local but part and parcel of the imperial regime.

As an ottomanist provincial society, the regional population continued to feature the traces of its diverse ethnic origins. In particular, many of the women in rural homesteads remained monolingual in one of the older Byzantine languages, Lazi, Greek or Armenian. However, many of the men (and in some places, most of the men) were affiliated with local militias or janissary regiments, or they were active as teachers or students in religious academies. An ottomanist provincial society featured normative uniformity in the domain of socio-religious practices but not a strict ethnic or linguistic uniformity.

The local elites were recognized by state officials. Sometimes they were appointed to state offices. Sometimes they rose to the higher ranks of provincial officials. At the same time, each member of the local elites was also a principal figure in a specific network of family, relatives, friends, and allies. And taken together, all these local elites composed a regional oligarchy extending across the coastal districts of the old province of Trabzon. This oligarchy was characterized by two important dimensions:

1. SOCIAL DISCIPLINE: A discipline of association was practised in the domestic salons and public coffee houses. The intimate face-to-face contracts formed on these occasions were the cement of regional social formations.
2. STATE ORIENTATION: The local elites were intermediaries between the local population and officials in the provincial capital. They regularly collected taxes from the inhabitants of the coastal districts. From time to time, they assembled groups of armed men.

This regional oligarchy was a double-edged sword. It was an instrument for supervising a large population dispersed over a mountainous terrain. At the same time, it was also a potential weapon for forcing high provincial officials to make concessions. Sometimes the local elites set siege to the provincial capital. Sometimes they forced the provincial governor to abandon the province altogether.

I want to insist on one point. The relationship between state and society was of a modern rather than a traditional character, at least in a certain sense of the term 'modernity' (Meeker 2004). In general, the population did not respect their primordial ethnic customs, not at all in many cases. Instead, they tried to conform to imperial norms, not the protocols of the palace, but rather to the norms of low-level military and religious institutions. In addition, the imperial regime was always responding to world conditions by institutional reforms. And the social formations of the regional oligarchy also changed in response to each new revision of state institutions. The local elites of Trabzon survived the abolition of the janissary institution (1826), the modernization of the imperial bureaucracy (1839–71), the Young Turk revolution (1908), the national revolution (1923), as well as the adoption of a multi-party electoral system (1950). By a succession of agreements, made and remade between local elites and state officials, a regional oligarchy adapted itself to a succession of radical reforms of state institutions. And each time, by making adaptations, local elites regained the capacity to bend and shape official policies and reforms.

Two centuries after the Ottoman conquest of the province of Trabzon, a large Christian majority had become a large Muslim majority in the eastern districts of Trabzon, sometime around the late seventeenth or early eighteenth century. This was partly the result of a gradual but steady immigration of Muslim peoples into the coastal region but also the result of the conversion of Christians to Islam. In the case of Trabzon, one remarkable fact is inescapable. A Christian population became more Ottoman and more Islamic than many other peoples of Anatolia, including those peoples who are conventionally considered to be Muslim peoples in some 'essential' sense of such a label. It would appear that the indigenous population of Trabzon, more experienced in the workings of official political and commercial systems than most Turkic-speakers, was in a favorable position for colonizing imperial state and market systems.

During the eighteenth century, thousands of soldiers and students were to be found in the eastern coastal districts of Trabzon. Moreover, the men of Trabzon were circulating in Anatolia as teachers or officers for hire. The Trabzonlus[6] colonized state institutions, and they did so by both legal and illegal means, by forged and genuine military commissions, forged and genuine academic diplomas, and forged and genuine permits for acting officially as an agha or a hodja. The Trabzonlus are well known for their legitimate accomplishments in various sectors, such as the army, business and learning. But also, the criminals of Trabzon have a reputation for their competence in counterfeiting, smuggling, gun running, arms manufacturing and mafia associations. In summation, the Trabzonlus deployed their knowledge of the state and the market for good and for bad.

The Exportation and Appropriation of the Palace System

As I have already mentioned, the Trabzonlus of the eastern districts were ready to participate in the empire, perhaps even at the time of the Ottoman conquest, but the Ottomans were not yet ready to open the doors of the imperial establishment. It was only two centuries later that the province became the homeland of a new ottomanist provincial society. Why did the Ottomans eventually permit, if not sponsor, the ottomanization of the Trabzonlus from the late seventeenth century onward? And why were the Trabzonlus so successful in colonizing the imperial regime in the ways that they did?

The first question cannot be definitively answered, since there is no detailed study of the state policies that were applied to Trabzon during the period in question. However, historians have discussed a number of broad social and political changes in the imperial regime that may have been of special importance for the eastern coastal region.

Firstly, by the seventeenth century, infantry and firearms were becoming increasingly important, especially in European military campaigns. As the feudal cavalry (*sipahi*) became obsolescent, the child levy was supplemented and finally replaced by recruitment of provincial Muslims as foot soldiers (Barkey 1994). This shift in military recruitment and training correlates with the militarization of the population in the coastal districts of Trabzon. By the later eighteenth century, many, if not most, of the men in these districts were associated with janissary regiments or local militias. The reports of travellers to the region also describe the men as armed with short rifles when they moved about the region (Meeker 2002: 166n42).

Secondly from the later seventeenth century, provincial notables began to assemble armies and challenge provincial governors, resulting in a decentralization of sovereign power in the imperial regime. The centralized government inadvertently contributed to this by adopting policies that strengthened local elites in order to counterbalance the rise of strong provincial governors (inalcık 1977). This imperial policy correlates with the rise of local power holders with armed followings everywhere in the coastal districts during the first part of the eighteenth century (Meeker 2002: 167–80).

Each of these developments exemplifies the way in which changes in state policies brought about changes in the structural relationship of state and society.[7] Each, therefore, represents the way in which *raisons d'état* played a role in the disorderly conjunction of state and society.

The second question – why were the Trabzonlus so successful in colonizing the state – is easier to answer in the light of long term social patterns in the coastal districts (Meeker 2002: 94–103). Each of the coastal districts of the old province of Trabzon forms a system of valleys running north and south from the coastline of the southern Black Sea to the high mountains of the Pontic chain. Each of these valley systems was a densely populated landscape whose inhabitants moved seasonally with their flocks from their lowland maize fields to their highland pastures. In this way, each valley system was also a social system that provided protection for the movement of goods between the sea routes along the coast and the land routes in the highlands. For centuries, even for millennia, the inhabitants of the valleys had a stake in the political and commercial structures beyond their little hamlets. For centuries, if not millennia, both men and women practised trades and crafts that exploited their relationship with the outside world, just as the men commonly left their families to look for employment in the towns and cities of the coastline and hinterland of the Black Sea area.

The Ottoman annexation of the Greek Empire of Trebizond may have disrupted these patterns but it did not destroy them. During the later Ottoman period, the population of the southern Black Sea coast features a social urbanism that flourished in spite of rural conditions. One can even say that the population of Trabzon was in some ways more an urban than a rural population, both before and after Ottoman annexation (Meeker 2002: 96).[8] It was multi-ethnic and multi-linguistic. It was the most densely settled rural landscape in Asia Minor. The hamlets of the coast were settled by soldiers and officers; students and teachers; merchants and transporters; masons, carpenters, weavers, dyers, metalworkers; manufacturers of textiles, weapons and boats. The population had become Muslim rather than Christian, but it was still a population with a range of *savoir-faires* oriented toward state and commercial markets.[9]

Local participation in state and commercial institutions was highly variable in the Ottoman provinces. As a consequence, the extent of the remaking of local societies by such participation was also variable. In this respect, the population of Trabzon lies at the extreme end of a spectrum. Circumstances both pushed and enabled the Trabzonlus to engage with the larger political and commercial world over the horizon of their little mountain hamlets.

An Ottomanist Provincial Society in the Age of Nations

In his famous book *Imagined Communities*, Benedict Anderson (1991) argued that a nation state claiming to speak and to act in the name of a nation as a people is a modern phenomenon. Examining the origins of such a state system, he placed a special emphasis on the psycho-political effects of the marketing of books in vernacular languages. But were there other paths to nationhood outside the Euro-American sphere, or at least other paths to something like nationhood?

The regional elites of the old province of Trabzon believed that high imperial officials were obliged to recognize their interests. The interpersonal networks the former represented were linked with imperial military and religious institutions. In these circles, it appears, the general population had the idea that the imperial regime should speak and act for them. Accordingly, the regional elites were able to mobilize thousands of men for the purpose of challenging the provincial government when it intruded upon their affairs. These regional elites, along with their relatives, friends and allies, were also hostile to foreign intervention in Ottoman affairs, because they believed (correctly) that their position and influence in the imperial regime would be compromised. The regional elites, again with the support of extensive interpersonal networks, also opposed reforms in the imperial regime for the same reason. During the first decades of the nineteenth century, the regional elites were even implicated in assassinations and rebellions that took place in the imperial capital itself.

Down to the present day, the population of the Black Sea coast has been known for its patriotism, formerly of an imperialist, more recently of a nationalist, character. In other words, there was something in Trabzon that brings to mind the Age of Nations. But this 'something' was already in place before such an epoch and had nothing to do with print-capitalism, even if it had a lot to do with other forms of exchange and communication. The population of Trabzon, either as a nation or at the very least a proto-nation, was based on a discipline of association, rather than the practised reading of novels or newspapers.

Following this same comparative logic, I want to mention two other analysts of the Age of Nations. The first is Clausewitz (1993) who understood that the means and methods of war-making were undergoing a sweeping change in Europe during his time. Aristocratic warfare had largely relied on mercenaries, that is to say, individuals who made a living as professional soldiers. Napoleonic warfare relied more heavily instead on drawing recruits and receiving support from the general population. This opened the way to total war, another feature of the Age of Nations.

Before the time of Napoleon, we already find something resembling mass mobilization in the province of Trabzon during the eighteenth century. But in so far as that description is appropriate, the Ottoman example was more closely linked with the dissemination of a discipline of association that was not directly inspired by battlefield strategies or weaponry. As a result, increasing popular participation in imperial military institutions was associated with the decentralization of sovereign power and, therefore, a decline rather than an increase in the military capacities of the centralized government.

The second analyst is Freud who was astonished by the savagery of the civilized peoples of Europe during the First World War. In his article, 'Thoughts for the Times on War and Death' (1957), he considered the phenomenon of 'ambivalence', that is to say, the mixture of love and hate that lies just below the apparent calm of everyday thoughts and feelings. According to Freud, one firmly believes that one loves those who are near and hates those who are distant, but one is mistaken. The intensity of one's love for some is linked with the intensity of one's hatred for others.

To make his point, Freud drew a comparison between what he termed 'primitive tribes' and 'civilized nations'. In both social conditions he found the same phenomenon of ambivalence as well as the same capacity for savagery. He also insisted that primitive tribes and civilized people featured what he described as a different psychological 'economy' of ambivalence. The tribesman, as Freud put it, is constantly embroiled in feuds and vendettas in defense of loved ones, while the citizen, in contrast, submits to norms of peace and order. Freud drew various consequences of this difference. For example, he saw civilized peoples as more depressed than primitive peoples, since norms of peace and order required a more thorough repression of instincts. Still, he observed, the citizen could occasionally shift from depression to mania, even to the point of condoning mass murder and wholesale devastation. The violence occasioned by total war among the civilized nations of Europe exceeded anything known to primitive tribes.

In Trabzon, we do not find the consolidation of a society of archaic tribes comparable to what is found in the Hadramawt, the Upper Nile valley, or the Atlas Mountains. The Trabzonlus escaped the condition of tribal particularism by identifying themselves with an imperial universalism. This would mean that a psychological economy of ambivalence of love and hate among the Ottoman Trabzonlus resembled that of the Age of the Nations. And yet, such a psychological economy had taken shape before the emergence of the Age of Nations. After the First World War, the Trabzonlus definitively entered the Age of Nations. During the 1920s and 1930s, many became activists in the Ataturkist revolution. Eventually, the Trabzonlus, by comparison with the citizens of other provinces, made a contribution to the Turkish Republic disproportionate to their numbers. The rapidity and completeness of this move from an imperial to a national society, not only in Trabzon but also in other Turkish provinces, has not yet been completely understood. With this summary account, I have hoped to indicate that the Turkish Republic had significant Ottoman foundations and so was not entirely the result of modernization through westernization.

For the purpose of insisting on differences, I have contrasted the relationship of state and empire in the Ottoman and European contexts. However, from a broader perspective, the core Ottoman provinces might well be considered to have been part of the state system of Europe from the early modern period. In this respect, the disorderly conjunction of state and society in the Ottoman Empire was never entirely isolated from the disorderly conjunction of state and society in Europe. Universal legitimacy, imperial architecture and ceremony, and military expansion in the Ottoman Empire were all driven in large measure by competition with specific European states. By this fact, the Ottoman Empire should be located inside, rather than outside, the passage from empires to nations in Europe.

Notes

1. A state order here refers to institutions of a centralized sovereign power. A social order refers to the diverse associational beliefs and practices of the groupings and communities that are subject to a centralized sovereign power. For the moment, I am begging the question of whether either state or society can be reliably considered as an 'order' at all.
2. Almost thirty years after its initial publication in 1975, the reception of *Discipline and Punish* bears little resemblance to its argument. The book is said to reduce history to the principle of state domination. The state holds a monopoly of power. It subjugates individuals to the status of its instruments. It reduces society to the status of its disciplinary mechanisms. This is a parody of the original argument.
3. The dates for the classical period are not definitive, since the periodization is disputed by Ottoman historians.
4. There were also Turkic-speakers in the Greek Empire of Trebizond at the time of its annexation by the Ottomans. They were a majority in many of the western districts but presumably only a minority in the eastern districts. Brendemoen (2002) has presented strong evidence that there was a number of Turkic-speakers in the eastern districts of the Greek Empire of Trebizond. Shukurov (1999, 2004) argues that some number of these Turkic speakers represented themselves as Christians. See Simonian (2004) on the Armenian-speaking Hamashen in the Greek Empire of Trebizond. See Hann and Beller-Hann (2001) on the Lazi-speakers.
5. This point opens up the large and shadowy question of the various 'channels' that linked the palace and regional elites. Elsewhere, such as Albania, the channel of religious brotherhoods was probably important. Still elsewhere, such as Kurdistan, the principal channel involved the relationship of tribal chiefs and sheikhs with provincial or palace officials. Still elsewhere, presumably in Bosnia, the channel of recruitment of local residents into the palace system was more important.
6. In Turkish, 'Trabzonlu' refers to someone from Trabzon.
7. I have not mentioned another change in the imperial regime associated with the lower echelons of the religious establishment during the seventeenth century. The Kadizadeli movement, supported by lower-level mosque preachers, opposed the 'innovations' of the Sufi orders and insisted on strict application of the sacred law of Islam (Zilfi 1986). The movement is one example of how the imperial regime was changed or influenced by 'popular' movements demanding certain kinds of imperial policies and institutions. The Kadizadeli movement may have been linked with the Islamization of eastern districts of Trabzon during the later seventeenth century, given that the Islam that came to predominate there did not favour the mysticism of the Sufi orders. The last prominent leader of the Kadizadeli movement, Vani Mehmet bin Bistam (d. 1685), a resident of Erzurum before coming to Istanbul, may be the key to a link with Trabzon. The religious professors and academies that proliferated in eastern Trabzon from the late seventeenth century had close ties with that town.
8. This is a non-intuitive observation, given that there were almost no towns in the coastal region until the contemporary period, especially in the districts east of Trabzon. I am obliged to add that the Trabzonlus have always been known in the cities of Turkey as coarse individuals, that is to say, as 'hicks'. They are outwardly-oriented rural dwellers, neither completely urban, nor completely rural in their outlook and behaviour.
9. For example, during the last century, sermons were given in Greek in the mosques and lessons were given in Greek in the district of Of. But also, it was a population that always benefited from newcomers who constantly added their own skills and learning to the repertoires of local *savoir-faire*.

References

Aksan, V. 1999a. 'Ottoman Military Recruitment Strategies in the Late Eighteenth Century' in *Arming the State: Military Conscription in the Middle East and Central Asia 1775–1925*, ed. E. Zürcher, New York: I.B. Tauris, 21–39.
—— 1999b. 'Locating the Ottomans among Early Modern Empires', *Journal of Early Modern History*, 3, 103–34.
Anderson, B.R.O'G. 1991 [1983]. *Imagined Communities: Reflections on the Origins and Spread of Nationalism*. 2nd edn. London: Verso.
Barkey, K. 1994. *Bandits and Bureaucrats: The Ottoman Route to State Centralization*. Ithaca: Cornell University Press.
Bentham, J. 1791. *Panopticon; or, The Inspection-house*. Dublin: T. Paine.
Brendemoen, B. 2002. *The Turkish Dialects of Trabzon: Their Phonology and Historical Development*, 2 vols. Wiesbaden: Harrassowitz.
Clausewitz, C. von. 1993 [1832–34]. *On War*, trans. and ed. by M. Howard and P. Paret. Princeton: Princeton University Press.
Foucault, M. 1977 [1975]. *Discipline and Punish: The Birth of the Prison*. New York: Vintage Books.
Freud, S. 1957 [1915]. 'Thoughts for the Times on War and Death' in *The Standard Edition of the Complete Psychological Works of Sigmund Freud*, vol. 14, ed. J. Strachey, London: Hogarth, 288.
Hann, C.M. and Beller-Hann, I. 2001. *Turkish Region: Culture and Civilisation on the East Black Sea Coast*. Oxford: James Currey.
inalcık, H. 1977. 'Centralization and Decentralization in the Ottoman Empire' in *Studies in Eighteenth Century Islamic History*, eds T. Naff and R. Owen, Carbondale: Southern Illinois University Press, 27–53.
Machiavelli, N. 1992 [1515]. *The Prince*, trans. W.K. Marriott. New York: Knopf.
Meeker, M.E. 2002. *A Nation of Empire: The Ottoman Legacy of Turkish Modernity*. Berkeley: University of California Press.
—— 2004. 'Greeks Who are Muslims: Counter-Nationalism in Nineteenth Century Trabzon' in *Archaeology, Anthropology and Heritage in the Balkans and Anatolia: The Life and Times of F.W. Hasluck, 1878–1920*, vol. 2, ed. D. Shankland, Istanbul: Isis Press, 299–323.
—— 2005a [1996]. 'Concepts of Person, Family, and State in the District of Of, Trabzon', reprinted in *Social Practice and Political Culture in the Turkish Republic*, collected papers, Istanbul: Isis Press, 165–82.
—— 2005b [1972]. 'The Great Family Aghas of Turkey', reprinted in *Social Practice and Political Culture in the Turkish Republic*, collected papers, Istanbul: Isis Press, 131–64.
—— 2005c. 'The Muradoğlu Family Line' in *Social Practice and Political Culture in the Turkish Republic*, collected papers, Istanbul: Isis Press, 183–203.
Necipoğlu, G. 1991. *Architecture, Ceremonial, and Power: The Topkapı Palace in the Fifteenth and Sixteenth Centuries*. Cambridge, Mass.: MIT Press.
Shukurov, R. 1999. 'The Byzantine Turks of the Pontos', *Mésogeios*, 6, 7–47.
—— 2004. 'The Crypto-Muslims of Anatolia' in *Archaeology, Anthropology and Heritage in the Balkans and Anatolia: The Life and Times of F.W. Hasluck, 1878–1920*, vol. 2, ed. D. Shankland, Istanbul: Isis Press, 135–57.
Simmel, G. 1978 [1900]. *The Philosophy of Money*. London: Routledge and Kegan Paul.
Simonian, H. 2004. 'Hamshen before Hemshin: The Prelude to Islamization' in *Archaeology, Anthropology and Heritage in the Balkans and Anatolia: The Life and Times of F.W. Hasluck, 1878–1920*, vol. 2, ed. D. Shankland, Istanbul: Isis Press, 93–121.
Tilly, C. 1985. 'War Making and State Making as Organized Crime' in *Bringing the State Back In*, eds P.B. Evans, D. Rueschemeyer and T. Skocpol, Cambridge: Cambridge University Press, 169–91.
—— 1990. *Coercion, Capital and European States AD 990–1992*. Oxford: Blackwell.
Zilfi, M.C. 1986. 'The Kadizadelis: Discordant Revivalism in Seventeenth Century Istanbul', *Journal of Near Eastern Studies*, 45, 251–69.

Chapter 9

ANTHROPOLOGICAL ORDER AND POLITICAL DISORDER

Jonathan Spencer

My theme in this chapter can be simply summarized in three juxtaposed quotes. The first is from F.G. Bailey's late 1960s introduction to political anthropology, *Stratagems and Spoils*: 'I have picked out in this introduction certain moral themes which ride between the lines of the book. Behind these themes – and behind the whole endeavour – is a repugnance for disorder, for the mere jumble of facts in which no pattern can be perceived, for "mere anarchy"' (1969: xiii). The second is from 'Thick Description' (Geertz 1973), probably the single most quoted anthropological essay of the 1970s: 'Nothing has done more, I think, to discredit cultural analysis than the construction of impeccable depictions of formal order in whose existence nobody can quite believe' (1973: 18). The third is from Nancy Scheper-Hughes' *Death without Weeping* (1992), a monograph which sums up the anthropological spirit of the 1990s as comprehensively as Geertz's essay evokes the decade of Watergate and large hair:

> The blurring of fiction and reality creates a kind of mass hysteria and paranoia that can be seen as a new technique of social control in which everyone suspects and fears every other: a collective hostile gaze, a human panopticon (see Foucault 1979), is created. But when this expresses itself positively and a state of alarm or a state of emergency is produced ... the shocks reveal the disorder in the order and call into question the 'normality of the abnormal', which is finally shown for what it really is (Scheper-Hughes 1992: 229).

On the surface, then, anthropology has progressed over the decades from a concern with social order to the celebration of the unruly capacities of disorder.

But beneath this apparently seamless move, rather more is going on. The 'order' of Bailey and his predecessors is primarily sociological: order as pattern or regularity – in institutional form, political behaviour or political process. Bailey's classic account of a certain style of political anthropology rests on his 'repugnance' for 'disorder'. The anthropologist's task is to bring out the order beneath the surface 'jumble of facts', to discern similarity within apparent dissimilarity. Here Bailey is continuing a line of argument traceable back to Fortes and Evans-Pritchard ('a comparative study of political systems has to be on an abstract plane' [1940: 3]) and Leach ('it is the underlying structural pattern and not the overt cultural pattern that has real significance' [1954: 17]). In this context, Geertz does not come out firmly against any interest in 'order', just against what he sees as excessive, and therefore implausible, delineations of order. His is a transitional position, midway between the scientism of the 1960s and the post-scientism of the 1980s.

In the work of Scheper-Hughes, like many of her contemporaries, a concern with disorderly institutions turns out to co-exist with a surprisingly straightforward vision of what might constitute a proper moral and political order. In this respect, Scheper-Hughes is writing within a very different structure of feeling: one concerned with disorder as disruption, as revealing the real pathology hidden beneath the surface of normal order. She is also writing with a very different voice, in her terms more 'engaged' and 'ethical' than the detached tone of the earlier writers (Scheper-Hughes 1995). I shall return to this issue of voice in the final part of this chapter, in which I try to delineate the structure of feeling within which Scheper-Hughes and many of her contemporaries are working: a structure of feeling organized around the antinomy of order and disorder, but with rather different values attached to each pole.

This progression can be seen most clearly in the anthropology of the political, a subject which has in its time been accorded a privileged, if sometimes rather puzzling, space in anthropological arguments about order. (Puzzling, because for many people the political is perceived as an arena of disorder and unpredictability, as I shall explain.) From the 1940s to the 1960s, the political was a central concern of social anthropologists, especially those trained in the British tradition of Malinowski and Radcliffe-Brown. In the 1960s, much political anthropology followed the lead of a political science concerned to be as 'scientific' as possible, while other anthropological currents were increasingly shaped by the interpretive sway of the humanities (Spencer 1997a). Then, in the 1970s, classic political anthropology ran out of steam, although a successor has recently emerged in the form of the 'anthropology of politics' (Vincent 1990, 2002, Nugent and Vincent 2004). Where 1960s political anthropology was concerned with more or less formal accounts of political processes (strategizing, dispute resolution) and political groupings (factions, lineages, action sets), the new anthropology of politics, as revealed for example in the recent Nugent and Vincent *Companion* (2004), is more concerned with the analysis of substantively political topics like nationalism, sovereignty and citizenship. A concern with the formal allowed anthropologists to discover evidence of the working of the political everywhere, even in the alleged absence of modern states and modern political institutions. The new concern with the substance of politics betokens a different kind of engagement with the object of study – a politically committed anthropology – and the abandonment of an intellectual world-view which categorized certain kinds of people in certain places (primitives, tribals, the indigenous, the colonized) into a space which was believed to be institutionally pre-political.

Perhaps the most central theme in recent anthropological work on the political is the analysis of violence and war, and the kind of contrast I want to explore in this chapter can be perfectly illustrated by two anthropological responses to violence, each perfectly capturing a certain moment in anthropological history. Here is Max Gluckman, broadcasting on the Third Programme of the BBC in 1955:

> Generally, over a limited area, there is peace as well as war in the feud. This peace arises from the existence of many kinds of relationships, and the values attached to them all by custom. These ties divide men at one point; but this division in a wider group and over a longer period time leads to the establishment of social order ... In this way custom unites where it divided, cooperation and conflict balancing each other. (Gluckman 1956: 23)

And here is Carolyn Nordstrom in her contribution to an edited volume on the anthropology of violence, in which she employs the textual oddity of a strike-through across the word 'reason':

> Based on my field experiences on the front lines of wars, I hope to challenge – to draw a line through – the epistemologies of Reason, with a capital R, as it applies to War. When War actually becomes a matter of life and death, Reason is replaced with a cacophony of realities. ... A concern with the reasons of war comes dangerously close to a concern with making war reasonable – which, of course, is a goal of the Enlightenment process. (Nordstrom 1995: 137, 138)

The contrast could hardly be greater. Gluckman's tone is calm and confident, soothingly putting the potentially upsetting facts of 'native' violence in their proper institutional context. Nordstrom's tone is somewhat less restrained: in place of Reason we are offered 'experience', the fieldworker's empathy, 'voices' and 'worlds'. The new anthropological order is warm rather than cool, empathetic, pluralistic and unafraid of the odd sweeping generalization (reasonable war as a goal of 'the Enlightenment process'?)

Over half a century, anthropology has moved then from soothing discoveries of 'social order' to impassioned engagement in 'world disorder' (Nordstrom 1995: 136). In doing so, as my subsequent comparison of 'voice' should make clear, there has been a shift in the substance and manner of anthropological writing about order and disorder. This shift is not merely a reflection of changed methods and epistemologies, it also constitutes a new version of the implicit 'we' embedded in anthropological argument, the taken-for-granted self-image of anthropological readers as an interpretive community. What follows in this paper draws on a much longer work in progress which, as will become apparent, looks at these issues not from the perspective of law and order, but in terms of politics and disorder. In particular, in this bigger project I am trying to highlight the disorderly operations of the political in order to destabilize some old ideas about the political as an ontologically privileged dimension of social life. In the case I discuss here, images of order are produced from the perceived disorder of unrestrained politicking. My example will be the tense relationship between the ideal of the nation and the practice of the political in Sri Lanka. So far so conventional, perhaps; but I also want to draw attention to some obvious emerging contradictions in recent appeals to 'ethical' (some might prefer 'moral') order in anthropological writing. These are evident in the writings of Nordstrom and Scheper-Hughes cited earlier, but are especially clear in a recent book by Michael Taussig, *Law in a Lawless Land* (2003), which provides the second example in my argument.

Political Disorder

One day in early 1983, some months before the anti-Tamil rioting in July which transformed Sri Lanka's politics, I went down to the tea shop in the Sinhala village where I had lived for about a year. The owner, who was a close friend of mine, was sitting behind the counter, engrossed in a pamphlet which he put down as I approached. The pamphlet in question was titled *Kavuda kotiya*? (Who is the Tiger?). On the front cover was a caricature of the leader of the main Tamil political party, the TULF (Tamil United Liberation Front), recoiling from a mirror out of which sprang a Tiger in place of his own reflection. The Tiger was a symbol of the biggest of the militant Tamil separatist organizations, the LTTE (Liberation Tigers of Tamil Ealam, or usually simply 'the Tigers'). The pamphlet itself, a crude anti-Tamil tirade, was the work of a Sinhala member of the Colombo government, Cyril Mathew, whose name was subsequently linked with the organized gangs which appeared in the 1983 rioting.[1]

'Hello', I said to my friend, 'I didn't know you were interested in politics'. 'Oh, this isn't politics', he hastily replied, 'this is about the national question'. The word I had used for politics was *desapalanaya*; my friend had used *jatika prasnaya* to denote the national question. The implication of his remark was striking: the 'national question' which, even then, dominated national political argument was somehow not 'politics'.

There are certain broad peculiarities in the pattern of rural politics in Sri Lanka in the 1970s and early 1980s which I can illustrate from my own field research. First of all there was a very high level of political participation, whether measured in terms of voter turnout at elections, or party identification in local communities. The 1982 elections transformed the village in which I was working. Compared to the only other countries where I have watched electoral politics (the U.S.A., Canada and Britain) attendance at political rallies was high, discussion of political issues was everywhere, roughly 90 percent of those eligible voted, and those who didn't were noticed and commented on. Moreover, before and after the election, the village could be divided into two large groups by party political identification: not everyone was known as either a UNP or a SLFP supporter, but a very large number of people were.[2] When the results of the presidential election were announced on the radio, a large crowd of government supporters set off in a ragged celebratory procession along the road through the village, pausing outside the houses of known opposition supporters to chant personal and party taunts at them.

But this high degree of political participation was not quite what we might expect from the usual label offered for it, which is rural 'politicization'. Few of those most actively involved in party politics attempted to explain their commitment in terms of party programmes or party ideology. More often than not they merely pointed out to me that the leaders of the other side were 'bad' people, liars, drunks and troublemakers. Most of my close informants were SLFP supporters. In the 1960s, when he did his field research, Richard Gombrich's neighbours were UNP supporters who had taught their children to sing a ditty referring to the party colour green which ran: *ape pata kola, api nä kalabola,* 'our colour is green, we are not troublemakers' Gombrich's UNP supporters' chief complaint about their political opponents 'was that they scolded too much' (Gombrich 1971: 266). Other observers have detected an unusually pronounced tendency to personal abuse and vilification in national political argument as well (Obeyesekere 1984: 508). In village politics, personal animosities seemed to far outweigh ideological preferences.

Along with this high participation and what, for now, I will call ideological innocence, there is a third characteristic of rural politics in Sinhala Sri Lanka: the sociological incoherence of party affiliation. Although there were reasonably wide disparities between rich and poor within the village, I was quite unable to correlate this in any way with visible party identification. Nor was caste a factor, although religion was for some: both the Christians and Muslims in the village supported the UNP with very few exceptions. Not surprisingly, in a constituency with a Buddhist majority but a UNP Muslim MP, the SLFP leadership was grouped around the monk at the village temple, but many Buddhist enthusiasts also supported the UNP. In other local studies in Sri Lanka caste, religion and class all emerge as factors affecting political identification in specific places. Some villages (but only a minority by the 1980s) even remained single-party villages. The general picture that emerges is that party identification is indeed high in all parts of Sinhala Sri Lanka (or was at the time of my original fieldwork), but that this identification is based on different factors in different places. In general people refer to their political opponents as above all personal enemies, and a major source of the sociological incoherence of party identification is the fact that party identification usually follows the contours of local arguments and local disputes. And this relates to people's idea of what politics is.

My final characteristic of rural politics in Sinhala Sri Lanka is the importance of state resources and patronage in the local economic order. Since Independence rural Sinhala areas have been net recipients of material resources from the state, which has creamed off surpluses from other parts of the economy, notably the plantation sector and more recently foreign development aid, and used them to pursue welfarist policies in rural Sinhala areas (Moore 1985). Relatively high quality education and health care, together with food subsidies, have given Sri Lanka disproportionately high quality-of-life indices for a country with its low per capita GNP. Over the years the distribution of these resources has been channelled more and more through the figure of the local Member of Parliament and, at village level, through local party leaders. A great deal of local political rhetoric is concerned to establish personal responsibility for the material boons of state largesse: look at the water supply *we* brought to the village, remember the school *we* built.

But this pattern of patronage explains less than it might appear. First of all, a lot of state resources have been devoted to general benefits – education, health care, food subsidies – which it is hard to personalize beyond a certain point. Second, patronage politics often function best in single-party settings, like the machine politics of Democratic Chicago, in which every appointment, and every contract, was carefully vetted by local officials; party division only confuses the issue. Third, in the cases I know best, local party bosses are careful to include some of their political opponents (and thus exclude some of their political supporters) in any distribution of limited rewards, sometimes to ensure the appearance of even-handedness, sometimes for more obscure and Machiavellian reasons of their own. Finally, in the one case where a genuinely limited but highly desirable good was distributed during my fieldwork – an allocation of plots of newly irrigated land under a repaired irrigation tank – it quickly became clear that the number of those disappointed was bound to exceed the number of those who actually received an allocation, and the party bosses who had drawn up the allocation went to great efforts to try to convince people that they were *not* responsible for the final distribution.

But this far from exhausts my friend's understanding of 'politics'. He was, after all, distancing himself – and his reading matter – from politics. So politics is not thought to be morally desirable. There is nothing in the word *desapalanaya* itself to suggest this; etymologically it refers to 'protection of the country' and, as far as I know, is a relatively recent neologism which has been taken up in village speech to denote a very specific form of life.

Let me list some of its characteristics. It is not about nationalism and the national question as my friend's comment makes clear. Nor is it something that people readily admit to being active in: it is always one's opponents who are involved in politics, rarely oneself. It is identified with division and trouble within the community. One of the first pieces of advice I was given when I arrived in the village came from a minor government official who asked what aspect of life I intended to study; he quickly answered his own question, 'You don't want to study politics, that is not a good thing.' In late 1982, during the months of campaigning for the presidential election and the subsequent referendum to extend the life of parliament, again and again people would apologize to me for the unseemly side of the village I was witnessing: this was all because of politics, and once the elections were over the village's troubles would end.

During the last months of 1982, in parallel with the elections, the village was absorbed by an extraordinary case of spirit possession involving an adolescent Muslim girl who had been possessed by a host of Sinhala demons which demanded that she be treated by Sinhala exorcists.[3] Some people felt the demons were responsible for the village's political troubles; others felt the trouble created by politics had rendered the village susceptible to demonic attack; still others thought the whole thing a fraud perpetrated by the Muslims in order to get money out of their Buddhist neighbours. The girl's case was taken up by a maverick Buddhist monk who prescribed a daily hearing of protective Buddhist verses (*pirit*) to keep the demons away; a few of her Buddhist neighbours came round every day to chant these in unison. On the day of the election I called round to see how the case was progressing. I found only one neighbour there and asked him why no one had come to chant *pirit*. These days, he explained, because of the politics in the village, people's minds are bad (*hita honda na*); for *pirit* to succeed, those involved should be clean, pure (*pirisiduvin*) and good. In other words, for this man, and I think in my other examples too, politics could be seen as a kind of collective moral disorder.

This kind of view finds ethnographic resonance across the South Asian subcontinent: we are in the presence of what Arild Ruud's 1990s Bengali villagers disapprovingly called the 'dirty work' of politics (Ruud 2001). It contrasts, though, with a set of assumptions that have a long genealogy in mainstream social science. These can be found, for example, in Edmund Leach's key heuristic, 'I assume that individuals faced with a choice of action will commonly use such choice so as to gain power, that is to say they will seek recognition as social persons who have power; or, to use a different language, they will seek to gain access to office or the esteem of their fellows which may lead them to office' (Leach 1954: 10). And they can be found, implicitly or explicitly, in the many versions of rational choice theory that have proliferated since Leach wrote in the 1950s. But whereas most critics have focused on the model of individual rationality in this sort of formulation, my ethnographic evidence should instead unsettle the moral assumptions behind it. The pursuit of individual interest – aggressively, in public – can make for a rather disturbing spectacle. Albert Hirschman, in his magnificent essay *The Passions and the Interests* (1977), reminds us of the intellectual work that went into the – now commonplace to the point of banal, but once revolutionary – idea that 'interests' were stable and potentially computable aspects of human action. This idea of human interest being under the sway of reason, and therefore predictable or computable, is at the heart of modern economics, as well as economistic strands of social theory such as rational choice theory. Hirschman's contrast is between these 'interests' and the 'passions' which, in the eighteenth-century arguments he analyses, became the area of uncontrolled and therefore unpredictable behaviour. But the village apprehension of the political ignores such niceties: the political is the space in which individual interests are pursued, but the results are far from stable. Instead the pursuit of political interest spills over into all areas of life in unpredictable and uncontrollable ways. We forget this perspective on the political at our own liberal peril.

This does not, though, exhaust the interpretation of my opening example. At this point I want to retrieve my earlier provisional formulation about the ideological innocence of village politics. In fact village politics are saturated in ideology; it is village political divisions which are ideologically innocent. The pamphlet my friend was reading was, after all, not only the product of a politician, it was the product of a politician who was often associated with the most unscrupulous and amoral political tactics. Politics may ideally be separate from the national question, but the ideological discourse of Sinhala nationalism is most often heard coming from the lips of politicians who sometimes seem to talk about little else. Indeed one of the most striking features of Sri Lankan political life in the early 1980s was something I have called ideological over-production (Spencer 1990: 10).

This takes two forms: quantitative and qualitative. The quantitative aspect is as hard to prove empirically as it is hard to escape ethnographically. Political functions are (or were) major public events attended by large numbers of people. Political figures use them as opportunities for speeches. These speeches usually work over well worn themes in the discourse of Sinhala nationalism. The newspapers and radio news reports carry lengthy accounts of similar speeches on similar themes from national political leaders; often they seemed to carry little else. James Brow has commented on the 'the sustained intensity and unprecedented explicitness with which authorities now proclaim their legitimacy' in rural Sri Lanka; whereas whole areas of life in the past 'went without saying because they came without saying', now 'the social prescriptions of Sinhalese Buddhist nationalism come in a barrage of saying that is almost incessant' (Brow 1988: 312, cf. Bourdieu 1977: 167).

Qualitative ideological over-production is a little easier to demonstrate: two examples might help. The first occurred a week after the UNP victory in a 1982 referendum; I remember looking up from the copy of Marquez's *Autumn of the Patriarch* I happened to be reading to see a front page newspaper story reporting one of President J.R. Jayewardene's characteristically magical realist speeches: the banner headline simply read 'I can do anything – J.R.'

The second comes from a paper by Michael Woost, based on research in an area close to the one in which I worked in the mid 1980s. The village in question had been singled out for attention by an idealistic Colombo-based farmers' self-help organization. The villagers went along with the organization's fanciful schemes as long as it kept providing free trips to Colombo, but were appalled when it was announced that the organization was to hold a meeting showing off the villagers' (non-existent) co-operative projects to various local VIPs. The villagers responded by hastily assembling a few compost heaps and quickly sowing a few chillies. The meeting was duly held and attended by local politicians and members of the Colombo organization. Amongst their speeches we find the following claims:

> Our (development) works show that we are the giants of today.
> This is indeed a historical landmark when one thinks of the 2,500 years since Prince Vijaya came and established our nation. All those who came with him were small farmers just like yourselves ... Thus this conference marks only the second time since Vijaya's arrival that there has been such a conference of small farmers.
> The ethical and hard-working qualities which have been revealed here in this village are indicative of the personalities of people born and brought up in our villages. No other country in the world has the spiritual development that we have. (Woost 1990: 176–78)

The villagers who were the subject of these panegyrics were quite unbothered by the discrepancy between the claims being publicly advanced on their behalf and what they knew to be the reality of the village projects.

They enjoyed the various speeches and calmly assessed their favourites, apparently on aesthetic grounds (Woost 1990: 179).

The political, in this example, contains within it both order and disorder. The village perception of party politics as an agonistic space of unseemly and disorderly activity serves as the ground against which images of proper national order are established. The regime in place at this time espoused a vision to build a *dhammika samajaya*, a society remade in the image of the Dhamma, the Buddha's vision of the order of things. Political rallies provide the occasion for the enunciation of utopian visions of the nation-that-was and the nation-to-be. Politicians write and disseminate pamphlets like *Kavuda kotiya*, all the while stressing that they write out of a sense of duty and not out of the pursuit of political interest. Buddhist monks intervene in the political arena, but always denying any political intent: their intervention is always said to be in the 'national' interest. In all this, the 'national' stands to the 'political' as anti-politics to politics, to employ Hansen's distinction: 'To denounce *rajkaraan* (politics), to separate the nation and its cultures from the realm of rational statecraft, and to adopt a moral, antipolitical critique of political leaders is possibly the most legitimate and the most common oppositional stance in contemporary India' (Hansen 2001: 229). Politics and anti-politics, the agonistic and the altruistic, individual interest and collective morality: seen from far enough away, these are only *rhetorical* alternatives, contained *within* the field of the political. In truth, there is no 'outside' outside politics, no safe space from which to mount a critique which is not itself a part of that which is being criticized.

Law in a Lawless Land?

Let me recapitulate the points made so far. My argument has perhaps gone no further than the distance from Bailey to Geertz, as revealed in the two quotes I have placed at the start of this paper. Bailey's horror of anarchy can stand (with some poetic license) for the wider intellectual project, shared by political anthropologists of his generation and political scientists alike, to treat the political as the pre-eminent domain of a 'scientific' social science. Despite all appearances of disorder, the political (like the economic) is the privileged zone of analytic order. The political anthropology of the third quarter of the twentieth century based itself on this confident apprehension of the political as a zone of intellectual certainty, a firm basis of knowledge wherever we might find it, irrespective of whether the foundation it provided was social structural (as in Fortes and Evans-Pritchard), or behavioural (the instrumental assumptions of Leach, and later F.G. Bailey). In both cases we could expect to isolate the political from the smoke-and-mirrors of culture, and use it as a safe object for comparison. Leach's

Political Systems of Highland Burma (1954), with its discernment of a common order behind the confusions of colonial sociology and the backwoods take on the politics of difference, remains the pre-eminent example of what can be achieved intellectually with a creative application of this heuristic.

Geertz's early suspicion of the appeal to implausible depictions of order may be directed less at political analysts, than at Lévi-Straussian structuralists, or Schneiderian accounts of key cultural symbols. (It is far from clear in the original who he has in mind.) But the sensibility behind his 1973 statement informs the coming 1980s aversion to grand theory and *grandes histoires*. For Geertz, the proper quest was for small signs of intelligibility, not big claims to order. For some who swam in his wake in the 1980s and 1990s, even intelligibility was a bourgeois vice to be avoided at all costs. As Michael Taussig reminisces:

> This was also a time when instability and contradiction were beginning to be valued – not devalued – by some of us working in the human sciences which, up to that point, had been geared to making sense of the social world as if it were like a machine responding to high pressure and low pressure, like the plumbing of a house, or like the plot of a nineteenth-century novel with its beginning, middle, and end. (Taussig 2003: 126)

The quote comes from Taussig's short book entitled *Law in a Lawless Land* (Taussig 2003) to which I will shortly return. Before that, I want to make one further connection: between 'instability and contradiction' in ethnographic description, and an accompanying lack of instability and contradiction in the moral judgements that inform that description.

Take for example, the following quote from Scheper-Hughes' harrowing account of shanty town poverty in Brazil, *Death without Weeping*:

> Most individuals trapped by their poverty in a cycle of sickness, worry, and despair are less aware, less critically reflective about their lives, lives that are, as one woman of the Alto put it, 'too painful to think about'. It is not surprising, then, that attempts to elicit discussions about *nervosa, fraqueza*, and *fome* [the somatic idioms of distress that were the focus of Scheper-Hughes' enquiry] so often resulted in popular interpretations that were fuzzy, inconsistent, and not infrequently contradictory. It is usual for the anthropologist to impose an order on her subject matter, to overlook the inconsistencies in the ways in which people make sense of the world in which they live. Here an analysis of 'epistemic murk' and contradiction is the task at hand. (Scheper-Hughes 1992: 175)

The allusion to 'epistemic murk' is a reference to Taussig's (1984) essay 'Culture of Terror – Space of Death', in which 'epistemic and ontological murk' in Roger Casement's account of colonial atrocities on the Putumayo is read as a response to the crushing weight of power and domination. So too in Scheper-Hughes' analysis: the women's apparent misrecognition of hunger as *nervosa* is revealed as the workings of a meaningful somatic idiom for expressing the unexpressible realities of the 'real "state of emergency" into which the community has been plunged' (Scheper-Hughes 1992: 187), again using another allusion to Taussig. By the end of the chapter in which this passage occurs, the author has taken us through a number of long, troubling stories of everyday suffering and out into the strong clear light of a concluding section headed 'Toward a liberation medicine'.

Murk and light; reality and illusion. One can, I believe, trace a very straightforward political-moral narrative through all of Taussig's work, although the sheer quantity of his output, and the extravagance of his expression, make him a difficult case to summarize. Instead I shall stick with Scheper-Hughes, whose work best exemplifies what I earlier called the structure of feeling within which much recent anthropology has operated. This is most vividly evoked in the 1995 article 'The Primacy of the Ethical' (Scheper-Hughes 1995) which sets out her programme for a new 'militant anthropology'. The article is based around her reflections on her Brazilian work, but rather more on her brief experience teaching and living in South Africa for a year in the early 1990s. At its heart is an exemplary moral narrative of her involvement in a tense situation involving the punishment by flogging of three young thieves in a squatter camp: a disturbing example of post-Apartheid 'popular justice'. Scheper-Hughes arranges medical treatment for one of the youths, and this raises tensions back in the camp. A community meeting is called and the anthropologist says her piece against the use of corporal punishment in popular justice. After the meeting, a number of suspiciously reasonable initiatives follow which combine to promise a better world, free of arbitrary violence, for all in the camp. Scheper-Hughes returns to Berkeley.

The argument is disarming in its moral clarity: what postmodern anthropologist would want to defend necklacing and flogging in the name of relativism, what positivist could ignore the plight of malnourished children in the name of scientific objectivity?[4] But despite the considerable criticism that followed publication of the piece – much of it summed up in the entirely reasonable response that the world is usually a great deal more complicated than *that* – I feel Scheper-Hughes' essay crystallizes a certain dominant mood in anthropology. Since the heyday of Leach and Evans-Pritchard, anthropology has somehow become a moralizing activity, its authors ever more inclined to wear their ethical hearts on their sleeves. For example, in a characteristic piece on the anthropological Zeitgeist 'circa 2004', George Marcus observes that 'Activism, or its challenge to the classic dispassionate scholar, has become a condition or circumstance of most fieldwork projects' (Marcus 2005: 677). Released from the bottle of old-time objectivist ethnography, the figure of the ethnographer has assumed heroic dimensions: at the heart of the action, a maker or remaker of moral order in a world of danger and disturbance.

Finally, this brings me to Taussig, a heroic ethnographer if ever there was one. *Law in a Lawless Land* is structured around a diary kept by Taussig during two weeks spent in a Colombian town, midway through a 'cleansing' operation by paramilitaries, in 2001. It is a remarkable book in many respects, not least for readers familiar with Taussig's previous anthropological contributions: the book is short, the tone cool and for the most part austere, the dominant mood morally troubled rather than morally confident. Diary entries report on bodies by the side of the road, interspersed with commentary on the history of the paramilitaries, reflections on violence and the diary form, and interjections from Taussig's graduate student seminar. The first half of the book is constructed round the unsettling motif of the *limpieza*, the 'cleansing' – a term invoked to explain and justify the killing of anti-social elements, petty thieves, drug addicts, the unruly poor. As Taussig explores the use of the term, bits of context swim into focus, most notably the corruption and uselessness of the police and the courts. Why do so many people apparently collude in the brutality and inhumanity of the paramilitaries? Mainly because 'the Colombian state cannot protect them from anything. From murder to traffic accidents, kidnapping or being mugged for your tennis shoes, the state is powerless whether you are rich or poor'. The police and the law, far from offering sanctuary or solution, are only 'likely to make things worse': if you make a complaint, you become a suspect yourself in the eyes of the police, with the threat of violence or the need for pay-offs; if a case should ever come to court, the punishment is likely to seem absurdly lenient (Taussig 2003: 30–31).

Taussig's diary builds to a climax of sorts with two consecutive entries for the 'Second Week' (22 and 23 May). In the first he returns to his notes from visits to the area in the early 1970s, and finds there other, older stories of bodies by the side of the road. What, if anything, has changed? This provokes a measured assessment of Colombia's history in the twentieth century, especially the entwining of local and national animosities in the capillary hatreds of everyday party politics, and the gradual revelation that the scenes he is witnessing are most intelligible if read in the register of the political, or that version of the political as performative disorder my village informants first warned me about.

At this point sobriety suddenly deserts the author, and his entry for the next day veers into an extended and hallucinogenic reminiscence of an attempt at shamanic healing years before, with invocations of Burroughs and Genet and other usual Taussigian suspects. It is as if the strain of dealing with a world which refuses to conform to the familiar moral dimensions of North American academic radicalism has finally overwhelmed him, and the only recourse is the aesthetic security blanket of his well worn shamanic riffs, first introduced in the brilliant and infuriating pages of *Shamanism, Colonialism and the Wild Man* (Taussig 1987). It seems to be the possibility that this is just another tale of small-town politics that tips him over the brink. Yet the story at the heart of the entry – which involves Taussig going into shamanic trance to heal a person he calls 'X.' – is in the end a retelling of the narrative of the ethnographer as moral redeemer and all-purpose righter of wrongs sketched in the central episode of Scheper-Hughes' paper: 'But when I returned to the house to perform the healing at 4:30 in the afternoon, X. was not there! So much for my self-importance! "I am playing God," I wrote in my 1977 diary' (Taussig 2003: 146). Indeed.

I find this recent work by Taussig fascinating because it seems to me to suggest that we might be in the middle of another transition in intellectual sensibility. *Law in a Lawless Land* contains within it exemplary expressions of the post-1980s ethnographic sensibility: the appeal to 'multiple realities' and the hallucinatory; the resistance to simplistic narratives with their – alas, 'nineteenth-century' – beginnings, middles and ends; but also the high moral and political tone, the striving for radical certainty which has been the, mostly unacknowledged, accompaniment to the anthropological celebration of the uncertain and shifting. 'The great theoretical advance of recent decades,' as Marshall Sahlins has dryly observed, 'has been the improvement in the moral character of the academy' (1999: 404). Tugging against the usual literary moves is the intractability of the story Taussig has to tell: the fact that his friends and informants seem to collude in the necessary 'cleansing' of local society, thus closing off the space of heroic resistance. This *is* above all a story of the disorderliness of the political, and at the very end he returns once again to a conventional historical summary of its political causes and political antecedents.

But Taussig does his best to maintain the exotic appeal of the violence – it is sorcery, he is told, it is like a drug. Just before the end of his diary he details his expedition to a slum area built on a huge mound of festering garbage – dangerous and toxic, it provides the necessary backdrop to his informants' desire for 'cleansing', but it also provides a characteristically Taussigian metaphor for what I have attempted to describe as the political. It is not just academics who construct images of order out of the disorder of the political.

To summarize: this chapter is about political theodicy and the ways in which we can respond to it. The political, at least in the form of modern mass politics, raises our moral expectations only to dash them on the rocks of unruly political disorder. As such, it carries within its own would-be negation, the claim to speak from outside the political altogether, as in the Sri Lankan appeal to the transcendent power of the nation which is somehow kept separate from the murk of the political. Analytically, in earlier political anthropology and much political science, the political has been privileged as a site of order – of models and projections and certainty. I find this just as counter-intuitive as the doomed attempt of my Sri Lankan friends to keep nation and politics separate. In more recent work, anthropologists have encouraged us to embrace the disorderly and transgressive, but only to find, hidden not so deep within it (and thus within us?) a political heart of gold. What is interesting about the positionality assumed by Taussig and Scheper-Hughes is that it is not merely difficult to argue against, but even those who do point out some obvious political and empiricial shortcomings find their objections simply ignored. (Who remembers the critics in the original *Current Anthropology* Comment accompanying Scheper-Hughes' original article?) I think this is because these arguments – with all their weaknesses and contradictions – are at the very heart of the structure of feeling within which many of us work today. Since the 1960s, anthropology has not abandoned order and certainty after all: it has simply reorganized the field in which they appear, such that they still dominate anthropological writing, only now as moral or ethical, rather than sociological, motifs.

Notes

1. On the background to the 1983 riots see Manor (1984) and Tambiah (1986, 1996). A flavour of Mathew's style can be found in the translated excerpts from his writing published in the journal *Race and Class* after the 1983 violence (Mathew 1984).
2. The right-of-centre UNP (United National Party) and the left-of-centre SLFP (Sri Lanka Freedom Party) have alternated in power since Independence in 1948.
3. I have given a fuller account of this case in Spencer (1997b).
4. Scheper-Hughes cunningly prepares a trap for her critics by offsetting her heroic account of the activist-ethnographer against a caricature of her Cape Town colleagues taking tea in the Department tea room. She who would criticize the larger argument must live forever in the ethical hell of the post-colonial tea room.

References

Bailey, F.G. 1969. *Stratagems and Spoils: a Social Anthropology of Politics*. Oxford: Blackwell.
Bourdieu, P. 1977. *Outline of a Theory of Practice*. Cambridge: Cambridge University Press.
Brow, J. 1988. 'In Pursuit of Hegemony: Representations of Authority and Justice in a Sri Lankan Village', *American Ethnologist*, 15(2), 311–27.
Foucault, M. 1979. *Discipline and Punish*. New York: Random House.
Fortes, M. and Evans-Pritchard, E.E. 1940. 'Introduction' in *African Political Systems*. London: Oxford University Press, 1–23.
Geertz, C. 1973. 'Thick Description' in *The Interpretation of Cultures*. New York: Basic Books, 3–30.
Gluckman, M. 1956. *Custom and Conflict in Africa*. Oxford: Blackwell.
Gombrich, R. 1971. *Precept and Practice: Traditional Buddhism in the Rural Highlands of Ceylon*. Oxford: Clarendon Press.
Hansen, T. 2001. *Wages of Violence: Naming and Identity in Postcolonial Bombay*. Princeton: Princeton University Press.

Hirschman, A. 1977. *The Passions and the Interests: Political Arguments for Capitalism before its Triumph*. Princeton: Princeton University Press.

Leach, E. 1954. *Political Systems of Highland Burma: a Study of Kachin Social Structure*. London: Athlone.

Manor, J. ed. 1984. *Sri Lanka in Change and Crisis*. London: Croom Helm.

Marcus, G. 2005. 'The Passion of Anthropology in the US, circa 2004', *Anthropological Quarterly*, 78(3), 673–95.

Mathew, C. 1984. 'The Mathew Doctrine', *Race and Class* (Special Issue: Sri Lanka – Racism and the Authoritarian State), 26(1), 129–38.

Moore, M. 1985. *The State and Peasant Politics in Sri Lanka*. Cambridge: Cambridge University Press.

Nordstrom, C. 1995. 'War on the Front Lines' in *Fieldwork under Fire: Contemporary Studies of Violence and Survival*, eds C. Nordstrom and A. Robben, Berkeley: University of California Press, 129–53.

Nugent, D. and Vincent, J. eds 2004. *A Companion to the Anthropology of Politics*. Oxford: Blackwell.

Obeyesekere, G. 1984. *The Cult of the Goddess Pattini*. Chicago: University of Chicago Press.

Ruud, A. 2001. 'Talking Dirty about Politics: a View from a Bengali Village' in *The Everyday State and Society in Modern India*, eds C. Fuller and V. Bénéï, London: Hurst, 115–36.

Sahlins, M. 1999. 'Two or Three Things I Know about Culture', *Journal of the Royal Anthropological Institute*, 5(3), 399–422.

Scheper-Hughes, N. 1992. *Death without Weeping: the Violence of Everyday Life in Brazil*. Berkeley: University of California Press.

——— 1995. 'The Primacy of the Ethical: Propositions for a Militant Anthropology', *Current Anthropology*, 36(3), 409–40.

Spencer, J. 1990. 'Introduction: The Power of the Past' in *Sri Lanka: History and the Roots of Conflict*, ed. J. Spencer, London: Routledge, 1–16.

——— 1997a. 'Postcolonialism and the Political Imagination', *Journal of the Royal Anthropological Institute*, 3(1), 1–19.

——— 1997b. 'Fatima and the Enchanted Toffees: an Essay on Contingency, Narrative and Therapy', *Journal of the Royal Anthropological Institute*, 3(4), 693–710.

Tambiah, S. 1986. *Sri Lanka: Ethnic Fratricide and the Dismantling of Democracy*. London: Tauris.

——— 1996. *Leveling Crowds: Ethnonationalist Conflicts and Collective Violence in South Asia*. Berkeley: University of California Press.

Taussig, M. 1984. 'Culture of Terror – Space of Death: Roger Casement's Putumayo Report and the Explanation of Torture', *Comparartive Studies in Society and History*, 26(1), 467–97.

——— 1987. *Shamanism, Colonialism and the Wild Man: a Study in Terror and Healing*. Chicago: University of Chicago Press.

——— 2003. *Law in a Lawless Land*. New York: New Press.

Vincent, J. 1990. *Anthropology and Politics: Visions, Traditions, Trends*. Tucson: University of Arizona Press.

——— ed. 2002. *The Anthropology of Politics: a Reader in Ethnography, Theory and Critique*. Oxford: Blackwell.

Woost, M. 1990. 'Rural Awakenings: Grassroots Development and the Cultivation of a National Past in Rural Sri Lanka' in *Sri Lanka: History and the Roots of Conflict*, ed. J. Spencer, London: Routledge, 164–83.

NOTES ON CONTRIBUTORS

Keebet von Benda-Beckmann is head of the project group 'Legal Pluralism' at the Max Planck Institute for Social Anthropology at Halle, Germany. She is Professor of Anthropology of Law at Erasmus University Rotterdam and an honorary professor at the universities of Leipzig and Halle. Her research focuses on legal pluralism, disputing, decentralization, social security and natural resources in Indonesia, Nepal and the Netherlands. Publications include *The Broken Stairways to Consensus: Village Justice and State Courts in Minangkabau* (1984); *Coping with Insecurity: An 'Under All' Perspective on Social Security in the Third World*, co-edited with Franz von Benda-Beckmann and Hans Marks (1994, 2nd edition 2000), and *Mobile People, Mobile Law*, co-edited with Franz von Benda-Beckmann and Anne Griffiths (2005).

Tilo Grätz completed his undergraduate studies at Free University Berlin and received his Ph.D. in sociology in 1998 from Bielefeld University. He has worked in the past on issues of ethnicity, local-level politics and media in West Africa. He is a research fellow at the Max Planck Institute for Social Anthropology in Halle, and has worked on a project on social and cultural aspects of artisanal mining in West Africa.

Peter Just is Professor of Anthropology at Williams College in western Massachusetts, U.S.A. He was educated at the University of Chicago and the University of Pennsylvania. He has conducted research in Indonesia since 1980 and is the author of numerous articles on the anthropology of law and the Dou Donggo of eastern Sumbawa, Indonesia. His most recent book is *Dou Donggo Justice* (2001).

Michael E. Meeker is Professor Emeritus at the University of California, San Diego, and Affiliate Professor at the University of Washington. He received his Ph.D. in anthropology from the University of Chicago (1970). He has done field work in Turkey in Trabzon, Antalya and Istanbul, principally from 1966–68 and 1986–88. He has written articles and books on poetry, society and religion among pastoral peoples as well as on social structure, local elites, nationalism and religion in provincial Turkey. Author of *Literature and Violence in North Arabia* (1979), *The Pastoral Son and the Spirit of Patriarchy* (1989), *A Nation of Empire: The Ottoman Legacy of Turkish Modernity* (2002) and *Social Practice and Political Culture in the Turkish Republic* (2004).

Fernanda Pirie was a post-doctoral research fellow at the Max Planck Institute for Social Anthropology from 2002 to 2005, where she carried out research on conflict resolution in eastern Tibet. This followed a doctorate in social anthropology at the University of Oxford. She is now a research fellow at the Centre for Socio-Legal Studies, University of Oxford.

Simon Roberts was educated at the London School of Economics (LLB, 1962; Ph.D., 1968) and has taught there since 1964, appointed Professor of Law in 1986. His early field research concerned local level disputing in Botswana. Latterly he has worked on dispute processes in the West. His current research includes work on alternative dispute resolution and a study of the growth paths of London commercial law firms (with Marc Galanter). Professor Roberts is on the editorial board of the Oxford Socio-Legal Studies Series and numerous law journals. He was General Editor, *The Modern Law Review*, 1988–95. His books include: *Order and Dispute* (1979); *Rules and Processes: The Cultural Logic of Dispute in an African Context*, with J.L. Comaroff (1981); *Understanding Property Law*, with W.T. Murphy and T. Flessas (1987, 4th edn 2004); and *Dispute Processes*, with M. Palmer (2005).

Jonathan Spencer is Professor of the Anthropology of South Asia at the University of Edinburgh. He has carried out fieldwork in Sri Lanka since the early 1980s, concentrating at first on rural change and local politics, but writing more recently on ethnic conflict, political violence and political non-violence. He has just completed a book on the anthropology of 'the political' in South Asia, and has been carrying out new research on the institutional history of British anthropology.

Bertram Turner studied social anthropology, physical anthropology and ancient history at the University of Munich and took his M.A. there in 1986. He received his Ph.D. in social anthropology from the University of Munich in 1996. He was academic assistant at the Institute of Social Anthropology and African Studies in Munich between 1993 and 2001 where he taught anthropology with special reference to legal anthropology. He has also held university teaching positions in Munich and Leipzig. He has been carrying out fieldwork in Morocco since 1996. Since 2001 he has been a senior researcher at the Max Planck Institute for Social Anthropology in Halle. Bertram Turner studies the management of natural resources in a plural legal constellation in south-west Morocco, and has recently published *Asyl und Konflikt von der Antike bis heute* (2005).

Aimar Ventsel received his BA in Anthropology and History at the University of Tartu and an MA in the same subjects at the Free University Berlin, Germany. In 2005 he received his Ph.D. in social anthropology from the Max Planck Institute for Social Anthropolgy, Halle and Martin Luther University, Halle, Germany. The focuses of Ventsel's research are social change and the transformation of property rights in Siberia, Russia. Ventsel is now a senior researcher at the Estonian Literary Museum and a member of the project group there studying changes in post-socialist societies.

INDEX

adjudication, 74, 115
administration, 2, 5, 31, 36–37, 56, 65, 92
    administrative control, 55–56, 62. *See* control
    village administration, 56
age, 5, 8, 35, 38–40, 43–44, 51, 56–58, 79, 118, 133–135, 137, 145–147
    adults, 38–40, 42–44, 49
    age groups, 35, 38, 44
    elders, 5, 11, 36, 38, 40–42, 49, 75–77, 82
    generations, 50, 102
    'kids', 6, 38–40, 44, 48–49
    youth, 5, 40, 42–43, 79
aggression, 5, 42, 53, 55, 65–69, 71, 73, 101
agriculture/agriculturalist, 24, 45, 92, 101
Amdo, 6, 8, 54–55, 62–63, 65–73. *See* Tibet
Anabarskii district, 35–36, 41–42, 50
Anderson, B., 149
authenticity, 9, 18–20, 23, 25–27, 29–30
authority, 4–5, 8, 10–11, 17–18, 20–21, 27, 29, 32, 39–40, 49, 57, 60–61, 65, 68, 71–73, 75, 82, 89, 95, 110, 113, 117–118, 124, 127–128, 130, 133, 137, 164
    and legitimacy, 4–5, 12, 17–18, 23, 26, 29–30, 71, 74–75, 77, 79, 81–85, 87, 104, 112–113, 124, 128, 134–135, 147, 158
    traditional authority, 10, 17–18, 32
autonomy/self-determination, 62, 66, 73, 76, 81, 51, 76

Bailey, F.G., 150, 159, 164
Benin, 75, 78, 83–84, 87–89
Bentham, J., 149
Buddhism, 59, 72–73, 164
    Buddhist lamas, 8, 65
    Buddhist monasteries, 55
    Buddhist monks, 159
bureaucracy, 143. *See also* state

centralization, 92, 149. *See also* decentralization
China, 62, 72–73
    Chinese government, 65
    Chinese rule, 63–64

Christians, 141, 143, 148, 154
citizenship, 88–89, 152. *See also* state
civil society, 9, 12, 18, 23, 25–26, 29–30, 102, 109
class, 8, 45, 51, 56, 114, 131, 135, 155, 164–165
    middle-class, 41
    working-class, 41
coercion, 6–7, 68, 149
collectivization, 36
colonialism, 163, 165
commercial competition, 1, 10, 18, 21, 26
commercial products, 30
community, 5, 7, 10–11, 25, 34–35, 37–46, 48–52, 54–56, 58–62, 69–71, 82, 89–91, 93, 95–96, 104–105, 107, 109, 115–117, 122, 127, 153, 156, 161
    local community, 5, 50, 82, 104–105
    village community, 46, 56, 61, 115
compensation, 60, 64–65, 77, 83, 96, 98, 102–103
conflict, 1–2, 5–6, 10–11, 15, 22–23, 25–26, 33–34, 40, 42, 44, 47, 50–55, 57–59, 61, 63, 65–66, 68–73, 77, 80, 82–83, 88, 91, 94–97, 99–102, 104–107, 110–111, 114, 130–131, 152, 164–165, 167–168
    conflict resolution, 6, 34, 44, 52, 54–55, 58, 61, 68, 70, 106, 110–111, 131, 167
    escalation of conflict, 96, 105, 107
    management of conflict, 91
    sources of conflict, 97
conformity, 57, 71, 97
consensus, 10, 15, 61, 69, 91, 97–101, 106–107, 127, 166
consumption/consumer goods, 9, 17–18, 28, 43, 53, 118
continuity, 8, 15–17, 25, 33, 77, 79, 81
control, 1, 3–6, 11, 14, 17, 34, 36–37, 39–40, 44, 47, 50, 55–57, 62, 64, 66, 73–79, 81–82, 84, 87, 90, 97, 103–105, 110, 131, 139, 150
    governmental control, 3, 11. *See also* state
    normative control, 64
    police control, 36. *See* police
    political control, 74, 105

psychological control, 139
public control, 78, 84
and regulation, 28, 93, 136
self-control, 136, 138
social control, 11, 34, 44, 47, 50, 73, 97, 110, 150
corruption, 74, 133, 162
court, 3, 11, 21, 31, 37, 49, 78, 86, 120–121, 123–124, 128, 131, 139, 162
creativity, 13, 15, 84
criminality, 37, 43, 78, 80
    crime, 35, 38–39, 41–42, 44–45, 47–48, 50, 83–84, 88, 120, 135, 149
    crime rates, 84
    trans-border crime, 83
crisis, 29, 32, 40–41, 75, 80, 92, 116, 140
    economic crisis, 40–41, 80. *See also* economy
culture, 8–9, 15, 17–18, 23–27, 30, 32, 35, 41, 48, 52–53, 67, 79, 85, 111, 119, 130–131, 149, 159–160, 165, 167
    cultural tradition, 23
    cultural heritage, 17, 19, 25, 28–29
    cultural presentations, 9, 24, 29–30
    and discursive productions, 18
    street culture, 41

decentralization, 81–82, 92, 140, 144, 146, 149, 168
democracy, 15, 88, 165
    bourgeois democracies, 135–137
    democratization, 81
development, 15, 34, 61, 71, 73, 78, 88, 91–94, 98–100, 102, 104, 106, 108, 110–111, 149, 155, 158, 165
    development agencies, 78, 94, 98, 104, 108
    development organizations, 61, 93, 102
    sustainable development, 98, 108
    transnational development agencies, 108
discipline, 60, 135, 138–140, 142, 146, 148–149, 164
disorder, 1–4, 6–14, 16, 18, 20, 22, 24, 26, 28, 30, 32, 36, 38, 40, 42, 44, 46, 48, 50, 52, 56, 58–60, 62, 64, 66, 68, 70–72, 76, 78, 80, 82–88, 90–92, 94–96, 98, 100, 102, 104, 106–110, 112–114, 116, 118, 120, 122, 124, 126–128, 130, 134, 136, 138, 140, 142, 144, 146, 148, 150–165, 168, 170, 172
    and alcohol, 40, 42–44, 47, 58
    and chaos, 3, 8, 10, 13–15, 89, 94, 106, 116
    and discourse, 26, 29, 79, 81–83, 85, 91, 94, 108, 124, 130, 157–158
    and disruption, 2–4, 10, 58, 70, 99, 105–106, 151
    dynamics of disorder, 13
    and fights, 37, 41–43, 47, 58, 73, 101, 104
    patterns of disorder, 4
    and prevention, 96
    ritualized disorder, 11
    and rumours, 44–47
    and state of emergency, 151, 162
    and war, 3, 15, 22, 53, 55, 73, 81, 110, 118, 124, 133–135, 139, 146–147, 149, 152, 165
    world disorder, 153
dispute, 15, 21, 25–26, 35, 40, 59–60, 63, 66, 68, 89, 93, 110, 112, 114–115, 151, 167
    dispute settlement, 60, 112, 114
Dou Donggo, 11, 52, 114–115, 119–120, 124–127, 130, 166
Durkheim, Emile, 12–13, 15, 18, 27, 32, 114, 128–129

economy, 26, 29, 33–34, 36, 41, 48, 52–53, 56, 72–73, 76, 94, 119, 147, 155
    economic crisis, 40–41, 80
    economic depression, 133
    economic life, 4, 78
    competition, 1, 3, 8–10, 13–14, 18, 20–21, 23, 25–26, 31, 80, 101, 104, 106, 134–135, 147
egalitarianism, 95
elites, 75, 79, 135, 141–146, 148, 167
equality, 56, 71, 96–97, 130. *See also* egalitarianism
ethnicity, 51, 138, 140, 166
etiquette, 112–113, 123, 128, 130
Europe, 2, 19, 28, 30, 118–119, 130, 133–137, 146–147
Evans-Pritchard, E.E., 73, 110, 164

feuds, 6, 8, 55, 65, 68, 147
    blood feuds, 6, 8, 55
formalism, 119, 122, 128. *See also* anthropological order
Fortes, M., 164
Foucault, M., 130, 149, 164
France, 19, 22, 109, 134, 137
    Bretons, 29
    Brittany, 19, 24–26, 29
    French grocery trade, 18
Freud, S., 129, 149

Geertz, C., 32, 110, 130, 164
gender, 8, 41, 56–58, 72–73, 99, 104
    and inequality, 37
    men, 5, 17, 37–40, 43, 46, 48–49, 55–58, 60–61, 63–64, 66–69, 71–72, 75, 77–80, 84, 99, 103, 117, 139, 142–145, 152
        boys, 40, 43, 48–49, 72, 80, 86, 88
        males, 38, 40, 42–47
        masculinity, 37, 41–42, 47, 50–51, 53, 66
        tough guy, 37, 42
        young males, 38, 40, 42, 44
    and violence, 1, 3–8, 10–11, 13–15, 32, 34–35, 37, 39, 41–45, 47, 49–55, 60, 62–71, 74, 78, 81, 83–84, 86–91, 95–97, 99–110, 113, 115, 117, 119, 121, 123, 125, 127, 129, 135, 147, 152, 161–165, 167–168. *See* violence
    women, 37–39, 42, 48, 60–61, 66–67, 69, 72–73, 78, 99, 103, 130, 139, 142, 145, 161
        females, 40, 43–44, 47
        girls, 21, 32, 40, 42, 45–46, 48, 72
genealogies, 23, 29
Gluckman, Max, 44, 114, 152
gold mining communities, 4, 75, 88
gossip, 44–47, 52
government, 17–18, 26, 29, 56, 61, 65, 73, 79–80, 85, 120, 131, 135–138, 140, 144, 146, 153–154, 156
    and governance, 34, 50, 81, 119
    governmental administration, 65
    governmental authorities, 65
    governmental institutions, 36, 134

habitus, 66, 91
Hassan II, 106. *See also* Morocco
hierarchy, 1, 38, 40, 55, 59, 71, 112
    social hierarchy, 38, 55
history, 3, 15, 21, 23, 26, 31–32, 52, 68, 73, 89, 93, 103, 109–110, 133–135, 148–149, 152, 162, 165, 168
honour, 5, 34–35, 37, 39, 41, 43, 45, 47, 49, 51–53, 96, 109–110, 113, 115, 117, 119, 121, 123, 125, 127, 129
hooliganism, 39
hospitality, 57, 61, 66
hostility, 26
household, 39, 57–60, 76, 99

identity, 28, 48–49, 51–52, 61, 73, 79, 89, 92, 97, 130, 164
ideology, 32, 63, 72, 104, 110, 115, 131, 154, 157
illegitimacy, 81. *See also* legitimacy
inclusion/exclusion, 12, 47, 92, 97
indeterminacy, 13
individualism, 54–55, 57, 59, 61, 63, 65, 67, 69, 71, 73
insecurity, 15, 78, 81–85, 87, 106–107, 166
    institutional insecurity, 82–83
    legal insecurity, 106–107
instability, 2–3, 9, 13–14, 65, 75, 106, 160
international donor organizations, 98
interventions, 77, 81, 98, 103–105
institutions, 2–5, 8, 12, 36, 50–51, 74–75, 77–79, 81–84, 86–87, 92–93, 95, 99–100, 105, 110, 112, 114, 117, 133–135, 139, 141, 143, 145–146, 148, 151–152
    formal institutions, 50, 87
    and governance, 34, 50, 81
    informal institutions, 12, 87, 92
    institutional creativity, 84
    institutional insecurity, 82–83. *See* insecurity
    legal institutions, 82, 84
    local institutions, 4, 82–83, 87, 99–100, 143. *See* locality
    political institutions, 87, 110, 152
    religious institutions, 141, 143, 146. *See also* religion
Islam, 5, 86, 88, 90, 93–94, 103–104, 110, 115, 140–141, 143, 148
    Islamic activism, 98
    Islamic law, 110
    Islamic legal order, 93
    Islamic legal regime, 93
    Islamization, 141, 148, 150
    kadi's courthouse, 126. *See* court
    and Muslims, 62, 141, 144, 149–150, 155, 157
    official Islamic doctrine, 93
    popularized Islam, 93
    and Salafiyya, 4, 103–105, 108, 111
    and Sufism, 93
    Sunni Islam, 140
    tarikat Islam, 141

judges, 11, 78, 114–115, 124, 128
jurisprudence, 52, 74, 110
justice, 3, 7, 15, 31, 47, 60, 77, 82–83, 86, 89, 91, 96–97, 101, 103, 106–107, 109–110, 118, 121–122, 124–129, 161, 164, 166
    communal justice, 82–83

local justice, 83, 103, 118
popular justice, 161
vigilante justice, 77, 89

kinship, 12, 22, 37–38, 53, 63–64, 73, 79, 94
and descent, 94
family, 19–22, 26, 34, 38–43, 50–51, 61, 63–64, 73, 77, 83, 100, 116, 122, 138, 140, 142, 149
lineage, 92, 102
matrilineal, 99
and networks, 35, 37–38
segmentation, 92, 94

Ladakh, 55–57, 62, 70–71, 73. See Tibet
language, 29, 32–33, 35, 52, 58, 69, 110, 112, 119, 123–124, 127, 129, 140, 157
law, 5, 7, 12–13, 15–17, 21, 37, 52–53, 72–73, 87, 91, 93–94, 98, 103, 108–115, 117–121, 123–129, 148, 153, 159–160, 162–163, 165–167
common law, 21
customary law, 113–114
legal authority, 21, 75, 82. See also authority
legal institutions, 82, 84. See institutions
legal practices, 93
legal proceedings, 112–113, 120, 124, 127
legal procedure, 112, 131
legal reasoning, 93
legal regime, 93
legal responsibility, 105
legal status, 119
legal symbolism, 120
legal system, 2, 61, 93, 107, 111, 122. See state
local law, 37, 87
and ritual, 2–3, 10–11, 14–15, 17–18, 23, 29–32, 34, 51, 53, 56, 60, 63, 72–74, 79, 106, 112–119, 122–123, 126–129. See also ritual
state law, 13, 37, 87, 93–94. See also state
violation of law, 37
Leach, E., 15, 165
leadership, 67–68, 88, 140, 155
and charisma, 79, 117, 125–127
party leaders, 156
and prestige, 34, 76–77, 79
religious leaders, 68
rulers, 3, 56, 62
legitimacy, 4–5, 12, 17–18, 23, 26, 29–30, 71, 74–75, 77, 79, 81–85, 87, 104, 112–113, 124, 127, 134–135, 147, 158. See also illegitimacy
liberalism, 81
liturgy, 123
local craft production, 24
locality / local knowledge, 8–9, 14, 17, 21, 23–24, 27, 61, 91, 130
loyalty, 66, 69, 72, 97, 106, 138
Luhmann, Niklas, 27, 31

Machiavelli, N., 149
Malaysia, 131
Mali, 75, 79–80, 84
Malinowski, B., 152
mediation, 54, 59–60, 63–65, 67–69, 73, 77
mediator, 59
Melanesia, 69–70
memory, 19, 32, 104
migration/migrants, 80, 93, 95, 75, 77, 81, 86, 88
military, 3, 71, 78, 86, 93, 133, 135–138, 141, 143–147, 149
militias, 74, 80–81, 142, 144
modernity, 8, 17–18, 20, 27, 30, 71, 111, 142, 149, 167
modern society, 30, 165
modernization, 133–134, 137, 143, 147
late modernity, 8, 30
Mohammed VI, 106. See Morocco
monasteries, 55, 62–64. See Buddhism
morality, 7, 13, 58–59, 61, 69, 91, 94, 100, 130, 159
collective morality, 159
and judgement, 21, 42
moral continuity, 77
moral narrative, 161
moral ontology, 117
moral rules, 59
moral standards, 91, 94
and norms, 1–2, 4–14, 16–17, 34, 38, 40–41, 45, 48, 55, 59, 63–71, 76–77, 83–85, 105, 115, 142–143, 147
moral standards, 91, 94
and obligation, 39, 58, 60, 67, 71
moral codes, 90–91, 94, 100
Morocco, 5, 7, 10, 90–93, 95, 97–99, 101, 103, 105–111, 168

nation, 2–3, 53, 134, 145–146, 149, 153, 158–159, 163–164, 167
and Age of Empires, 133, 137
and Age of Nations, 133–135, 137, 145–147

nationalism, 134, 149, 152, 156–158, 167
nationality, 3
nation-state, 114, 126. *See* state
nationhood, 145
NGOs, 102
norms, 1–2, 4–14, 16–17, 34, 38, 40–41, 45, 48, 55, 59, 63–71, 76–77, 83–85, 105, 115, 142–143, 147
   normative system, 12
   norms of aggression, 55, 67–68, 71
   norms of retaliation, 7, 66, 68
   social norms, 5, 10–14, 34, 40, 45, 55, 66, 71, 83, 115
   shared norms, 1–2, 5–7, 13, 55
   violation of norms, 40
   norms of restraint, 55, 69

obedience, 137–140
oppression, 11, 13
order, 1–14, 16–42, 44–52, 54–74, 76, 78, 80, 82–114, 116–120, 122–124, 126–132, 134, 136, 138–140, 142, 144, 146–148, 150–165, 167–168, 170, 172
   anthropological order, 150–153, 155, 157, 159, 161, 163, 165
   breach of order, 11
   civil order, 119, 122, 128
   communal order, 10, 84
   concept of order, 61
   cosmic order, 11, 116, 122, 127
   and discourse, 26, 29, 79, 81–83, 85, 91, 94, 108, 124, 130, 157–158
   and disorder, 1–4, 6–14, 16, 18, 20, 22, 24, 26, 28, 30, 32, 36, 38, 40, 42, 44, 46, 48, 50, 52, 56, 58–60, 62, 64, 66, 68, 70–72, 76, 78, 80, 82–88, 90–92, 94–96, 98, 100, 102, 104, 106–110, 112–114, 116, 118, 120–124, 126–128, 130, 134, 136, 138, 140, 142, 144, 146, 148, 150–165, 168, 170, 172. *See* disorder
   economic order, 67, 100, 155. *See* economy
   and harmony, 7, 60, 70, 91, 96–98, 100, 104, 109–110, 115, 131
   legal order, 56, 91, 93, 106, 122
   maintenance order, 2, 34, 44, 59, 68–69, 90–91
   models of order, 7, 12–13, 70, 90, 93, 95, 98, 106
   moral order, 4, 13, 61, 101, 107, 151, 153, 162
   natural order, 116–117, 119
   negotiation of order, 10, 90
   ordering institutions, 8, 12, 75. *See* institutions
   and peace, 2, 6, 9, 14–15, 51, 60, 69–71, 73, 84, 104, 107, 110, 116, 147, 152
   perception of order, 9, 82
   political order, 10, 13, 69, 105, 118, 150–151, 153, 155, 157, 159, 161, 163, 165. *See* politics
   processes of order, 4, 14, 108
   public order, 48, 74, 76, 82, 87–88
   and regularity, 4, 8–9, 16, 89, 113, 123, 151
   religious order, 4, 71, 93–94, 103, 105
   restoration of order, 60
   state order, 2–4, 11, 78, 106–107, 132, 134, 138–140, 148
   and structure, 5, 9, 12, 32, 34, 36–38, 53, 70, 113–114, 117, 119, 124, 151, 161, 164–165, 167
organizations, 61, 74, 79, 86, 88, 93, 102, 154
   informal organizations, 93
Ottoman Empire, 2, 133–134, 137, 147, 149, 167
   and Turkey, 149, 169

panopticon, 136–137, 139, 149–150
parliament chamber, 3, 11
pastoralists, 8, 54–55, 62, 71–73, 101
piety, 103–104, 129
police, 8, 36–37, 56, 59, 64–66, 75–77, 79–80, 114, 128, 162
politics, 1, 3, 13, 33, 51, 73, 75, 81, 84, 86–89, 130–132, 140, 151–157, 159–160, 162–167
   anti-politics, 159
   informal politics, 81
   mass politics, 163
   political change, 81–82
   political organization, 38, 92
   political participation, 154
   political theodicy, 163
   political culture, 8, 85, 149, 167
   political movements, 74, 93
   political domination, 23, 26, 29–31
   political office, 23, 118
   political ascendancy, 3, 10, 26
poverty, 98, 100, 160
power, 1–2, 6–7, 14–16, 37–38, 49, 62, 65, 67–68, 71–74, 76–77, 79–81, 84–86, 89–90, 92, 95, 103, 105–107, 110, 118, 126, 128–129, 133, 136–140, 144, 146, 148–149, 157, 161, 163–165

and domination, 1, 13, 23, 26, 29–31, 62, 68, 90, 134, 148, 161
and hegemony, 1, 75, 79–80, 82–83, 103, 164
juridical powers, 77
legislative powers, 83
political power, 79. *See* politics
power relationship, 136
and sovereignty, 4, 81, 121, 152. *See* leadership
predictability, 1–2, 4, 6, 8–9, 12–14, 84, 107, 113, 122–124
prestige, 34, 76–77, 79
pride, 34–35, 37, 39, 41, 43, 45, 47, 49, 51, 53, 65, 113, 115, 117, 119, 121, 122, 124, 125, 127, 129
processes, 2–4, 6, 8–9, 11–15, 25–26, 30, 39, 54–55, 57, 60–61, 65, 70, 74, 81, 85, 93, 96, 108, 112, 114–115, 117, 151, 167
and dynamics, 13–14, 42, 54, 61, 65, 69–71, 91, 114
juridical processes, 85
processual approach, 9
processes of order, 4, 14, 108
social processes, 8–9, 12, 96, 114–115
producers/suppliers, 17–18
production, 9, 17–19, 21–22, 24, 27–28, 74–75, 92. *See also* consumption
public services, 78, 81
public sphere, 22, 29
punishment, 4–5, 47, 49–50, 64–65, 82, 161–162
corporal punishment, 161
retributive punishment, 4
Radcliffe-Brown, A.R., 152
rationalization, 129, 134
reciprocity, 6–7, 45, 53, 95–98, 100–101, 104–107, 109, 138
reconciliation, 59–60, 87, 116–117
religion, 7, 32, 59, 91, 94, 104, 114–115, 128, 129, 141, 154–155, 167
and ritual, 2–3, 10–11, 14–15, 17–18, 23, 29–32, 34, 51, 53, 56, 60, 63, 72–74, 79, 106, 112–119, 122, 127–129. *See also* ritual
religious authority, 72
religious events, 93
religious movements, 86, 93
representations, 9, 17–18, 24–25, 27–31, 91, 139, 165
and discourse, 91
ritual and symbolic representations, 30

reputation, 34–35, 38, 42–47, 49–50, 127, 143
resources, 1, 10, 23–24, 26, 32, 38, 41, 50–51, 57, 75, 77–78, 84, 86, 93, 98–99, 101–102, 104, 108, 155, 166, 168
natural resources, 93, 98, 108, 166, 168
resource management, 98–99
respect, 6, 17, 23–24, 28, 39–40, 46, 61, 68–69, 76–77, 79, 83–84, 98, 100, 109, 142, 145, 147, 151
responsibility, 39, 49, 54–55, 57–59, 61, 63, 65–69, 71–73, 85, 91, 93, 95, 102, 105, 155
shared responsibility, 95
retaliation, 7, 9, 54, 66, 68, 71, 83, 95–96, 98, 101–102, 107
revenge, 47, 54–55, 59, 63–64, 66, 70, 72, 96. *See also* punishment
rights, 11, 38, 41, 50, 60, 82, 87, 89, 96, 100–102, 105, 107, 109, 116, 118–119, 168
exploitation rights, 100–102
individual rights, 50, 60
inheritance rights, 100–101
property rights, 41, 50, 118, 168
ritual, 2–3, 10–11, 14–15, 17–18, 23, 29–32, 34, 51, 53, 56, 60, 63, 72–74, 79, 106, 112–119, 122, 127–129
and law, 114, 129–130
performance of a ritual, 10
rites of passage, 11
secular ritual, 118, 131
rule-breaking, 5–7,9, 13–14, 55, 66, 69
breach(es) of rule(s), 3, 10, 23, 25–26, 60, 72, 97. *See also* law
Russia, 35, 38, 49, 52, 168

Sahlins, M., 73, 131, 165
Sakha, 35–38, 40–41, 48, 51–52. *See* Siberia
sanction, 54, 60, 77, 83. *See also* punishment / communal sanctions, 83
Scheper-Hughes, N., 15, 110, 165
Scott, James, 44–45, 53
security, 1–2, 6, 9, 11, 14–15, 39, 50, 78, 84, 86, 88, 91, 106, 162, 166
sexual behaviour, 46–47
Siberia, 5, 34–35, 38, 40, 51–52, 168
Siberian anthropology, 34
Simmel, Georg, 13, 25
society, 2–10, 12, 14–15, 18, 23, 25–26, 29–30, 32–33, 40, 44, 51–54, 65, 69, 73, 75, 83, 87, 102, 109–110, 114–115, 117, 126, 127–137, 139–145, 147–149, 159, 163, 165, 167
complex societies, 1, 128

and social behaviour, 8, 34, 55, 57, 112
and social capital, 5, 52, 56, 58, 71, 96
and social continuity, 8, 15, 17. *See* continuity
and social control, 11, 34, 44, 47, 50, 73, 97, 111, 151. *See* control
and social groups, 4, 14, 62, 97–98
and social networks, 39, 107
and social stratification, 95, 98, 105–106
and social structure, 34, 36, 38, 53, 70, 114, 132–133, 166, 169
solidarity, 92, 97, 100–102, 105, 128, 137–140
Souss, 92–95, 98, 102, 106, 108–110
sovereignty, 4, 81, 121, 152. *See also* power
Soviet ethnography, 34
Soviet officials, 36
Soviet Union, 34, 36
spontaneity, 13, 128
Sri Lanka, 3, 153–155, 158, 164–165, 167
    Independence, 56, 99, 103, 105, 155, 164
    local communities, 80, 84, 154
    LTTE (Liberation Tigers of Tamil Ealam), 153
    party politics, 154, 159, 162
    political participation, 154
    presidential election, 155, 157
    Sinhalese, 158
        Sinhala Nationalism, 158–159.
        See also nation
    SLFP (Sri Lanka Freedom Party), 154–155, 164
    TULF (Tamil United Liberation Front), 153
    UNP (United National Party), 154–155, 158, 164
    village politics, 154, 156–157
stability, 2, 4, 9, 65–66, 70, 84
state,1–5, 7–9, 11–15, 17, 32, 35–37, 39, 48, 50, 54, 56, 61, 72–75, 77–94, 96, 98, 101–102, 104–107, 115, 117–119, 121–122, 127, 131–145, 147–150, 155, 161–162, 165–166
    and administration, 2, 92
    citizens, 4, 75, 87, 102, 124, 125, 131–132, 140, 147. *See also* citizenship
    hegemony, 1, 75, 79–80, 82–83, 103, 164
    central state, 75, 80–82, 87–88
    margins of the state, 80
    modern states, 137, 152
    public services, 78, 81. *See* public
    and society, 3–4, 8–9, 14, 132–137, 140, 142, 144, 148, 166
    state agents, 8, 77–80, 86
    state officials, 36, 39, 93, 142–143
    state enterprise, 36
    state formation, 72–73
    state institutions, 5, 81, 83, 87, 105, 117, 143, 145
    state law, 13, 37, 87, 93–94
    state representatives, 90, 102
    weak states, 74, 89
status, 5, 11, 39, 58, 61–62, 65, 67–68, 71, 73, 102, 119, 124, 148
strangers, 8–9, 64, 77, 82, 86
Strathern, Marilyn, 14–15, 54, 62, 70, 73, 108, 111

Taussig, M., 15, 165
taxation, 74, 135
    taxes, 56, 77, 134, 137, 142
territory, 7, 35, 41, 63, 79–80
    territoriality, 79, 94
theft, 41, 63–64, 70, 77
    stealing, 38–39, 41, 44, 64
    thief, 64, 72
Tibet, 6, 8, 55, 62, 71, 73, 167
Tilly, Charles, 134
Trabzon, 132–133, 135, 137, 139, 141–149, 167. *See* Ottoman Empire
tradition / 'tradition', 8, 14, 16–20, 23–24, 27–32, 49, 79, 87, 93, 110–111, 133, 151. *See also* 'modernity'
    and invention, 30, 32
    and quality, 19
    traditional authority, 10, 17–18, 32
    traditionalism, 119, 122
transnational actors, 98–99
trust, 6, 8–9, 14, 17, 27–28, 73, 94, 97

unemployment, 37
UNESCO, 94
Uurung Khaia, 35–39, 42–49. *See* Siberia

values, 41, 44, 51–52, 54–55, 69–70, 91, 151–152. *See also* norms
    collective values, 91
    moral values, 55. *See also* morality
vigilantism, 87–89
vigilante groups, 4, 8, 74–75, 77, 79–89
vigilante justice, 77, 89
village, 5, 10, 15, 24–26, 33–40, 42–49, 51, 53, 55–61, 66, 68–73, 75–77, 80–83, 87–88, 94–95, 99, 101–102, 105–106, 109–110, 115–116, 118, 128, 153–159, 162, 164–166
    village councils, 82–83, 87, 105, 109

violence, 1, 3–8, 10–11, 13–15, 32, 34–35, 37, 39, 41–45, 47, 49–55, 60, 62–71, 74, 78, 81, 83–84, 86–91, 95–97, 99–110, 113, 115, 117, 119, 121, 123, 125, 127, 129, 131, 135, 147, 152, 161–165, 167–168
acceptable violence, 5–6, 8, 96, 103
collective violence, 34–35, 37, 39, 41, 43, 45, 47, 49, 51, 53, 113, 115, 117, 119, 121, 123, 125, 127, 129, 131, 165
death, 15, 22–23, 26, 34, 42, 52, 59, 64, 78, 102, 106, 116, 146, 149–150, 152, 160, 165 / homicide, 102

destabilising violence, 65
group violence, 47
monopoly of violence, 74, 78
organized violence, 3
retributive violence, 65

Weber, Max, 127
West Africa, 4, 17, 74–75, 77, 79, 81–83, 85–89, 166
Westernization, 133–134, 137, 147
witchcraft, 25, 78, 83 / demons, 156